THE LAST AGE
OF MISSIONS

THE LAST AGE OF MISSIONS

A Study of Third World Missionary Societies

LAWRENCE E. KEYES

William Carey Library

Library of Congress Cataloging in Publication Data

Keyes, Lawrence E., 1944–
   The last age of missions.

   Bibliography: p
   1. Missions--Societies, etc. 2. Church and
underdeveloped areas. I. Title.
BV2365.U53K48 1982   266'.063'1724   82-22006
ISBN 0-87808-435-5

Published by
William Carey Library
P.O. Box 40129
1705 N. Sierra Bonita Ave.
Pasadena, California 91104
Telephone (213) 798-0819

In accord with some of the most recent thinking in the academic press, the William Carey Library is pleased to present
this scholarly book which has been prepared from an author-
edited camera ready copy.

PRINTED IN THE UNITED STATES OF AMERICA

To Shirley Joan Keyes
Wise counselor, wife, mother and friend
in appreciation for
her partnership in ministry.

CONTENTS

FIGURES

PREFACE

One of the fastest growing areas in missions today is the non-Western missionary movement. A study of it helps to balance our view of world missions and to understand one of the ways God proclaims His message to all peoples in the whole inhabited world (Matthew 24:14). A study of non-Western missions also demonstrates the increasing maturity resident within the Third World evangelical church, a development often ignored by many believers within our traditional Western congregations.

Within the West, such organizations as Wycliffe Bible Translators, Missionary Aviation Fellowship or the Foreign Mission Board of the Southern Baptist Convention are well known. Yet there are hundreds of lesser known agencies located within the non-Western world, mature groups like the All Nations Frontier Missions, Omega World Missions, the Indonesian Missionary Fellowship, or the Caiua Mission of Brazil. There are even specialized service groups such as the Hong Kong Association of Christian Missions or the Brazilian Center of Missionary Information in Rio de Janeiro. These are some of the strategic and complimentary counterparts to North American and European evangelical associations, without which we would never accomplish the Great Commission. Since 1972, the number of Third World agencies has grown 81%, and they continue to increase rapidly. In order to be an effective World Christian, the other half of the story of world missions must be told.

In three sections, *The Last Age of Missions* describes the growth and importance of the non-Western missionary movement. The first section defines and contrasts the Third World mission societies

with the West.   The second presents the results of a year-long
international research project which up-dates any previously published material on the subject.   The statistics in this section
were carefully researched and verified by additional field informants, and reflect the situation as accurately as possible as of
1980. Yet, with a project of this size it is impossible to present a report without any error or misinterpretation. The back
page of this book provides the necessary feedback sheet for any
corrections or clarifications which one might find. The third
section sketches modern missions as a cooperative venture, suggesting the kind of participation which should involve all societies everywhere. The four appendices are included for those
students of mission interested in additional specific data on the
non-Western world.

The purpose of this study is to partially describe the missionary cooperation which would result if Third World missions
were taken seriously. Ever since participating in the Berlin
World Congress on Evangelism in 1966, my hope for a substantial
cooperative witness has grown significantly. And now as I work
within the non-Western world, I observe the continued necessity
for such cooperation. With limited funds for outreach, duplicated
activity on the field, and the imbalance of shared researched information, the new age of missions must be one of partnership.
Not an organizational union between a few Western agencies, nor
an unequal superiority between Western and non-Western societies,
nor even a cooperative effort where evangelistic fervor is sacri-
ficed, but it should be a task oriented association whereby all
participants are equals, firmly dedicated to the purpose of reaching the thousands of yet unreached people groups worldwide. The
body of Christ is a missionary cooperative and we can give God
glory by our interdependent obedience.

Lawrence Keyes
May 23, 1982
Sao Paulo, Brazil

FOREWORD

The Last Age of Missions is a highly appropriate title for this
book. Many trace the development of modern missions back to the
days of William Carey, about 180 years ago. It is true that the
message of the gospel has spread around the world at an unprecedented rate since then. Christianity has become a truly universal
religion. But it is also true that until quite recently the missionaries who were the bearers of the Good News were white men and
women from the North Atlantic, Western cultures.

What, then is the "last age?"

The last age of missions is a term describing the highly significant development of missionary sending agencies among the churches
of the Third World. While the phenomenon of missionaries from the
Third World is not itself new, up until the decade of the sixties
they have constituted a mere trickle in the missionary stream. Now,
however, the movement of missionaries from churches in Asia, Africa
and Latin America is a substantial tributary. Some feel that the
movement is so strong that by the turn of the century as much as
half of the world's Protestant missionary force may be non-Western.

Lawrence Keyes has been observing this trend for years. Convinced that Third World missions is a major force for world evangelization being raised up by God, Keyes decided to dedicate a
considerable block of his time as a trained missiologist to researching the facts. Using the facilities of the Fuller Seminary School
of World Mission and of the MARC ministry of World Vision International, Keyes has taken the study of the missionary movement from the
Third World far beyond anything else that has been done in the past.
The publication of the data and Keyes' perceptive analysis of it is
a milestone event in contemporary missiological literature.

The Last Age of Missions has come just at the right time. The decade of the eighties is already seeing the most massive ingathering into the Kingdom of God that history has ever known. Never before have there been so many people in the world who desire to open their hearts to Jesus Christ. Never has missiological theory been so highly developed. Never have material and technological resources been so plentiful and available to the missionary enterprise. The major hinderance to the completion of the Great Commission is personnel. While there does seem to be an upsurge in missionary interest and dedication among young people from the Western countries at the present time, Westerners alone are not sufficient for the task. Only as the Western missionary force is at least matched by missionaries from the Third World can the task be completed. A powerful stimulus for motivating Third World churches, mission agencies, and Christian people for cross-cultural and international involvement has now been provided by Lawrence Keyes in the form of *The Last Age of Missions*.

The impact of this book can hardly be overestimated. It should be used by professors of mission in their classes to inspire students with news of what God is doing. It should be translated into twenty other languages and spread abroad as a challenge and encouragement to those for whom the missionary call is a relatively new aspect of their Christian experience. Tens of thousands of black, brown, red and yellow missionaries will join the whites in preaching the Gospel of the Kingdom to every people -- and then shall the end come. Even so, come, Lord Jesus!

C. Peter Wagner
Fuller Seminary School of World Mission
Pasadena, California

PART ONE
THE MATURING CHURCH
IN THE THIRD WORLD

1

THE LAST PHASE

In 1978, Theodore Williams, General Secretary of the Indian Evangelical Mission said:

> A significant development in the history of the Church in our age is the rise of indigenous missionary movements in Asia, Africa and Latin America.... The winds of change blowing across Asia, Africa and Latin America and the wind of the Holy Spirit moving upon the church in these continents indicate we are in an exciting period of mission history.... Third World missions have just made a beginning.(1)

No longer is Nigeria just a country that receives missionaries; it is a missionary sending country as well. Nor is Brazil only a nation that receives North American missionaries, but a nation that sends missionaries to the uttermost parts of the earth. The beginning of a new dimension in missionary involvement has come. The initiative in world evangelization is moving toward the emerging nations of the Non-Western world.

THE FOUR PHASES - A DESCRIPTION

As we look back across the centuries, however, we can observe other areas that have in their turn held the initiative. There have been at least three preceding phases which evidenced significant missionary activity. Each succeeding phase has contributed personnel for a witness in an expanding world.

Phase One

The initial phase of world missions centered primarily in the middle East. It began in the first few pages of the Bible, when a
special missionary nation was called to "be a blessing...to all
the families of the earth" (Genesis 12:1-3). This understanding
of the Bible, while not new, has only recently been emphasized in
evangelical scholarly circles by Walter Kaiser, Jr. of Trinity
Evangelical Divinity School. Missiologists such as Ralph Winter,
Don Richardson and Paul Pierson espouse this understanding of the
Old Testament period as a period in which Israel was not only
supposed to attract the nations to the Living God but was intend-
ed to reach out as well.

Thus when our Lord commissioned the Twelve, this new beginning
did not negate the years of witness recorded in the Old Testament
(i.e., 2000-400 B.C.). Israel indeed had prophets and kings, many
of whom were faithful witnesses to His Name. The Psalmist exhorts,
"Let all kings bow down before him, all nations serve him" (72:11);
"Ascribe to the Lord the glory of His name; bring an offering and
come into His courts" (96"7, 8). Isaiah stresses that "...It is a
light thing that thou shouldest be my servant, to raise up the
tribes of Jacob, and to restore the preserved of Israel: I will
also give thee for a light to the Gentiles, that thou mayest be my
salvation unto the end of the earth" (Isaiah 47:6).

FIGURE 1

PHASE ONE: The Middle East

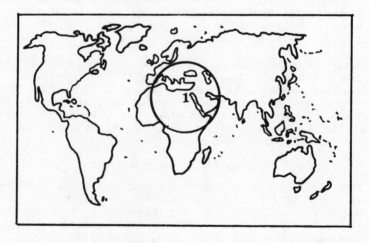

With Christ, however, an expanded new nation composed of the
children of Abraham by faith began to *reach out* and witness to
the ends of the known earth with the gospel. Thus, the Apostle
Paul probably went as far west as Spain. Peter may have traveled
to Rome (as did many others), the Apostle Thomas, an active missionary, might have evangelized as far east as India (as did Bar-
tholomew). John and Timothy worked at Ephesus and Titus evangelized Crete - all in preparation for the continued outreach by the
Apostolic Fathers and their disciples the first four centuries
after Christ established a firm foundation for what was to follow.

Phase Two

The geographical center of world missions moved northward and re-
mained in Europe for well over one thousand years. The international structure of the organized church developed rapidly, often
with the help of the proliferating monasteries. The one genuine
missionary thrust into the pagan world during the first five
hundred years of this second phase (beginning in the fifth century), was carried out by Celtic missionaries.(2) From Ireland,
many circled through northern Europe evangelizing the barbarians.

There were other significant achievements as well emanating
from Europe. In 910 A.D., the Cluny monastery was founded and
the monks later established over 700 daughter houses throughout
Europe. The thirteenth century brought the Friar movement, or
Mendicant orders; first was the Waldenses (from Peter Waldo), a
conservative group whose influence spread all over Europe. Next

FIGURE 2

PHASE TWO: Europe

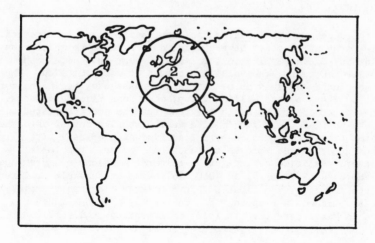

came the Franciscans (1209 – from Francis of Assisi) who preached
in city streets to the masses. Dominic then formed the Dominicans
(1216), an intellectual order which worked among Europe's urban
and educational centers. Much later Ignatius of Loyola initiated
the unique Society of Jesus (Jesuits – 1534), an order historically identified with creative missionary methodologies worldwide.

Another significant influence during this second phase, comes
from the movements of the Spanish and Portuguese *conquistadores*
(primarily 16th century), whose ships routinely carried missionaries. Furthermore, the forerunners of today's Protestant missionary agencies were formed such as The Paris Society (1663),
the Danish-Halle Mission (1705), and Herrnhut (1722). Even the
launching of the so-called "modern missionary movement" by William
Carey in 1792 can be considered a part of this phase. Between
1792 and 1825 at least fifteen separate societies, located primarily in England, were formed. They backed the efforts of such
notable missionaries as Carey, Ward, Marshman, Judson, Morrison,
Moffet, etc.

Today, the presence of British and European missionaries
blanket the world, significantly assisting in the growth of God's
Kingdom. Theological liberalism or parish professionalism in the
home countries have not diminished the missionary fervor among
many continental agencies for history demonstrates their faithfulness. Furthermore, funds and personnel for world evangelization are increasing much due to several special continental congresses and conferences on personal witness. Even though the
central locus of foreign missions eventually moved from that continent, Western Europe continues to represent a strong force in
cross-cultural missions.

Phase Three

The third geographical center has been focused in North America.
While European churches have continued to send out missionaries
worldwide, North America in the last 150 years has become the
greatest source for the voluntary thrust of world mission. The
true beginning of this phase overlapped phase two, beginning more
than 150 years before William Carey, when John Eliot and Thomas
Mayhew preached to the North American Indians and translated the
Bible. Settlers in North America were virtually thrust into the
mission fields constituted by the aboriginal peoples. Literally
dozens of organized efforts to reach the Indians by colonial
believers qualified as true cross-cultural missions and preceded
William Carey. Finally, in 1810, following the example of Carey's
efforts in India, the first American foreign missionary society
was established in response to a request by mission-minded students in Massachusetts. In 1812, this society, the American
Board of Commissioners for Foreign Missions, sent out its first

group of missionaries. Originally organized by Congregationalists,
the ABCFM from the beginning served many denominations (Presbyterian, Dutch Reformed, German Reformed, etc.) until each group began
its own denominational endeavors. Within the first fifty years
of its existence, ABCFM missionaries traveled to the Near East,
Asia, Micronesia, Hawaii and Africa, being greatly hindered only
by the American Civil War.

FIGURE 3

PHASE THREE: North America

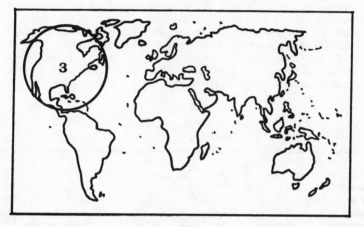

By 1865 the Civil War was over and North American missions
began to develop rapidly. By the first decade of the twentieth
century, historian Robert T. Handy writes:

North America was then supplying about a third of the
total world Protestant missionary staff and almost half
of the financial backing for the whole enterprise....
The achievement of the missionary movement, in which
American Protestantism had become so deeply involved, was
a major event in Christian history. In many parts of
the world churches were planted where they had not been
before - institutions which later became strong and
independent, able to restate the faith in indigenous
terms. The movement also did much for educational,
medical, and social service, making contributions to
human welfare that were often later copied by new
nations as they took shape in the twentieth century.(3)

Today North America (along with Europe and the Orthodox Church
of the East) continues missionary work of all types. However, in
1967, believers in North America alone contributed $317 million

for the work of missions. In 1975, the total had increased to
$656 million (4) which was and continues to be more money freely
given to evangelical missions than from any other continent in
the world. By 1979, the total had increased to $1,148 million!

However, three-fourths of the world remains non-Christian.
One-half of the world lives in areas presently untouched by any
gospel witness.(5) In terms of North American activity, 90% of
our missionary engagement assists already existing churches; only
10% of the missionary force is actively involved in pioneer evangelism - in reaching the unreached located in totally non-Christian people groups. (6) It is obvious that a new thrust is needed
to penetrate those thousands of Muslim, Hindu, Chinese, tribal and
other pockets of people that do not now have an indigenous inter-
nal witness (see Chapter 4). We are beginning to see the emergence of this new thrust from among those countries and peoples
considered to be in the "Third World." This new thrust, we see,
as a fourth phase of world missions.

FIGURE 4

PHASE FOUR: The Third World

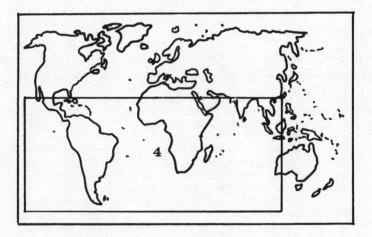

Phase Four

The acknowledgment of this new locus of mission sending activity
in the Non-Western world in no way ignores the valuable contribution which Western countries must continue to make toward world
mission. The experience, funds, and personnel from Western believers are constantly needed due to escalating demands. But decisive
additional effort must be forthcoming from somewhere if we are to
fulfill the Great Commission. An editorial in *Christianity Today*
points to this fact:

Donald McGavran has estimated that a single missionary
family cannot work with a community numbering more than
five thousand people. If this is true and if there are
at least two billion who have not heard of Christ, then
it follows that not thousands or tens of thousands, but
hundreds of thousands of missionaries are needed to
finish the task of world evangelization. And if the
population of the world continues to increase at the
present rate, then it is likely that seven or eight
hundred thousand missionaries will be needed.(7)

In God's wise guidance, the missionary focus is beginning to
turn towards the Non-Western World - not to supplement Western
activity but to complement the present outreach worldwide. The
"younger" church is maturing. It is assuming responsibility for
mission while forming its own missionary structures. Ralph Winter
writes, "The great new fact of *our* time must be the emergence of
Third World missions. This is the next phase of missions today."
(8) Many now agree with this statement. For this reason, it is
important to look more closely at the very concept of the "Third
World."

THE THIRD WORLD - DEFINITION

The term "Third World" became popular in the early 1970's.
Initially it referred to an economic category describing the poor-
er nations in contrast to the richer, more developed nations. In
1975, *U.S. News and World Report* defined the term "Third World"
as consisting of "'have not' nations, still undeveloped, whose
interests don't jibe with those of developed nations in the other
two worlds - that is, the communist and non-communist world."(9)
Closely connected with this economic definition is a political
one which Dennis E. Clark illustrates. "The Third World is popularly used to refer to the independent nations of Asia, Africa and
South America who increasingly want to determine their destinies
apart from the influence and pressures of the so called great
powers."(10)

In 1976, Walbert Buhlmann cast a slightly different light on
the meaning of the term "Third World." "Some distinguish (it
economically or) sociologically: the way society is divided into
the rich, the middle class and the poor, or capitalists, tradesmen
and proletariat...others politically: NATO, the Warsaw pact and
the non-aligned; others geographically: east, west and south.
The last is preferable today."(11) In application, he continues,
"According to our view the Third World church is, as a general
rule, identified geographically with the Third World, with the
tropical zone extending right around the world but also a little

beyond the tropics and with the three continents of Latin America,
Africa and Asia (including Oceania)."(12)

Opinion is mixed concerning this term "the Third World." However, in an attempt to be fair, an economic usage is prohibitive
because it omits Japan, Brazil and Saudi Arabia – nations for our
purpose normally associated with the Third World, yet which cannot
be considered "poor" or "underdeveloped." If we use the phrase
"Third World" with a geopolitical meaning, it omits the many non-
anglo cultural units living within the boundaries of the United
States who are more closely identified with their own homeland
than with the cultural patterns of North America (this is true for
many groups within the boundaries of many countries). Also, this
geopolitical definition would probably include Australia and New
Zealand within the Third World, countries geographically close to
Asia, but psychologically more closely identified with Europe and
North America. And, if we assume that all Third World countries
have a general desire to be considered politically non-aligned
with the two great world systems (communist and capitalist), what
does this mean with regards to China? Is China, then, excluded
from the Third World? or is Japan? or Cuba? The problems with
either a geopolitical or economic definition are many.

The definition of Third World which I choose to use, therefore,
is a social-psychological explanation. It is the mental identification with some grouping or country other than that of the two
great Western powers. It includes not only the majority of African,
Asian and Latin American peoples, but also the Cambodians in Canada,
the Hispanic Americans in the United States and the Africans in
Europe. The Third World consists of those peoples that possess a
greater affinity with their own people than with either the capitalist or communist countries. They cultivate their own national
independence and when abroad, prioritize the maintenance of
personal relationships "back home."

Therefore, to label these peoples "the Third World" is not meant
in any way to be derisive. The adjective "third" is *never* to imply
inferiority or submission. On the contrary, what we refer to as
the Third World is a separate and powerful force in and of itself
and is distinct because of the self-identity of those peoples com-
posing it. As C. Peter Wagner writes, "the mentality of a people
classifies it in the Third World."(13)

THE IMPORTANCE OF THE THIRD WORLD – AN ANALYSIS

No less than 3.3 billion people live in the Third World; and
from among them Christians are increasingly conscious of their own
responsibility to be involved in world mission. In 1975, for
example, Bishop James Sangu of Mgeya, Tanzania said:

One of the clearest signs that a church has matured is
the fact that it is not the object of missionary activity
but becomes the subject of it. From a mission church it
becomes a missionary church. With the changeover of
responsibility from the missionary congregation to the
African churches themselves, we should start surveying
the continent to consider the missionary work to be done
and plan a mission strategy.(14)

During the same year, when the Asia Missions Association (the
first regional association of mission agencies to be formed in
the Third World) was inaugurated, Dr. Philip Teng of Hong Kong
"called on the delegates to look to new horizons in missionary
endeavor which lie before the Asian churches."(15)

These statements were not the first indication of an interest
by the Third World in mission activity. In 1833, Ko Tha Byu
evangelized several regions of Burma and in 1843 Joseph Merrick
from Jamaica worked cross-culturally in Cameroon Africa. Later
in our generation, the Third World evidenced increased involvement in mission outreach through such·diverse entities as the
Hindustan Bible Institute of Madras, the Christian and Missionary
Alliance Churches in Argentina, and the Tzeltal Indian tribe in
Mexico. In his December 2, 1971 prayer letter, Samuel Moffett
of Korea wrote:

The Korea Presbyterian Church already has nineteen
missionaries spread from Ethiopia to Brazil and more are
waiting to go.... The seminary has just sent one of its
best professors, Dr. Park Chang-Hwan, the foremost Bible
translator in Korea, as this country's first missionary
to Indonesia.(16)

In Guinea-Bissau (formerly Portuguese Guinea), missionary
Leslie Brierley (Worldwide Evangelization Crusade) reported that
beginning in 1945:

One man of the Manjaco tribe went to the unevangelized
areas of the *Bisagos* tribe - a totally different type of
people.... Another of the *Papel* tribe crossed the frontier
from Guinea to neighboring Senegal. Although a Portuguese
subject, he evangelized *Balanta* tribesmen of Senegalese
nationality who had never previously heard the Gospel.(17)

One example from the West Indies is the International Missionary
Fellowship. Organized in April, 1962, the I.M.F. trains nationals
and sends them to various Latin fields in cooperation with other
existing societies. By 1974, over 35 missionaries had been sent
out with Jamaican support including a couple to Papua, New Guinea.
And in 1975, a Ghanian missionary was sent to the United States,

under the auspices of the Presbyterian Church U.S., to work in new
evangelistic and educational endeavors.(18)   The Third World has
been active in missionary outreach for many years.

Yet today there are four reasons why this fourth phase could
become the greatest missionary sending age ever. These considera-
tions are anthropological, financial, missiological and organizational, and while not comprehensive, are significant and reside
within the Third World itself.

1) First, considering Third World potential in terms of anthropology, its efforts could become strategically important because
certain Third World societies are highly respected by various
other unreached peoples of Asia, Africa and Latin America. This
respect encourages a greater receptivity to the messenger resulting in benefit for the message he proclaims. For example, within
China there is a cultural similarity to and a psychological
respect for Chinese from other Asian lands that few Westerners
could expect to receive. This "respect" involves a certain
willingness to hear what the Chinese evangelist might have to say,
a certain level of openness to his message. This level of openness is what is meant by "respect" and there are thousands of
similar situations throughout the world. These relationships
enhance the working out of the Great Commission.

Another illustration of this might come from one very respon-
sive area of the world. In India, Andhra Pradesh, a central
territory of over 50 million people, is open to the gospel message.
The majority of Christian activity in Andhra Pradesh has been
focused upon the *Harijan* (untouchable) community, even though 65%
of Andhra Pradesh is comprised of a middle class community called
the *Shudra*. Becoming a Christian for the *Shudra* often meant a
social "lowering" and a personal identification with *Harijan*.
Thus Indian evangelists from *Harijan* had little success among the
Shudra or even among the high *Brahman* or *Kshtriya* communities.
Yet recent experience has indicated that the *Shudra* do respond to
the message in a much more positive manner when it is conveyed by
other means. Specifically, the Bengalis (who have a similar
culture though a different language), the Keralas (southeast India),
or even the Fijians (many have Indian roots) or the Australians
(because of past British influence), are able to communicate in
a meaningful way to the *Shudra*.(19)

Such mutual respect exists among all peoples everywhere. Guate-
malans have their preferences; Nigerians also have theirs. Very
often these preferences are for peoples who are part of the Third
World, particularly because Westerners have so often been identified with colonialism and imperialism. It is, therefore, nothing
less than good mission strategy to look to Third World missionaries to tap the great potential for evangelization that exists

among the thousands of mutually respected relationships throughout the world.

2) Secondly, this fourth phase of world mission could become crucially important because of finances: money often goes further if given to a Third World missionary.

In 1972, an average income for a North American missionary overseas was $10,926. In 1975, it rose to $17,754.(20) Yet Theodore Williams estimates that the yearly salary of an Indian missionary is approximately $601.(21) In Brazil where approximately 746 national missionaries serve in both foreign and domestic endeavors, many receive $400 to $600 monthly, or $4,800 to $7,200 yearly - and some receive much less.(22)

C. Peter Wagner asks, "How can they do it so cheaply?" Concerning the Evangelical Missionary Society of Nigeria (which reported 213 cross-cultural missionaries in 1979), he writes:

> I have some clues from a series of mimeographed reports I have recently received from survey teams led by the E.M.S. secretary, Panya Baba. The report describes new areas, attempts to locate the most responsive peoples, makes recommendations for church planting, suggests the number of missionaries needed, and then a section follows: "How the Evangelist Might Make a Living." This report assumes that the missionaries will so identify with the people that they will make their own living right where they minister. Among the possible occupations are poultry raising, vegetable gardening, growing fruit trees, tailoring, and merchandising. A report like this wouldn't recruit many white-footed missionaries, but apparently large numbers of black-footed missionaries are accepting the challenge.(23)

While the issue of finances is never a simple one, it must be acknowledged that many Third World missionaries can be supported for a much lower amount than their Western counterparts.

3) The third consideration for judging the Third World to be a great missionary force is a missiological one: the potential for missionary recruitment is greater in the Third World than anywhere else. This is true not only because of the large masses of people among whom societies can evangelize and recruit, but also because of the already large churches from which there are believers presently demonstrating a responsiveness to God's call.

It is estimated "that by the year 2000, 60% of the world's Christians will be non-white."(24) Ready to work toward making that become a reality are such churches as the Full Gospel Central

Church in Seoul, Korea with over 160,000 members. Also proclaiming
its desire to reach the world for Christ is the Asia Theological
Association with Korean Joon Gon Kim estimating that six new
churches are being started each day in Korea by various denominations.(25) The present expanding base for missionary recruitment
in Korea is significant.

The largest Protestant sanctuary in the world has been built
in Brazil by the Brazil for Christ *(Brazil para Cristo)* denomination; its seating capacity is 25,000. It has also been reported
that nearly 3,000 new evangelical congregations have been planted
each year by various Brazilian groups.(26) In Guatemala, because
of its large and expanding church, some report that it could
become the first "majority" Protestant country in Latin America.
In fact, the church growth *and* potential for missionary recruitment throughout Latin America is extremely impressive.

David Barrett, research secretary of the Anglican Consultative
Council in Nairobi, Kenya, estimates that two-fifths of the total
African population is identified as Christian (with more than six
million Africans being added to Christianity each year, at an
astonishing rate of 16,000 believers a day).(27) One illustration
of Africa's large Christian church is found in Nigeria. Here the
Church of Christ has been rated as one of the fastest growing
churches in the world. "The church has grown by 400% in ten years
to a total strength of half a million, with only 350 full-time
African pastors and 3,000 part-time evangelists."(28) Connected
with this large Christian segment is the fact that in 1979
Nigeria's Evangelical Churches of West Africa (ECWA) added 138
married couples to their missionary force (an impressive feat by
any standards), and collected contributions from Nigerians during
1978 totaling nearly $250,000.(29)

Many Third World church contexts are large and growing, providing a platform from which to recruit missionaries. Some, however,
are much smaller. Yet even in Japan (.5% of the total population
being Christian), the believers have organized more missionary
societies than any other Asian country except India. In Burma,
a poor country with 3.5% of its 32 million population identified
as Protestant, the believers have sent at least 900 missionary
evangelists.(30)

With the facts listed in the book *Operation World*, it is possible to estimate that the total Protestant population in the Third
World is almost 158 million believers.(31) This is a striking
base for missionary recruitment. But, in order to understand the
significance of this fact, let me suggest a paradigm. If we
suppose that an average missionary recruitment percentage is 4%
of a total church membership (as it actually is in many U.S. sending societies, with some even higher, i.e. Assembly of God with

10% or Christian and Missionary Alliance with 9%), the potential missionary total would be 631,872 missionaries within the Third World Protestant church. Sadly, the actual number of missionaries is much lower. Nevertheless, the present and expanding potential for reaching the unreached by Third World Christians is a fact which is significant for the total future picture of world evangelization.

4) The last theme indicating the importance of this fourth phase of missionary endeavor is an organizational one: Third World missionary societies are not bound to follow Western organizational structures. Some seem to be involved in mission with little or no structure (i.e., Tzeltal Christians of Mexico; Chinese Christians in Burma). Others possess a simplified structure to complete one mission (i.e., Aymara Indians to the Navajo Indians in the States). There is no obligation on the part of Third World mission societies to pattern themselves after Western forms. In characterizing societies from the Third World, simplistically, Asian societies (particularly Indian) seem to follow more closely the independent "faith mission" structures (i.e., Voice of Gospel and Church Growth Missionary Movement in India, The Philippine Evangelical Mission, The Asian Evangelistic Fellowship of Singapore). African societies seem to be developed not as independent societies, but more as part of denominational communities (whether Protestant or African Independent); while Latin American missionary activities are often centered upon individual or small group outreach (although Brazil, like India, has developed many denominational and independent faith mission structures). Within these three regions, there is quite a diverse arrangement of organizational forms.

Specifically, some are supported by various individuals, some by a church or denomination. Some report monthly to the receiving community, some to the sending society. Some agencies employ "tentmaking" practices, some supply a limited specialized service to the existing church. As we shall see later, the diversity is enormous and such diversity enhances cultural adaptability and effectiveness. There might be many more societies which do not receive mention even in these pages because they have a form unrecognizable to Western eyes. Take, for example, the numerous Argentine missionaries who are ministering in dozens of locations throughout Latin America, yet who are not listed in these pages for lack of a known label and structure. Such diversity is hard to tabulate, yet indicates that Third World missionaries can operate under many circumstances, an important factor contributing towards the role which they are beginning to have in world evangelization.

God desires than no one perish without having a chance to accept His Son's redemption. The fourth phase of missionary endeavor indicates that his *whole* body is engaged in presenting Christ's

message. No longer are there only certain sending countries and
no longer are those that receive only receiving countries. Each
nation (including the United States) is both a sending and a receiving country. Missions is no longer dominated by the West; it
involves the whole world. However, one key question for us is,
"Are we of the West prepared to trust the Holy Spirit to lead the
Christians of Asia (Africa and Latin America)...or must a control-
ling Western hand be permanently resting on the Ark of God?"(32)
Our answer to this question will largely determine how we participate in God's ever expanding kingdom in the years to come.

2

FROM PATERNALISM
TO PARTNERSHIP

Chapter 2

FROM PATERNALISM TO PARTNERSHIP

For God so loved the world, that He gave His only
begotten Son, that whoever believes in Him should not
perish, but have eternal life. For God did not send
the Son into the world to judge the world; but that the
world should be saved through Him. He who believes in
Him is not judged; he who does not believe has been
judged already, because he has not believed in the name
of the only begotten Son of God (John 3:16-18).

The words of Jesus are clear and precise. Mission is central
to God's plan. Throughout Scripture, God reveals that redemption
is His major concern. The Psalmist writes, "Proclaim good tidings
of His salvation from day to day. Tell of His glory among the
nations, His wonderful deeds among all peoples" (Ps. 96:2-3).
Isaiah the prophet declares, "In the last days, the mountain of
the house of the Lord will be established as the chief of the
mountains, and will be raised above the hills; and all the nations
will stream to it" (Is. 2:2). Matthew, in his book directed to
Jewish hearers, states that "This gospel of the kingdom shall be
preached in the whole world for a witness to all the nations; and
then the end shall come" (Matt. 24:14). Mark also writes, "Go
into all the world and preach the gospel to all creation" (Mark
16:15). It is within this framework that Jesus reveals God's
plan. Jesus came to this world so that "the world should be saved
through Him." It is this message which comes from God and which
must be proclaimed. In the words of theologian Johannes Blauw,
the mission of the church is to be considered"...not as an historical phenomenon but as a commission from God."(1)

The Apostle Peter informs us that our Lord is "not wishing for
any to perish, but all to come to repentance" (II Pet. 3:9). This
means that the scope of our mission is the *world*. God wills that
the Bangaru people of India, the Xavante of Brazil and the race-
track residents of the United States come to repentance. He wills
that each of the estimated 16,750 separate peoples who have not
yet heard His name (some 2/3 of the world's population) recognize
His Son as Savior and Lord. This is a momentous challenge, a near
impossible task. The only way it can ever be achieved is if we
humble ourselves before God and spiritually join hands with
Christian believers everywhere. If it is important to plant "a
growing cluster of churches for every people by the year 2000"(2)
we in the West must work interdependently *with* those from other
lands.

Today there is a growing openness on the part of Western missionary agencies for evangelistic partnership with their non-Western
counterparts. In evangelical circles, this awareness hardly
existed even ten years ago. As Warren Webster, General Director
of the Conservative Baptist Foreign Mission Society writes, "We
look forward to the 1980s as a decade of partnership with Third
World churches and mission societies, confident that our Lord
will fulfill His promise that, if He is lifted up, He will draw
all people to Himself."(3)

With the great potential for missionary partnership, we could
conceivably be entering one of the greatest decades ever for world
evangelization. Yet the prospects have not always been so favorable. In order to be faithful to all opportunities, it is
necessary to have an understanding of God's biblical model for
cooperation as well as the historical attempts at cooperation in
the past. Hopefully, this will make it possible to avoid the
mistakes of the past and within a biblical framework maximize
present opportunities.

PARTNERSHIP - A BIBLICAL EXAMPLE

One of the most developed metaphors in Scripture portraying the
Christian church is the Body of Christ. In almost every New Testament book, the Holy Spirit uses the symbol of the human body to
clarify deep spiritual truth. God wants the nature of His Church
clearly understood. Thus He has delineated His character by using
one of the most familiar of His creations - the human body.
Certainly this symbol is a major factor in understanding what the
church is, from God's point of view.

In I Corinthians 12:12-27, the Apostle Paul begins by making
the comparison between one's physical body and Christ's spiritual
body of believers. Within this passage he cites three basic

components of the illustration. First in verses 12 and 13, he
reminds his readers that just as each person has only one physical
body, so the church of Jesus Christ consists of only one universal
spiritual body. The *unity* of Christ's church is highlighted by
the number of times the word "one" is used within just these two
verses. This oneness is not necessarily an organizational union
but rather an organic unity. Union is an external structure unit-
ing individuals through a binding organizational form or system;
unity is an inherent cohesiveness which makes the many essentially
one in God's Spirit. Thus, union is an external bond; unity a
relational, innate oneness. Within the body of Christ, the
members possess a spiritual unity, an imparted spiritual oneness
which is centered upon the body's leader, Jesus Christ.

The second basic component cited in this passage is *diversity*
(vs. 14-20). While on the surface the "diversity" of the body may
seem to contradict the "unity" of the body, Paul clarifies the
emphasis by writing, "For the body is not one member, but many"
(vs. 14). The subject here is not the whole church but rather the
specific members. Each Christian has received different spiritual
gift(s), natural talents, ethnotheological insights, and
culturally-oriented personalities, all of which contribute towards
the body. Christ's local *and* universal body is composed of these
multi-diverse elements.

The third basic component of Christ's body mentioned in I Corinthians 12:21-27 is the key to the previous two. It is the dependence which each member has upon the other for overall balance and
maturity (vs. 21-27). This interdependence between believers can
be called *mutuality*. It is the quality of life experienced when
various members of the body work together for mutual encouragement, fellowship and training. The capstone to Paul's illustration is verse 27: "And if one member suffers, all the members
suffer with it; if one member is honored, all the members rejoice
with it." Elsewhere Paul writes, "For just as we have many members
in one body and all the members do not have the same function, so
we, who are many, are one body in Christ, and *individually members
of* one another" (Rom. 12:4-5).

Although there are human limitations to the total application
of "body mutuality" nevertheless God's ideal continues to be our
goal - to experience as many interdependent relationships as is
humanly possible. And if we apply this principle to international
missions, the idea of "organizational mutuality" becomes valid.
If each Christian missionary is part of Christ's one body, diverse
in his or her own way, yet essential for continual balance and
growth of the church, then it should be valid to display this
spiritual mutuality by inter-organizational cooperation. However,
in the world of Christian missions, this truth has only rarely

been put into practice. When the countries of the Third World
began to develop their own national mission sending agencies, all
too often the attitude of those in the West was not one of antici-
patory partnership, but of paternalistic superiority. It has taken
decades for Westerners to recognize what God has already developed
within the Third World. So a review of the historical development
of missionary partnership is important in order to avoid such
mistakes in the future and to enhance the manifestation of "body
mutuality."

PARTNERSHIP - A HISTORICAL DEVELOPMENT

The story of early Third World missionary activity is exciting!
It includes societies much older than the Sudan Interior Mission,
the Southern Baptists or the Overseas Missionary Fellowship. As
Wagner writes:

> In the 1820's, for example, missionaries like Josua
> Mateinaniu were hopping from one island to another in the
> Pacific. This is one reason why Oceania is almost entirely
> Christian today. In the 1830's, some Jamaicans, led by
> Joseph Merrick, pioneered the missionary movement to the
> Cameroons. By 1884, Methodist missionaries were going out
> from India to Malaysia. In 1907, the Korean Presbyterians
> began sending missionaries, among the first being Kee Pung
> Lee. One of history's most effective missionary societies
> called the Melanesian Brotherhood, was organized in the
> 1920's in Oceania.(4)

One of the most famous of India's nearly one hundred societies is
the Indian Missionary Society, founded in 1909 to evangelize other
cultures within the country. Also, in 1925, the unique Dipti
Mission for tribal evangelism was formed. In 1939, the Apostles
Revelation Society was formed in Ghana to reach Ghanians and
eventually Togoans. For over 150 years, the Third World has
been quietly active in cross-cultural evangelistic endeavors! Yet
only in the last fifty years have Western churchmen received these
Third World leaders as equals in "near-neighbor" evangelism, and
only in the last ten years has the topic of mutual ministry for
world evangelism been widely discussed. What Paul illustrates in
Scripture is only now finding fulfillment.

The reasons for this lag are many. Communication worldwide has
not always been easy. Travel and personal acquaintance with these
foreign societies was often difficult. The natural concern has
always been with one's own work. Yes, there were some informed
people, knowledgeable of these indigenous endeavors. Often they
themselves were influential in establishing additional new missions.

But the official relationship for more than one hundred years
between Western and non-Western mission sending societies was
generally one of paternalism. This is apparent from both the ecumenical and evangelical missionary histories - a relationship
which has only slowly become full partnership in both cases. As
a brief study of these missionary histories reveal, Paul's
Apostolic teaching is difficult to obey.

Phase One: Church-Centered Relationships

The year 1910 was a highlight in Western mission history.
North American societies were in their early formative stages.
In considering this period, Kenneth S. Latourette, dean of
Christian historians, praised "the courageous initiative of
missionaries, who singlehanded or by two's and three's dared to
bring their faith to areas hitherto untouched by Christianity."(5)
The goal of those who went out was obedience to the Great Commis-
sion; much of the impetus in their movement came from one of North
America's greatest missionary statesmen, John R. Mott.

In 1890, Mott founded the World Student Christian Federation
which began to enlist students for evangelistic causes. In 1900,
under Mott's leadership, 1400 students from 200 colleges gathered
in London for an International Student Volunteer Missionary Movement Conference. And it was Mott eight years later who sent out
questionnaires to missionaries overseas in an attempt to prepare
for one of the most decisive conferences ever held in the 20th
century.

In 1910, at the height of North American missionary interest,
over 1200 delegates met in Edinburgh for the First World Missionary
Conference. This gathering was to become the "model" for mission
conferences, the birth of ecumenism, the incentive for evangelizing the world in one generation. It attracted the attention of
world political leaders such as His Majesty King George V of
England and ex-president Roosevelt who both sent messages of
commendation. Edinburgh 1910 has been labeled "a watershed."
"It gave to missions a new outlook, that the whole world is the
mission field, and there is no church that is not a church in
the mission field."(6)

Unfortunately, Western relationships with the already existing
Third World mission agencies left much to be desired at Edinburgh
1910. "Only 18 participants were from the younger churches and
these were not representatives of their own churches, but of
Western missionary societies."(7) As Ralph Winter writes:

The most incredible single error of judgment in mission
strategy in the 20th century is the fact that although there

were in fact by 1910 a handful of younger missions (what
we now call Third World Missions) - not merely younger
churches - it is a simple matter of historical fact that
not a single one of these precious little green shoots
springing up was invited.(8)

Evangelistic outreach was ethnocentric, viewed essentially as
something to be performed by trained Western churchmen. Although,
respect for younger churches was expressed, full independence was
granted to them only when they were "qualified." Unconsciously
and unfortunately, paternalism dominated the proceedings. It was
apparent in the language used (i.e., "older, mature churches" vs.
"younger, immature churches"). And, one of the flagrant examples
of paternalism involved the "mature" churches establishing *for*
the "younger" churches the necessary guidelines for church discipline. Edinburgh 1910 also designated the national leaders from
these "younger" churches to "become the agents of Christianizing
(Westernizing?) their national life."(9)

    As time went on, there were other church-centered conferences
which slowly progressed in accepting and implementing full, interdependent partnership. This aspect begins with the missionary
conference of 1928 held in Jerusalem, sponsored by the newly
established (1921) International Missionary Council (I.M.C.), the
continuation committee of Edinburgh 1910.

    At Jerusalem in 1928, the meeting of the Council brought
    together a larger number of representatives of the "younger"
    churches than had ever before attended an ecumenical gather-
    ing. They were not merely the nominees of missionary
    societies, but were the chosen representatives of the
    National Christian Councils which had grown with vigour
    since Edinburgh 1910.(10)

Of 230 delegates, 111 were from the "younger churches" of which
54 were national leaders. In comparison with Edinburgh 1910 which
invited 1% of its delegation from the Third World, Jerusalem had
48%, 23% of the total being Third World leaders rather than
missionaries. During the post-World War I era, many countries
were beginning to experience a new sense of national unity and
pride. Demands for self-determination were heard. Many "leaders
of the so-called younger churches were very much in the vanguard
of this struggle"(11) and for them to participate together with
Western leaders made visible the interdependent nature of Christ's
body.

    Because of Jerusalem, the relationship between the "younger"
and "older" churches began to change. From paternalism to partnership, a new mutual identity emerged. The mission of Christ was

defined as the "mission of the church" in which all participate.
Partnership was the new theme. As missiologist Jerald D. Gort,
professor at the Free University of Amsterdam writes:

> Mission is never "finished", for it belongs to the very
> being of the church. (At Jerusalem) it was not an euthanasia
> of mission that was needed, but a mercy killing of missionary
> imperialism, paternalism, superiority complexes; mission
> itself however - church-centric mission - must remain every-
> where.(12)

The next step in world missionary relationships came in 1938
when the Western-oriented International Missionary Council chose
a Third World country for its global gathering. The place was
India. In the words of Charles W. Ranson, a General Secretary
for the I.M.C.:

> At Tambaram, near Madras (India)...the delegates from
> the younger churches were approximately equal in number
> to those from the older. This conference produced a
> wealth of detailed and explicit thought and planning
> concerning the main aspects of the missionary task. It
> gave striking expression to the strength and solidarity
> of the world church. The representatives of China and
> Japan - whose countries were at war - and of the western
> powers, whose relations were strained almost to the break-
> ing point, shared together in a common fellowship of
> thought and worship.(13)

The central theme of the Madras Conference was "the upbuilding
of the younger churches as a part of the historic universal Christian community."(14) Although paternalistic in title (i.e.,
"younger"), the proceedings demonstrated a true partnership in
both planning and missionary practice. Like Christ's interrelated
body, churches of both "older" and "younger" traditions were
committed to preach the evangelistic message of the New Testament.
To many, this meant the spreading "of the *evangelion,* the saving
message of Jesus Christ and the Kingdom of God, in the whole world,
among all men and nations."(15)

At last, within this first phase of church-centered structures,
partnership had become the central theme expressing active missionary relationships worldwide. And it has continued both in the
other major conferences (Whitby, 1947; Willingen, 1952; Ghana,
1958; New Delhi, 1961; Uppsala, 1968; Nairobi, 1975), and in the
major assemblies sponsored by the more limited Commission on World
Mission and Evangelism (Mexico, 1963; Bangkok, 1973; Melbourne,
1980). Since Edinburgh 1910, the unceasing concern has been to
include, in a growing percentage, participants from all churches
everywhere. The strength of the ecumenical position, therefore,

has been its inclusiveness. It has consciously worked to produce
a functional partnership. On the other hand, however, the inherent
weakness within this inclusiveness has been its willingness to
tolerate diverse theological persuasions. While strong on partnership, the Lordship of Jesus Christ has been interpreted in a limit-
less variety of ways. Such issues as biblical authority, the
uniqueness of Jesus Christ and the unwavering and universal need to
proclaim his saving atonement have been given exclusively humanistic
interpretations.

The inherent weakness of the ecumenical stance become visible
during the historic 1961 world gathering in New Delhi, India when
the International Missionary Council merged into the World Council
of Churches. The I.M.C. represented missionary societies and
received direct representation from them. The W.C.C. represented
churches and pastoral concerns. Ideally both needed to remain
distinct and project a separate, strong emphasis for balance and
growth. Yet the tragedy occurred when missions was redefined and
absorbed into parish priorities. As the desire for worldwide
partnership among churches continued, missions and direct missionary representation lost their unique identity and voice.
Furthermore, a new socio-political definition of evangelism was
developed at the World Conference on Church and Society (1966)
and officially accepted at the Fourth General Assembly of the
World Council of Churches in Uppsala (1968). This pattern of
thought represented a significant departure from the historical
position of Biblical evangelism and caused a reaction among many
Christian leaders worldwide. This departure prompted the formation of an alternate group which stressed theological conservatism
and missions as their two strengths. But worldwide partnership
among the proponents of this evangelical group was slow to
blossom.

Phase Two: Mission-Centered Relationships

The history of North American evangelical missionary endeavor,
while spanning more than seventy years, began its ascendancy after
the Second World War with the founding of the Evangelical Foreign
Missions Association in 1945. The event which widely publicized
the evangelical movement, however, was the World Congress on
Evangelism, held in Berlin in 1966. For ten days, 1200 participants from over one hundred nations discussed the urgency of
presenting a clear evangelistic message; the stated goal (like
Edinburgh 1910) was "the evangelization of the human race in this
generation by every means God has given to the mind and will of
men."(16) While Berlin was significant in the fact that it
brought together so many Christian workers from all parts of the
globe, the true reflection of evangelical missionary relationships
during this period preceded Berlin by six months and was labeled,

"the largest ecumenical strategy conference of Protestant missionaries ever held in North America."(17)

In April, 1966, in Wheaton, Illinois, 938 delegates from 71
countries met at Wheaton College for the Congress on the Church's
Worldwide Mission. Of major importance is the fact that this
gathering was sponsored by the two great North American evangelical missionary organizations: the Interdenominational Foreign
Mission Association (I.F.M.A.) and the Evangelical Foreign Mission
Associations (E.F.M.A.). In 1966 these two groups represented
13,000 missionaries who worked in more than 120 nations. Because
of several factors, including the theological inclusiveness of the
church-centered movement, these two primary sponsors called for a
congress to assess the rapidly developing evangelical missionary
enterprise. Like the Berlin Congress soon to follow, the central
concern throughout was theological. The call to the congress
stated that "its compelling aim (was) to bring into focus the
Biblical mandate to evangelize the world."(18)

Of significance to us is the way in which the congress was convened. It was both proper and necessary that the sponsors confront
the grave issues of the day. Communism, theological liberalism
and evangelical attempts at self-identification were pan-cultural
realities. But at Wheaton, essentially North American versions
were the only interpretation given. The "fulness of time" had not
yet arrived for thinking in terms of reciprocal Third World missionary relationships. What Madras (1938) voiced did not yet
affect the Wheaton delegates. Thus, of the 87 committee members,
program personnel and consultants listed, only six (or 7% of the
whole) were Third World leaders without financial and/or organizational ties to the West.(19) It was a North American conference
convened for North Americans.

Under the historical circumstances, this paternalism can be both
understood and accepted on the basis that it is necessary to come
to terms with one's identity before entering into broader missionary participation. This is what Wheaton accomplished. The
genuine dismay comes when, just five years later, at another major
strategy conference, the agenda *once again* reflected shortsighted
paternalism.

In 1971, over 400 leaders from various E.F.M.A. and I.F.M.A.
related organizations (representing 16,000 missionaries by that
time), met at Green Lake, Wisconsin for a week-long conference.
The theme was central to our present concerns: church-mission
tensions and relationships. Yet, like Wheaton in 1966, Green Lake
virtually ignored national Third World leadership. There were no
non-Western spokesmen among the 16 chosen major contributors and,
in fact, of the 378 participating delegates, only 17 (or 4% of the
total) were non-Western leaders.(20) This can be seen as a real
tragedy since the discussion centered on East-West relationships.

With that as a theme, the conference included all too few representatives from the nearly 200 already existing Third World
mission sending organizations. Even the representation from the
myriad of national "receiving" churches was generally considered
inadequate. As Pius Wakatama, one African evangelical leader,
wrote:

> The Green Lake Conference could have had far-reaching
> results because of its timeliness. What most limited its
> effectiveness was,...that it was an Americans-only confer-
> ence. The few nationals attending were mostly students
> who happened to be in the country. They were not invited
> as full participants but as "resource personnel." None
> of them presented major papers even though many of them
> had strong opinions on the subject and were well-qualified
> to speak since they were leaders in their own countries.
>
> The structure of this conference reflected the same
> paternalism and short-sightedness which is making some
> nationals call for a moratorium. Here were four hundred
> American missionaries and mission executives discussing
> such a key issue affecting their relationships with
> churches overseas, and yet the leadership of those
> churches was not included in the discussions. It was a
> one-sided conference.(21)

From the North American perspective, Ted W. Engstrom, currently
Executive Director of World Vision, Inc., reported:

> Delegates were urged often by the conference leader-
> ship to "listen" to the voices from overseas, but,
> unfortunately, the few men representing national church
> leadership were a minority and the "listening" process
> was pretty much more one of mission leader "listening"
> to fellow-mission-leader.(22)

Hector Espinoza from Mexico was one of the few national "consultants." He expressed one reason North American missionaries have
difficulties:

> By the end of the conference it was easy to discover
> at least one of the causes of (missionary) tension: out
> of fifteen national "consultants," only six received the
> opportunity of addressing the conference in a general
> session, and then, it was obvious to some mission execu-
> tives and nationals, that unfortunately there still
> widely prevails the old mentality of having the mis-
> sionary do all the talking and let the national do all
> the hearing.(23)

One glimmer of change from paternalism to partnership can be
seen in Dennis Clark, itinerate missionary with the Bible and
Medical Missionary Fellowship. In 1971, he published a book
entitled, *The Third World and Mission*. This popularly written,
well-timed emphasis on Third World missions immediately influenced
North American leadership towards missionary partnership. Less
than one year later, C. Peter Wagner edited the follow-up treatise
to Green Lake '71 entitled, *Church/missions Tensions Today*.
Surprisingly, many of Clark's concerns were mirrored in a rapid
about-face only months after Green Lake. For example, Warren
Webster, General Director of the Conservative Baptist Foreign
Mission Society, wrote:

> The establishment of indigenous churches is no longer
> seen as an adequate end and goal of biblical missions
> unless such churches become "sending" churches in, and
> from, their own milieu. The New Testament knows nothing
> of "receiving" churches which are not also in turn to be
> "sending" churches. To this end the founding of national
> mission societies and the entrance into mission of national
> churches on every continent are cause for profound grati-
> tude and continued encouragement.... We are beginning to
> see churches in Japan, as well as in Taiwan, Korea, the
> Philippines, Indonesia, India and elsewhere accepting
> the missionary responsibility which of necessity lies
> upon the church in every place, not just in western
> lands.(24)

In the same chapter, Webster calls for partnership, not paternalism; "the key word for mission/church relationships," he says,
"is partnership."(25)

Another contribution in Wagner's book is a case study from
Vietnam written by T. Grady Mangham, Jr., a mission executive with
the Christian and Missionary Alliance. He reports on the missionary sending nature of the pre-war Vietnamese church and how
this might be an example of partnership. The key question was
raised by Ralph D. Winter in his stimulating chapter, "The Planting
of Younger Missions." "What I would like to know," asked Winter,
"is why the sending of missionaries by the younger church is so
relatively rare a phenomenon, and, if discussed, is so widely
conceived to be a 'later on' type of thing."(26) What he suggested was additional study to produce a "directory of the missions
originating in the non-Western world."(27)

The advice was heeded! In the same year (1972), at the Fuller
Seminary School of World Mission, in Pasadena, California, C. Peter
Wagner coordinated a first-of-its-kind research project. With
student assistance from Peter Larson, James Wong and Edward Pentecost,

questionnaires were sent to Africa, Asia and Latin America resulting in a directory of 210 agencies which reportedly sent out a
total of 3,404 missionaries.(28) This information helped to open
wide the door of missionary partnership.

A year later, in his opening statement to the International
Congress on World Evangelization, Billy Graham set the mood by
saying that the world "will never be reached by 'near-neighbor'
evangelism." Before 2,700 participants in Lausanne, Switzerland
in 1974, Graham continued:

> To build our evangelistic policies on "near-neighbor"
> evangelism alone is to shut out at least a billion from
> any possibility of knowing the Savior.

> Churches of every land, therefore, must deliberately
> send out evangelists and missionaries to master other
> languages, learn other cultures, live in them perhaps
> for life, and thus evangelize these multitudes. Thus
> we should reject the idea of a moratorium on sending
> missionaries.... The Christians in Nigeria are not
> just to evangelize Nigeria, nor the Christians in Peru
> just the people of Peru. God's heartbeat is for the
> world.(29)

To this end approximately half of the major papers and reports
were presented by national Third World leaders. There was even
a functional report entitled "Third World Missions." One of its
summary statements was "National cooperation is needed for the
purpose of sharing of ideas, fellowship, prayer support, and
financial assistance wherever the need arises."(30) The report
also felt sufficient liberty to state that "the structure should
be formulated and directed by the national mission church people
and should not be a carbon copy of Western mission structure."(31)

As a significant follow-up to these thoughts, 900 pastors,
evangelists, denominational executives, missionaries, professors
of mission and religious journalists met in Pattaya, Thailand to
discuss partnership in world evangelization. During ten days,
from June 16 to 27, 1980, representatives from 87 countries
studied how to define and select a "people grouping," and how
to win the chosen "people" to Christ. The majority of the
participants were Third World leaders - thus implying that within
the worldwide evangelical partnership, the major responsibility
for world evangelization lies upon the Third World church. It
is essentially their task to discern "people groupings," to
contextualize the Gospel without jeopardizing its uniqueness,
and to preach it unashamedly. The hope for achieving an evangelized world lies with them!

Specifically Third World *mission* leaders, however, were then the highlight of the World Consultation on Third World Missions, held four months later at Edinburgh, Scotland. This was a smaller conference of 275 leaders who were, as in 1910, exclusively delegates of mission agencies (whether denominational or interdenominational). An astonishing third of the delegates (and a third of the 171 agencies represented) were Third World. Three of the four major plenary addresses in the morning were assigned to Third World leaders (George Samuel, Petros Octavianus and Panya Baba). One half of the popular evening plenaries were carried by Third World mission leaders (N. J. Gnaniah and Thomas Wang). For the first time in history, a large number of Third World mission leaders worked together with their Western counterparts as equals in a world-level conference of mission leaders. In history's only other world-level conference made up exclusively of mission leaders, in 1910, as Ralph Winter has noted (see above, page 21), the only Third World mission leaders then existing were apparently overlooked and not even invited. It is to be recorded that although a larger number of agencies were represented at Edinburgh in 1980 than in 1910 the 1980 gathering represented a smaller proportion of the total number of agencies worldwide. The mission structure itself, in 1980, was being more widely questioned in World Council circles and even in some Evangelical circles.

The 1980's

History reveals that it is difficult to develop both partnership in world mission and balance in the Christian message. Only once before has a similar dynamic combination existed. That began in 1910 at Edinburgh and continued for approximately twenty-five years during the initial stirrings of the ecumenical movement. However, the significance of the 1980's is that once again there is just such a combination. Not only is there balance in a widely recognized message (i.e., The Lausanne Covenant) but the idea of partnership is the conscious concern of those connected with Lausanne and Pattaya. Knowledge regarding *what* must be done is widely dispersed. The missing element is *who* specifically will do it and *how* will they mutually cooperate together for greater effectiveness.

African Pius Wakatama is concerned that mission organizations worldwide be aware "that the body of Christ is international and interracial in nature."(32) As Michael C. Griffiths of Overseas Missionary Fellowship once said concerning his organization:

We in OMF today are not only international, but interracial, so that "missionary" is no longer synonymous with "Western". We have Chinese missionaries from Hong Kong, Singapore and Malaysia. We have Japanese, Filipino, Maori and Fijian missionaries.... The missionary body is

increasingly international, so we are not saying, "Do you
want a Western missionary?" but rather, "Do you want an
international missionary?" These may be of any race or
color, and I think this is a very positive approach to
missions in the 20th century.(33)

The key to the 1980's is not paternalism but partnership. It
is not only a Western partnership among those of like kind, but
an international partnership among those of different kinds; not
a denominational partnership, limited to one's own group, but one
based cross-denominationally upon one's personal confession of
Jesus Christ as Lord. It is God who honors such reciprocal
partnerships with the evidence of much fruit; and it is each of
us who is responsible to learn from the past, apply biblical truth
and maximize present opportunities for world evangelization.

3

VARIETIES OF
NON-WESTERN MISSIONS

The "renewed mind" is one of the Apostle Paul's most prominent
themes. Throughout his letters, he encourages Christ's followers
to think on God's truths and to meditate upon His ways. In Romans
12:2, Paul expresses his basic challenge for Christian maturity,
"Do not be conformed to this world, but be transformed by the
renewing of your mind, that you may prove what the will of God
is, that which is good and acceptable and perfect."

According to Paul, each believer is responsible to study God's
written word and to understand God's actions. He uses words such
as "knowledge," "learning," "believe," or "understand" to indicate
an important truth: a follower of God can be judged by what he
thinks and how his thoughts influence his actions. A Christian is
one who believes (Rom. 10:9-10), who exercises faith (Eph. 2:8-9;
Heb. 11:6), who mentally recognizes Jesus as Savior and volition-
ally accepts Him as Lord (Acts 16:31). He is the one whose
righteous actions find their origin in righteous thoughts (Eph.
4:17-24), whose growth and maturation takes place through mental
renewal (Col. 3:10; II Cor. 3:18). When Paul writes that a transformed life comes from a renewed mind (Rom. 12:2), he is not merely
giving advice, but stating the basis for personal Christian development. As Solomon so aptly summarizes, "For as a man thinks within
himself, so he is" (Prov. 23:7).

Often within the Third World, God's perspective on the Christian
life has been clothed in Western garb. The "renewed mind" and all
that it entails has been seen through Western eyes. Definitions,
insights, interpretations, even applications of God's truth have

been suggested by those foreign to the non-Western countries and
context. The historical roots for many of the Protestant denominations within the Third World, the sources for nearly all sacred
hymns and Bible translations, the patterns of ministry and of
ministerial training generally originate in the West. And along
with this, there has been introduced into most non-Western countries the same polarization which separates social concerns from
evangelistic work. The mark of "foreignness" is stamped upon many
churches and mission agencies originating within the non-Western
world; for them "renewal" has meant the acceptance of Western
"Christianization."

One of the more recent and significant developments within the
Third World, in a natural reaction against "Westernization" has
been the rise of an indigenous searching of God's Word. When
evangelical North Americans began serious recognition of non-
Western missions, many national Third World leaders were already
involved in their own critical reflection of Scripture. Their
desire has been to formulate a "regionalized" renewed mind, to
interpret God's Word for themselves in their own context in an
attempt to personalize the Bible's authority to their unique
situations.

Though little known to Western believers, the explosive growth
of Third World theologies is presently incalculable. Instead of
Geneva, London, Wheaton or Pasadena being key Protestant centers,
other cities have now become prominent. Singapore, Buenos Aires,
San Jose, Nairobi and Jos are all places in the forefront of
evangelical Third World thought. No longer are non-Western missionaries solely dependent upon Europe or North America for their
biblical interpretation. There are many active "national" scho-
lars who influence the structure and scope of missionary service.
Believers in Africa, Asia or Latin America can now look to their
own national brothers for biblical training and understanding.

Throughout these pages, many of these Third World voices will
be quoted. Yet it must be emphasized that although a wide variety
of authors and theological positions are presented, they are cited
to demonstrate the dynamic of Third World critical reflection without necessarily approving of their whole theological line. Indigenous Biblical expertise is vast and varied; both liberal and
conservative positions exist. But they are reported only to
portray the present panorama, not to project any one particular
philosophy.

CONTEXTUALIZATION

An Explanation

Leslie Newbigin, a prominent Anglican leader and mission strate-
gist believes that mission "is an acting out of fundamental
belief."(1) The fundamental belief to which Newbigin refers can
be almost anything. Whatever one believes structures the way he
or she performs and proclaims the gospel. In essence, this is the
Scriptural principle of the renewed mind applied to mission.
Whatever we hold dear concerning the Christian faith will directly
mold the nature of our witness. If the Gospel is viewed horizon-
tally, emphasizing primarily the cup of cold water given in Jesus'
name, missionary endeavor obeys this premise and follows this
pattern. If the Gospel is understood vertically, emphasizing the
centrality of Christ's cross and the need for each person to
accept God's sacrifice, then mission is structured in this fashion,
communicating Christ's redemptive act and encouraging a personal
response. This fundamental belief is for mission what fuel is for
a fire. Without it there is no flame or heat.

Significantly, the one fundamental belief among both evangelicals
and those of ecumenical persuasions is an anthropological one. The
one constant directive which affects Third World mission everywhere
is the concept of contextualization. The word means the continual
appropriation of God's revealed Word to the specific location,
wherever that location might be. Like the word "indigeneity," it
assumes that one's biblical study is rooted *in* and identified *with*
a specific culture. However, unlike indigeneity, contextualization bridges one's past with his present real needs. In other words,
contextualization is a dynamic term, recognizing the need for constant update, while attempting to be culturally relevant with God's
unique message.

From the Third World, Shoki Coe, one of the original proponents
of contextualization and past principal of Tainan Theological
College in Taiwan defines contextuality as "that critical assess-
ment of what makes the context really significant in the light of
the *Missio Dei*."(2) Simplifying this, Japanese Yoshinobu Kumazawa
uses the word "relevance." "When we discuss relevance as a theological issue, we have to think of it in terms of relevance to
the Word of God and relevance to the situation in which we live.
That means there must be relevance to the text and the context."(3)

In Lima, from October 30 to November 9, 1979, the Second Latin
American Congress on Evangelism (or CLADE II) affirmed the need
for understanding Scripture within a particular historical context."(4) This conference, which could be one of the most significant for Protestants in Latin America, vibrated with this theme.

C. Rene Padilla affirms that, "The concern for the contextualization of the gospel reflected in that first address (by Prof. Emilio
Antonio Nunez) became one of the dominant notes throughout the
congress."(5) Contextualization, he suggests, is one of the
greatest needs within Latin America today.

In an address given at the triennal general assembly of the
Association of Evangelicals of Africa and Madagascar, General
Secretary Tokunboh Adeyemo states:

> The theological prospects and religious movements in
> Africa resemble the world of the second and third centuries
> of the Christian era. Theirs was a time of doctrinal strife
> that called for ecumenical efforts to formulate creeds and
> a positive Christian apologetic. Likewise, evangelicals
> in Africa need a system that will express theological con-
> cepts in terms of African situations. Theology in Africa
> should scratch where it itches.(6)

In the same light, the Rev. Gottfried Osei-Mensah, General Secretary of the Lausanne Committee for World Evangelization suggests
that there might be "...a serious setback within the next decade
unless this generation of Christian leaders takes steps now to
contextualize the gospel and its ethics in all areas of African
life."(7)

Although Asia has seen attempts to indigenize since the 16th
and 17th centuries (e.g., Robert de Nobili in India; Matthew
Ricci in China), the same concern for contextualization remains
in evidence today. Dr. Lien-hwa Cho, professor of New Testament
Studies at the Southern Baptist Seminary in Taipei, mentions
"points of contact" between Christianity and Confucianism as one
viable contextualized theme.(8) Kosuke Koyama, former Japanese
missionary to Thailand now serving as senior lecturer in Religious
Studies at the University of Otago, New Zealand, proposes "reflection," and the "raising of issues."(9) Gerald H. Anderson in his
introduction to Asian theological thought writes that "the great
new fact of our time...is the break from Teutonic captivity by
Christian theologians in the Third World as they seek to recon-
ceptualize the God of biblical revelation within the context of
their different cultures."(10)

Application

The influence contextualization has upon Third World mission
is extremely significant! The desire of most Third World
Christians is to organize and finance their own missionary outreach. As the paper "Let My People Go," (published by three
executives of the Christian conference of Asia in December, 1974)

reveals, "We often feel dependent (on the West)..., and act in a dependence which inhibits our imagination to see ways in which mission can proceed with our given scarcity of such resources."(11) Probing more deeply, the paper presents several critical financial issues:

- Does the extent to which we use foreign funds hinder us from developing our own stewardship?
- People's commitment is related to how we give ourselves, what we put into the cause, what it costs us to do it.
- Do foreign funds affect adversely the depth of commitment to Christian causes among our people?
- Do they create a style of church life which is not ours and inappropriate to our situation?
- Do they create structures which we cannot maintain ourselves?
- Should we be more self-reliant and live more on the basis of our scarcity of resources?
- What are the guidelines which help us to be selective about how much of such resources we are ready to use and how we use them?(12)

The dialogue on missionary "self-support" is only beginning. Many desire financial independence and are willing to sacrifice and maintain a lower standard of living in order to be financially free from the West. Others permit occasional gifts while rejecting monthly ties. Some believe that if there are any funds used, by necessity they come from the West. Whatever the persuasion or need, financial independence is rapidly becoming an important consideration. Chapter 6 will discuss this key subject in greater detail.

Another issue raised by contextualization is the increasing tendency to center missionary training in non-Western area. African John Mbiti gives a forceful illustration to this point:

He returned to his home after nine and a half years of theological training with a Th.D. and excess baggage in theology to confront the realities of his people whose hopes he incarnated. At the peak of the celebrations marking his return, his sister fell to the ground, possessed by the spirit of her great aunt - and they looked to him to exorcise the spirit. But all he could do was to demythologize her suffering according to Rudolf Bultmann.(13)

In virtually every Third World country today there are local Bible schools for the purpose of training Christians in God's Word. In addition, and perhaps more exciting, are contextualized training programs sponsored by the various indigenous mission

sending agencies. In a recent preliminary study based on personal
correspondence with 87 separate individuals from throughout the
non-Western world (spread somewhat equally between the three major
regions of Africa, Asia and Latin America), I found that African
countries seem to favor longer periods of orientation for mission
candidates (often two years or longer), Latin American countries
incorporate the shortest training periods (4 months to one year)
and Asian countries vary from four weeks to four years. All
regions want their candidates to receive biblical training (generally at the Bible Institute level), and in almost half of the
cases, additional language and/or seminary training is desired.
One example of a localized training program comes from the Right
Reverend Bishop Albert Yawoah, Patriarch of the Church of the Lord
Aladura in Ghana, who has assisted in the sending of sixteen missionaries (in 1980) and plans to send out five more in 1981:

> A regular basic training or preparation is given to
> missionaries before they depart for the field. The
> training is requisite to the nature of their mission,
> such as Bible institute, language learning (English and
> local), explanation or interpretation of the Gospel on
> the lines of a training college for priests or ministers
> of the Christian Church. The length of time of training
> is not less than three years.(14)

There are a number of aspects within non-Western missions which
differ from traditional patterns as a result of contextualization.
In addition to finances and education, there are other practical
areas affected such as a preference for contextualized literature
and the tendency towards a loosley structured mission organization.
However, two prominent areas seem to arise as *central* to any potential differentiation between Western and non-Western missions.
They are *community* and *completeness* (or wholeness). The first
involves *how* mission is performed while the second deal with *what*
is proclaimed. The *Last Age of Missions* involves both.

Community

Although few sociologists claim that the community experience
is central to Western society (i.e., Nisbit), many more admit that
the teaching of individual competition, the attraction of "the
self-made man," or the spirit of "frontier independence" permeates
society and stands in stark contrast to non-Western patterns of
communal sharing. In this manner Marie-Louise Martin, university
lecture in Lesotho writes:

> We westerners are used to thinking in terms of individ-
> ualism. Easterners - amongst whom Jesus lived - as well as
> Africans emphasize much more the community aspect.(15)

Confirming this, Rev. Bongamjalo Goba, a congregational minister
in Capetown, identified the African personality with ancient
Israel's because both possess a sense of group solidarity, a
world view in contrast to the Western philosophy of "personal
rightism."(16)

Community is a way of life for Africans in general. In East
Africa, Tanzania has developed the national policy of "Ujamaa,"
the philosophy of communal sharing. Bishop Christopher Mwoleka
of Rulenge, Tanzania confesses, "I am dedicated to the ideal of
Ujamaa because it invites everyone, in a down to earth practical
way to imitate the life of the Trinity which is a life of sharing."(17) John Pobee, a theological professor in Ghana, demonstrates that one of the two foundational pillars among the *Akan*
society, a large matrilineal people of Southern Ghana is that of
sensus communis. "Descartes spoke for Western man when he said
cogito ergo sum - I think, therefore I exist - *Akan* man's ontol-
ogy is *cognatus ergo sum* - I am related by blood, therefore I
exist...." (18) Thus Margaret Traub, a Liberian writes:

> To an African unaccustomed to sophisticated city life,
> it is inconceivable that in some places a man can be
> stabbed to death on the street and people hurry by as
> if they had not seen it - or that men and women can live
> together in apartment houses for years and never get to
> know each other. Such aloofness is completely foreign
> to the African nature and culture.(19)

Similar themes are also apparent in Latin American cultures.
There, where people are more important than programs, small groups
or "Basic Communities" (of Roman Catholic origin) develop rapidly.
These small groups:

> ...truly spring from the need to live the church's life
> more intensely, stressing greater personal relationships,
> reflections on life and the Gospel with greater commitment
> to family, work and neighborhood. They are inspired by the
> sincere desire for a more human dimension in Christian
> life.(20)

In Asia, one example comes from Choan-Seng Song who expresses
annoyance with some missionaries who attempt to witness without
truly knowing people. To him, as with many Asians, it is "the
heart" which makes the difference.(21)

The value placed upon personal relationships is incalculable.
Whether familiar or fraternal, the natural tendency is to filter
one's meaningful existence through the grid of horizontal relationships. This produces certain non-Western distinctives inherent

within Third World missionary endeavors. Three such distinctives
are relational evangelism, relational education and relational
worship.

Distinctives Resulting
From Communal Concerns

1. Although it is imperative to proclaim Christ's good news,
the methodology chosen often reflects the importance of one's
personal relationships. Kosuke Koyama writes:

> Our neighbors in Asia are not interested in Christology,
> but can be concerned with our neighborology. This means
> that our neighbors in Asia are ready to hear our message
> of Christ if we put it in "neighborological" language,
> though they would reject Christ if we were to present him
> in Christological language.(22)

This points to the reality observed in many towns and villages
throughout the Third World. Friendship evangelism demonstrates
concern for more than one's soul; and the responsibility to witness is given to more than merely the pastor or trained evangelist.
There exists a built-in respect for horizontal relationships. The
concerns are for family units and friendship ties. Although friendship evangelism never neglects the crossing of cultural frontiers
in order to reach an unreached people, nevertheless it places the
emphasis on community once a missionary crosses a frontier as a
witness.

One interesting observation made by Donald McGavran which illustrates the importance of communal structures in evangelism is that
of the multi-individual conversions, or "people movement." This
is the winning of large social groups, the collective response of
whole "families" who make a favorable decision toward Christ all
at the same time. It occurs often among non-Western peoples as
church growth history reveals. In fact, from my own correspondence
with Third World leaders, I have recently received personal notice
of four such "multi-individual, mass movements" occurring at the
present time: one in India (the Meitei tribes), one in Bolivia
(the Aymaras), another in Peru (the Quechuas), and the last in
Kenya (the Masai tribe). Certainly there are many others.

2. Another interesting parallel which also illustrates communal
concerns comes from the Peruvian Enrique Guang. He writes criti-
cally concerning the Western missionary who goes:

> ...to the land of savages where updated teaching methods
> aren't so necessary. The predominant teaching method has
> been vertical, setting a distance between the teacher and
> students, the one who knows and the one that doesn't, whose

extremes are wisdom and ignorance. Because of this vertical nature, the missionary-teacher is inaccessible and from this position says, *I know, I can, I decide.* The student is placed on a level where he has to listen, be quiet, repeat, and say: *I don't know, I can't, I mustn't.* This is how sterilization is produced. In other words, in past missionary work, little has been done about fruitful horizontal teaching methods.... In the Third World, and especially in Latin America, we speak of Paulo Freire's "problem-creating education", Gutierrez's "total language" method and others.(23)

Another illustration of this same character comes from India. Here the religious pluralism has enhanced the evangelistic method of dialogue. Although one tendency inherent within relational dialogue is to weaken the uniqueness of Jesus Christ, nevertheless J. R. Chandran, Principal of the United Theological College in Bangalore, clarifies that dialogue is one essential pedagogical tool:

One of the most obvious frontiers of the church's mission in India is the meeting with people of other living faiths.... In the fulfillment of the evangelistic and missionary task of the church on this frontier, the evangelists or missionaries do not simply carry the reality of Christ with them. They go to witness to the reality of the gospel of Jesus Christ, and this process includes the discernment of the presence of that reality in the frontier situation or even in the other faiths. It is this realization which has been expressed through the dialogue approach.(24)

3. A third difference or distinctive between Western and non-Western missionary endeavors caused by communal concerns is that involving Christian worship. Many nationals agree with Enrique Dussel, the Argentine theologian when he rejects a "privatized" individualistic religion in favor of a more communal, social-oriented Christianity.(25) Thus baptism is not viewed exclusively as an act between convert and Christ, but also between convert, Christ and Christian community: "I am received into a prophetic body by baptismal consecration."(26) Church discipline is seen relationally, "understood as relating to what goes on between persons rather than following rules and being categorized."(27) Relationships are critical in Third World missionary endeavor.

The important New Testament word "brother" is repeated over 120 times in the epistles, and reflects a "deep responsibility and concern for one another."(28) Many Third World cultures possess a natural understanding of this concept and easily incorporate communal concerns into both Christian witness and worship. To the

missionary, the fact that one is related to another, either biolog-
ically and/or spiritually is important. This provides an inherent
basis for "bearing one another's burdens" (Gal. 6:2) which many in
the West do not possess. Perhaps one goal for non-Western believers
might be to teach Western Christians new insights into scriptural
injunctions such as, "love one another as I have loved you" (John
15:12). Just as the West has proclaimed the importance of personal
Bible study, perhaps the non-West could reciprocate and proclaim
the importance of interpersonal relationships. The hope is that
together we all receive the mature "mind of Christ" while reaching
the yet unreached worldwide.

Completeness

   The second significant issue which surfaces because of the emphasis on contextualization is that of completeness, or of personal
wholeness. An individual is not viewed as a divided being, nor is
he or she participating in a divided world (i.e., sacred vs.
secular). Generally, in the non-Western world, man is understood
as a unit, he is considered in "holistic" terms. And it is this
concept which affects the message of many Third World missionaries.

   To present an adequate backdrop, psychiatrist Abraham Maslow
writes concerning his study of Western man. After years of
research, he concludes that:

      ...for most people a conventional religion, while
   strongly religionizing one part of life, thereby also
   strongly "dereligionizes" the rest of life. The experience of the holy, the sacred, the divine, of awe, of
   creatureliness, of surrender, of mystery, of piety,
   thanksgiving, gratitude, self-dedication, if they happen
   at all tend to be confined to a single day of the week,
   to happen under one roof only of one kind of structure
   only, under certain triggering circumstances only, to
   rest heavily on the presence of certain traditional,
   powerful, but intrinsically irrelevant, stimuli, e.g.,
   organ music, incense, changing of a particular kind,
   certain regalia, and other arbitrary triggers. Being
   religious, or rather feeling religious, under these
   ecclesiastical auspices seems to absolve many (most?)
   people from the necessity or desire to feel these
   experiences at any other time. "Religionizing" only one
   part of life secularizes the rest of it.(29)

Then Maslow concludes with an important statement:

   I noticed something that had never occurred to me, namely
   that orthodox religion can easily mean de-sacralizing much
   of life. It can lead to dichotomizing life into the

trancendent and the secular-profane and can, therefore,
compartmentalize and separate them temporily, spatially,
conceptually, and experientially.(30)

It is this separation of life into different and distinct categories which many Third World leaders reject. This rejection
focuses upon many issues, but primarily upon the salvation message.

Hugo Assmann writes:

> The concept of salvation has been historicized to the
> point where one has to ask the question: "Saved in this
> world or the next?" That is, horizontalism versus verti-
> calism...(In light of our holistic theme) the old dualism
> of natural-supernatural, nature-grace, and so on, no longer
> express opposites....(31)

Orlando E. Costas, a more evangelical spokesman from Latin
America writes:

> The crucial problem in mission today is whether we
> can overcome our particularities, get a glimpse of its
> totality and maintain its integrity; or in other words,
> whether we can repossess earnestly and urgently the
> biblical vision of a holistic mission, carried out
> faithfully and consistently in crossroads of life. We
> are experiencing a crisis of wholeness and integrity.
> The fundamental missiological question before the
> Christian church is not whether mission should be
> conceived of as vertical, horizontal, or both; not
> whether it should be thought of either as spiritual
> and personal or material and social.... It is rather
> whether we can recover its wholeness and efficacy,
> whether we can see it as a whole and live up to its
> global objectives.(32)

Elsewhere, Indian D.S. Amalorpavadass argues that salvation is for
"the whole Person,"(33) while Chinese Jung Young Lee believes in
"the category of wholeness rather than of partiality" for Christian
living.(34) And, one typical spokesman for Africa is John S. Pobee,
a conservative theologian from Ghana. While linking cultural
traditions with Christianity, he argues that, "it is difficult to
distinguish sharply between the religious and the non-religious,
between the sacred and secular. In African societies, religion
stares people in the face at all points...."(35)

To be sure, the issues at stake here are serious ones. During
most of the 20th century, the West has been polarized - the ecumenical side strongly advocating social concerns while the

evangelical side proclaiming personal salvation. Yet it is interesting to note that during the last decade, and largely due to a
few sensitive Westerners and several Third World spokesman, these
two dichtomized positions at times have begun to merge together
and become more inclusive.

For example, on the ecumenical side, Bishop Mortimer Arias
from Bolivia spoke at the gathering of the world Council of Churches
in Nairobi (1975) pleading for a more "balanced" evangelistic position on mission. Speaking on behalf of the Commission for World
Mission and Evangelism (CWME) on "That the World May Believe,"
Arias reminded the Council that "the initial purpose behind the
creation of the World Council of Churches was to 'support the
churches in their task of evangelism.'"(36)

On the evangelical side, a comparison of the Berlin Congress on
World Evangelism (1966) with the Lausanne Congress on World Evangelization (1974) shows development in the inclusion of holistic concerns in evangelization. Berlin mentions the importance of social
involvement; Lausanne stresses its integral participation in
evangelistic outreach. As in Nairobi, Lausanne included strong
comments from Latin America, particularly from the ad hoc group
advocating "Radical Discipleship", led by Rene Padilla and Samuel
Escobar. Other Third World leaders also voiced strong opinions
concerning holistic themes (i.e., Festo Kivengere, Juan Carlos
Ortiz, Orlando Costas). The Lausanne meeting saw particular emphasis given to socially-oriented themes on Christian life-styles.
The Lausanne Covenant may be considered as one of the most balanced
documents ever produced on mission in the 20th century. Much of
this is a result of Third World participation.

Ghanian theologian Kofi Appiah-Kubi perhaps sums up the general
feeling among many Third World leaders. In his writing concerning
the rapidly growing indigenous African Christian churches, he
comments:

> ...the most significant and unique aspects of these churches
> is that they seek to fulfill that which is lacking in the Euro-
> American missionary churches, that is, to provide forms of
> worship that satisfy both spiritually and emotionally and to
> enable Christianity to cover every area of human life and
> fulfill all human needs.(37)

Distinctives Resulting
From Holistic Concerns

The most obvious application of this theme to Third World mission
is that among the national missionaries who proclaim a "holistic"
message, Jesus Christ not only saves from sin but also is the one

who helps reap a good crop, who heals the sick, defeats the invis-
ible enemy, and alleviates personal guilt. In practice, besides
the proclamation of Chirst's "good news" some Nigerian missionaries have given assistance in agriculture and pecuaria while many
Brazilians preach Christ and teach literacy. Historically, one
difference between John Wesley and these modern Third World
preachers is that social reform *followed* Wesley's revival, whereas
social reform often *accompanies* non-Western missionary activity.
Men and women are not divided into separate compartments, but
viewed as integral wholes. Salvation touches the whole person.

The Apostle Paul wrote encouraging the early church to develop
"holistically." He said, "we are to grow up in all aspects into
Him" (Ephesians 4:15). Elsewhere he wrote about the position we
have in Christ: "...in Him you have been made complete" (Colossians 2:10). Wholeness is a biblical teaching. It is part of
God's "renewed mind." Not only is completeness needed in our
message but also balance is required in our methods. The Third
World possesses unique strengths in these areas. Therefore, could
not our non-Western brothers and sisters help us to become more
balanced, more social, more involved in "body mutuality?" As
Paul wrote, "Let this mind be in you, which was also in Christ
Jesus" (Philippians 2:5).

PART TWO

THE MISSIONARY OUTREACH
OF THE THIRD WORLD

4

A NEW IDEA FOR
NEW INFORMATION

Thomas Wang, an Anglican churchman in Hong Kong says:

The Europeans have run their course; the Americans have
run their course. They have all to various degrees paid
their gospel debt. Now it is the Asians' turn to run the
course and pay the debt. Let all Chinese Christians
unite.(1)

Donald A. McGavran and Norman Riddle, after extensive research
in Zaire, wrote a book entitled *Zaire, Midday in Missions*. Their
evaluation: "The collapse of Western empires and the rise of
hundreds of self-governing young churches, far from ending Christian Mission, usher in the time of its flowering."(2) The authors
recognize that one of the great new facts of our time in Zaire is
the emergence of indigenous mission structures and that 284
Zaireans are beginning to "pay the debt."

Theodore Williams, Vice-Chairman of the Asia Missions Association
and General Secretary of the Indian Evangelical Mission, says, "A
strong tide of missions is rising in India and throughout Asia
today. Third World missions have just made a beginning."(3) To
complement this, historian Stephen Neil writes that in the Christian world during the last fifty years, one immense change is
"the shift of the center of control in the Third World churches.
At the beginning of the century almost everything was in the hands
of the foreigner, now everywhere the control has passed into the
hands of the indigenous leaders."(4) It is an uncontested fact
that church and mission agencies are rapidly developing within the
Third World.

Yet missions leaders everywhere are wondering just *how* fast are
these agencies and churches developing? How many Third World missionaries are there *now*? To which countries do these workers go?
In which "foreign" languages do they speak? Upon what basis are
they supported? From which countries are they sent? How long,
on the average, do they stay? There are many questions concerning Third World outreach for which little widely known information was available. Mission leaders from all regions have
described this new development, yet virtually no one had recent
data for regions other than his own. There was a great need for
an updated picture of the new, almost explosive, growth of Third
World missions so that missionary funds and personnel might be
employed toward maximum results.

FIRST EVALUATION

As has previously been mentioned, the first project undertaken
to survey the rise of non-Western missions worldwide was coordinated
by C. Peter Wagner in 1972. At the Fuller School of World Mission
in Pasadena, Wagner invited three men, Peter Larson, Edward Pentecost
and James Wong, to survey the strength of Protestant missionary
activity among the African, Asian and Latin American peoples. They
sent out 697 questionnaires around the world and received a response
of 34.1%. They discovered that, in 1972, there were at least 210
missionary societies which were sending out a minimum of 3,404 missionaries. The significance of their study pointed to the startl-
ing discovery that there was a formidable force of missionary
personnel daily involved in evangelistic endeavors which previously
had been virtually ignored!

In 1976, Marlin Nelson continued the research by focusing his
Fuller Doctor of Missiology research specifically upon various
Asian countries. His data are much more complete than the 1972
study due to his limited scope. With responses from 53 societies
in eight countries, 1,293 Asian missionaries were reported to be
on the field at that time. This finding was significant to world
missions because Nelson reported a 30% increase in the number of
missionaries. Also, his results indicate that of these nearly
1,300 missionaries, "631 or 49% are foreign missionaries working
in another country."(5) Concerning part of the other 51%, Nelson
concludes that, "we must not neglect the urgency of cross-cultural
home missions. This must be recognized as a valid mission work,
and a type that can be done with a *minimum of logistical
problems*."(6)

The 1976 study raises several new questions. Is the exhortation
concerning cross-cultural home missions being understood and valued?
Are the Asian missionary agencies presently fulfilling their potential with proper strategy and personnel deployment? Are the African

and Latin American agencies growing like those in Asia and are
they following the same Asian structural patterns? Are these fulfilling their present potential with strategy and personnel deployment?

The need continued for an additional comprehensive study into
Third World missionary societies. Not only were there many
unanswered questions, but since 1972 little had been done to
survey all three regions of Third World activity. The 1972 report
stated the need for further study while the 1976 report suggested
reevaluation of present ministries. Furthermore, if the completion of the Great Commission partially depends upon the effectiveness of "their" recruitment, deployment, strategy and even cooperation with the Western church, then a new study of non-Western
indigenous missionary agencies was demanded. The needed research
was conducted and completed in 1980.

THE 1980 STUDY

Purpose Statement

The goal of the 1980 survey was to research Third World Indigenous
missionary societies for the purpose of better understanding their
strength, involvements, direction and potential, so that, the body
of Christ, worldwide, can better cooperate for the more efficient
accomplishment of world evangelization and Christian growth.

Scope and Limitations

In order to understand fully the above purpose statement, it is
necessary to define and clarify the terms used. The explanation
of these terms is as follows:

Third World. There is much dialogue concerning the definition
of this term. As chapter one explained, some use it to denote an
economic relation (e.g., rich vs. poor countries); others imply a
geo/political meaning (e.g., nations not aligned to either capitalist or communist countries). But the meaning used in this research
is essentially a psychological definition. "The mentality of a
people classifies them in the Third World. This mentality means
that a certain people feel themselves independent to some significant degree of the two great Western power blocks...."(7) This
definition includes the African, Asian and Latin American peoples,
but it would also include the Vietnamese of Los Angeles or the
Turks in West Germany - those who might live in Western nations
yet who identify more with their own homeland than with their
present living habitat.

Indigenous. Indigeneity means that the society or agency origi-
nated and developed as a natural part of *or* as a natural response
to the national church and her faith in Christ. Obviously, some
groups began through foreign missionary advocacy. These will be
included within the study if they report significant *national*
leadership. Other societies were both established and developed
by national leaders (i.e., the "Foundation of the Fellowship for
Evangelism in Indonesia"). It is to this double degree of indigeneity that this study will devote much attention, for this kind
of missionary advancement must be continually reproduced throughout the world.

Missionary. The word "missionary" historically encompasses
almost any good activity performed in our Lord's name while living
away from home. This has included jungle aviation, medical assistance, radio technicians, and a host of other important support
ministries. To limit the scope of our study, however, I have chosen
to define the word "missionary" as any person or agency performing
primarily evangelistic, pastoral, or teaching activity in cross-
cultural situations. This implies that the major emphasis is not
placed upon E-0 evangelism (proclamation within one's home church)
nor upon E-1 evangelism ("near neighbor" evangelism, witnessing
to those who are within cultural reach of one's home church). But
the major emphasis will be placed upon E-2 and E-3 evangelism
(cross-cultural outreach), the only difference between the latter
two being how foreign the situation is to the one sent. The reason
for this selective emphasis is clearly explained by Ralph Winter.

At the Lausanne Congress on World Evangelization in 1974, Winter
spoke on the topic, "The Higest Priority: Cross-Cultural Evangelism." He said:

> The master pattern of the expansion of the Christian
> movement is first for special E-2 and E-3 efforts to cross
> cultural barriers into new communities and to establish
> strong, on-going, vigorously evangelizing denominations,
> and then for that national church to carry the work forward
> on the really high-powered E-1 level. We are thus forced
> to believe that until every tribe and tongue has a strong,
> powerfully evangelizing church in it, and thus an E-1 wit-
> ness within it, E-2 and E-3 efforts coming from outside are
> still essential and highly urgent.(8)

Because it is difficult to discern the difference between E-1
and E-2 evangelistic efforts within certain regions of the non-
Western world, both the final tabulation of Third World Missionaries
(Chapters 5 and 6) and the Third World Agency Directory (Appendix)
include workers from both categories. However due to the primacy
of cross-cultural efforts, the vast majority of the reported missionaries are involved in E-2 or E-3 endeavors only.

Societies. Wherever Christianity grows and develops, there will always be at least two basic kind of structures. The first is the best known and most widely used throughout the world. It is the church structure, the diverse fellowship of believers consisting of both young and old, male and female, mature and immature, rich and poor, committed and not-so-committed. The church accepts them *all* on the basis of their belief in Christ the Lord. It makes no difference who the believer is nor where he or she lives. The church structure possess a purposeful plurality.

The second structure, however, is more selective. It is the missionary society consisting of singularly-minded personnel. It places parameters upon membership and limits upon activity. The commitment level of each worker often is higher than within the first churchly structure as are also the demands placed upon the participant by the society. It is this second structure, the society which specializes in missionary activity, which is the primary focus of the 1980 study.

Historically, the term some missiologists use for the first structure is "modality" - a sociological word which labels groups whose inclusiveness involves people regardless of age, temperament, color or sex. It is all encompassing and multidimensional in activity. In contrast, the term some missiologists use for the second structure is "sodality" - another sociological word which describes voluntary associations where only qualified and/or interested persons join and participate. Sodalities usually are goal oriented groups, being either denominational or interdenominational, but selective in their activities and procedures. Normally they recruit from the modality (or local church) and train personnel as opportunities and funds permit. Ralph Winter, the one who originally applied these two sociological terms to the Christian missionary movement(9) believes in the "legitimacy of *both* structures, and the necessity for both structures not only to exist but to work together harmoniously for the fulfillment of the Great Commission, and for the fulfillment of all that God desires for our time."(10) However, instead of using the technical term sodality, this study employs the more common word *society* (or agency) and focuses its interest on this second structure.

Also, the scope of the 1980 study excludes all Catholic societies, as well as those pertaining to the Orthodox, Mormon, Jehovah Witness and Seventh-Day Adventist churches. It includes, however, Anglican and Independent (i.e., African) societies. Each society, in order to be included in the study must have a majority of non-Western workers, receive a majority of funds from Third World peoples, and be directed by one or more non-Western believers. The primacy of cross-cultural work is explained above under the heading "missionary."

*...of better understanding their strengths, involvements,
directions and potential.* Because, little contemporary knowledge
exists regarding Third World indigenous missionary societies, the
purpose is to list who they are, their geographic location, their
primary ministries, which languages are involved, projections and
goals, as well as their problems and hindrances, established terms
of service, financial status and general theological persuasions
in order to understand better this great missionary force which
God has developed.

... so that the body of Christ, worldwide, can better cooperate.
We desire to obey our Lord and participate in both world evangelization and holistic church growth. Could it be, through the results
of this research, that our knowledge will increase concerning other
parts of Christ's body? That new insights will be gains concerning
the diversity of our God and the creativity of our brothers? That
growth will be experienced as we discover new areas of God's faithfulness and that our stewardship of God's resources will be more
effective as we learn and mature together in the task of world
evangelization? If so, the time and effort spent on the 1980 study
will have been profitable.

Procedure

The research project began in September 1979 as Wagner and I
discussed together various present needs in world evangelization.
As the importance of this project surfaced, a procedural outline
was laid out and funding secured from three interested sources:
the Lausanne Strategy Working Group, Missions Advanced Research and
Communication Center (MARC) of World Vision, and Mission To The
World, the missionary arm of the Presbyterian Church of America.
Also, an advisory committee was formed consisting of C. Peter
Wagner, Dean Gilliland of the School of World Mission, Fuller
Theological Seminary, and Samuel Wilson of MARC. Special mention
must be given to O.C. Ministries, Inc. (formerly Overseas Crusades)
for helping me with secretarial assistance and for allowing me an
extended furlough from my ministry in Brazil to complete the
research.

The procedure involved four basic phases. First, because there
was no accurate and complete list of contemporary Third World
mission agencies, the immediate need was to compile one. One
hundred and forty three initial letters were sent out in an attempt
to update the 1972 working list. A 53% response was received from
this first phase. A copy of the first questionnaire can be found
in the appendix.

The next step was to formulate the primary "Mission Agency
Questionnaire" which was sent to all the newly discovered mission
agencies (a copy of this also appears in the appendix). The

questionnaire itself went through three revisions. Because of the author's close proximity to the School of World Mission, it was possible to test, correct and validate the questionnaire with the help of two dozen Third World church leaders. The questionnaire requested information concerning geographical areas of missionary involvement, support sources, theological persuasions, future projections and possible suggestions for our mission agency list. Many additional newly formed societies were suggested through this source. English was used as the primary language with a Portuguese version added due to the author's permanent Brazilian residency. Very possibly this is the reason Brazil figures so prominently in the data received from Latin America.

The third procedural phase involved two complete mailings of the questionnaire: the first in early January and the second (as a reminder) in late April of 1980. Along with this, additional correspondence was carried out in an attempt to discover missionary movements which the questionnaire itself was not designed to detect. Several unstructured, non-Western missionary movements have been identified and included in these pages.

The last phase is the reporting of the research. This includes the first three chapters of this book (general background information) along with the next three (specific findings). The goal is to report what has been discovered in such a way that it might have the broadest exposure.

In the February, 1980, issue of the *Kansai Mission Research Center News Report*, the following statement is made: "The main purpose of KMRC is to give inspiration, insights and contacts that can further the discipling of the millions of Japanese not yet reached by the Gospel."(11) We trust the information contained in the following pages will, likewise, give "inspiration, insights and contacts" for the further discipling of millions not yet reached by the Gospel.

5

INFORMATION FOR
WORLD CHRISTIANS

On March 28, 1980, Rev. Dicky J. Palandeng, vice-chairman of
the newly named Fellowship of Baptist Churches of Indonesia wrote,
"We praise God for the continual growth in West Kalimantan (Borneo)
through the ministry of our missionaries. The members of the
churches there have increased 900 percent during the past four
years."(1)

Another report comes from Rev. Chhawnzinga, chairman of The
Seekers of Lost Souls, an indigenous Indian Mission. He writes
concerning the growth of his agency to its present size of 51
members. In 1972:

>...a few voluntary evangelists went to the tribal people
of Tripura and Cachar to preach the gospel. There were
different clans of those tribal peoples worshipping different gods. The most surprising and challenging tribe
among them was the Muolshoum. Because they worshipped an
idol which claimed Mizo origin called Zobawmthanga, and
because they claimed that the Mizo people would free them
from their bonds and bring them the light, many voluntary
evangelists came forward to teach these people and to
help alleviate them from their bad economic conditions.(2)

Thus The Seekers of Lost Souls became a cross-cultural mission.

Throughout the non-Western world, indigenous missionary activity
like this is growing explosively. On the one hand, much of this
growth occurs among *unstructured* endeavors. These are groups of

believers who spontaneously proclaim the "good news" without any
formal organization defining and directing their activity. The
Quechua Movement for Christ in Bolivia, the Tzeltal Christians and
the Chol Indian Church of Mexico, The Apostolic Church of Ghana,
the independent evangelistic outreach by Mr. Peter Yang and Prof.
Sutira Ariapongse of Bangkok, Thailand or the many Chinese Christians in Burma are examples of effective unstructured missionary
endeavors. They are independent movements, spontaneous in their
outreach.

Yet a good portion, if not most, of world evangelization today
is being carried out by missionaries who belong to organized or
structured societies. The above mentioned Fellowship of Baptist
Churches of Indonesia or The Seekers of Lost Souls are only two
of at least 368 Third World Missionary Agencies presently active.
They all possess a non-Western chief officer, some system for
raising and maintaining financial support and several ministerial
plans for the future. Each is involved in cross-cultural activity,
employs a majority of non-Western workers and receives a majority
of funds from Third World peoples. These 368 active agencies do
not include Mormon, Jehovah Witness or Seventh-Day Adventist
Churches, but *do* include Anglican, and Independent (i.e., African)
Church Societies. They vary greatly in character but are united
in the fact that they are organizationally discernable. By using
this list of 368 active agencies (see Appendix II), with supple-
mental information from the completed questionnaire (see Appendix
I), a description of the present status of structured Third World
missions becomes possible. This description will be divided into
two parts: 1) The Emerging Missions (this chapter), and 2) The
Emerging Trends (Chapter 6).

The Emerging Missions

In early 1980, a list of 462 potentially active missionary
sending agencies was formed and used as a basis for discerning
Third World missionary activity. As correspondence was maintained
with many on the list, 80% of the total list of 462 agencies was
confirmed by either returned questionnaire or personal letter.
Because of this, an important difference is being made between
the "Total List" of 462 agencies and the "Total *Active* List" of
368 agencies. Each one of the 368 agencies has been mentioned by
one or more of the 282 contributors worldwide confirming their
existence. Furthermore, because 45% of all mailed questionnaires
were filled out and returned (thus giving a significant 56% return
rate for these 368 active listings) the following information is
considered authoritative.

Number of Missionary Agencies. In 1972, James Wong, Edward
Pentecost and Peter Larson reported that there were at least 203
structured missionary societies resident within the non-Western

world. Eight years later, I found 368 active agencies. This represents an 81.28% increase. During the same eight year period, *Asia* and *Oceania* together increased 92.59%, from 108 to 208 agencies. *Latin America* decreased by 8.19%, from 61 to 56 agencies; while *Africa* grew a significant 285.18%, from 27 to 104 agencies. *Africa* not only doubled in the number of mission sending countries (twelve to twenty-four), but the region attributes much of its rapid agency growth to the lively expanding Independent Church movement. Most of these new agencies are the result of the already existing Independent Churches which now are entering the cross-cultural missionary arena. Many of these newly established societies are departments of mission within denominational structures.

Latin America, reported a decrease in the number of agencies. Perhaps this can be attributed to one or more of three reasons. First, is the issue of correspondence. Even though I received a commendable 50% return rate from Latin America, based upon the Active Agency List, it was still the lowest percentage received from any Third World area. Second, is the issue of the initial Latin American list. The original list of Latin American agencies, out of the 462 Total Agency List, contained less names for this continent than for any other major region. In comparison, the 1972 study began with 301 possibilities and validated 61. In 1980, the research began with only 76 listings, of which 56 were confirmed. Yet dozens of additional letters were received from church leaders throughout the Latin region seeming to confirm that there had not been great new growth in the number of organizations. The third reason is the issue of independent missionaries. Mention has been made of the many unstructured, independent cross-cultural agencies. Obviously, they do not appear in the data, yet are vitally important. In 1972, Larson, Wong and Pentecost wrote, "with the acquired data for newer agencies, the growth of missionary activity in Latin America seems to be increasing."(3) This did occur for awhile, and perhaps continues with these independent missionaries. Yet the surprise is that during the whole eight year period, the number of structured missionary sending agencies declined. Figure 5 presents a chart of these findings. Please notice that these data *do not* include specialized support ministries (i.e., Bible schools, literature distribution, communication or transportation endeavors) and also that they are within the limits for inclusion as described in Chapter 4.

Figure 5: TOTAL NUMBER OF ACTIVE MISSIONARY AGENCIES

(Listed by country and compared with the 1972 Study.(4)
The last column records the "Total List" of 462
agencies, even those presently unconfirmed.)

Country	1972 Total Active List	1980 Total Active List	1980 Total List
Africa:			
Angola	2		1
Cameroon		2	2
Chad	1		
Dahomey			1
Egypt (U.A.R.)	2	2	5
Ethiopia		1	1
Gabon		1	1
Ghana		23	29
Ivory Coast			1
Kenya	2	16	22
Liberia	1	1	1
Madagascar	2	2	5
Malawi	2	1	2
Nigeria	4	16	31
So. Africa	6	6	13
Swaziland	1	1	1
Tanzania		3	4
Togo			1
Uganda	1	1	2
Zaire	3	14	14
Zambia		6	7
Zimbabwe		8	15
Sub-Total	27	104	159
Asia:			
Burma	2	5	5
Hong Kong	6	9	10
India	26	66	68
Indonesia	1	13	13
Japan	32	27	38
Korea	7	22	22
Malaysia	2	3	3
Nepal	1		
Philippines	13	30	30
Singapore	4	7	8
So. Vietnam	1		
Sri Lanka	2		

Figure 5: Continued

Country	1972 Total Active List	1980 Total Active List	1980 Total List
Asia:			
Taiwan	3	7	8
Thailand	3	3	6
Sub-Total	103	192	211
Latin America:			
Argentina	7	3	5
Bolivia		1	1
Brazil	26	29	38
Chile	2		2
Colombia	2	5	7
Costa Rica	3		
Dom. Republic		1	1
Ecuador	1	3	3
Guatemala	3	7	9
Jamaica	3	2	2
Mexico	5	2	2
Peru	2	2	2
Puerto Rico	3		2
Trinidad	1		
Uruguay	1		
Venezuela	2	1	2
Sub-Total	61	56	76
Oceania:			
Amer. Samoa	1	2	2
Fiji	2	3	3
Guam		3	3
P. New Guinea		5	5
Solomon Is.	1	2	2
Tonga Is.	1	1	1
Sub-Total	5	16	16
			462
Western Countries:			
New Zealand	1		2
U.S.A.	6	5	9
Sub-Total	7	5	11
Grand Total			472

Note: These listings represent primarily cross-cultural frontier
        mission agencies. The additional specialized support
        ministries such as medical or educational activities are
        not included. Agencies listed under Western Countries,
        although listed here, were received too late for inclusion
        into the 368 Active Agency total.

New information is received when we list together all the agencies in order of size. Eight years ago, Japan represented the
nation with the most mission sending agencies. In 1980, out of
100 different mission sending countries, India confirmed sixty-six
cross-cultural agencies, while the Philippines placed second, with
thirty. It is significant, in view of the "Latin decline", that
Brazil is third with twenty-nine confirmed cross-cultural groups,
over one-half of Latin America's listings. Figure 6 presents the
ten leading mission sending countries by number of reported agencies in comparison with 1972.

Figure 6: THE TEN LEADING MISSION SENDING COUNTRIES

Based upon the number of Reported Agencies and
compared with the 1972 Study.(5)

1972	Number of Active Agencies	1980	Number of Active Agencies
1. Japan	32	1. India	66
2. Brazil	26	2. Philippines	30
3. India	26	3. Brazil	29
4. Philippines	13	4. Japan	27
5. Argentina	7	5. Ghana	23
5. Korea	7	6. Korea	22
7. Hong Kong	6	7. Kenya	16
7. So. Africa	6	7. Nigeria	16
7. U.S.A. (Third World)	6	8. Zaire	14
8. Mexico	5	9. Indonesia	13
8. Oceania	5	10. Hong Kong	9

This data is based upon the Active Agency List only.
No specialized ministries are included (i.e., Service
or Support groups). A listing of these 1980 Agencies
appear in the Appendix II.

In 1972, a relationship was suggested between the Third World
countries which have the greatest number of mission agencies and
the number of foreign missionaries present in those same countries.
Bill Needham, then working in Brazil, intimated that the presence
of foreign missionaries in a country assist in the development of
new indigenous agencies;(6) that where there are the most foreign
missionaries, there will be also the eventual establishment of many
new societies.

In order to understand the truth of this relationship, two
sources were compared: the Eleventh edition of MARC's *Mission
Handbook* which contains data of North American missionaries worldwide, and the Third World data as recorded here.   In 1969, according to the *Mission Handbook*, the three Third World countries which
listed the highest number of North American missionaries were Brazil
(2,170 workers), Japan (1,864 workers), and India (1,517 workers).(7)
Interestingly, these same three countries appear on top of the list
in Figure 6 for 1972.   In 1975, the four countries with the most
North American missionaries were Brazil (2,170 workers), Japan
(1,644 workers), Mexico (1,232 workers), and the Philippines (1,181
workers).(8)   Although five years passed until the 1980 study was
completed, still three of the four countries listed in 1975 are
among the largest in Figure 6 for 1980.   In the case of India,
while being omitted in the *Mission Handbook's* top four listings
for 1975 (it represented only 871 North American missionaries(9)),
nevertheless India is listed first in the 1980 chart (Figure 6)
suggesting that great spiritual benefits are being reaped today due
to immense labors in the past.

Thus, there seems to be a direct relationship between the number
of foreign missionaries present in a country and the number of
mission agencies produced by the believers in that same country.
This does not imply that the mere presence of foreign workers is all
that is needed to encourage the development of new societies.   But
this data appears to confirm the value of missionary presence as
one strong contributing factor.

The fact that Japan went from first place in 1972 to fourth in
1980 may be explained by the difficulty I faced in receiving
replies.   Like Latin America, Japan was slow to answer.   Out of
38 potential names of agencies, only nine questionnaires were
returned.   An additional 18 agencies were confirmed by letter with
little extra information.   Another six replies were received but
they represented specialized support groups.   Because the purpose
of this list is to report only cross-cultural mission societies
whose primary functions are prophetic or evangelistic (see Chapter
4), these other support groups are excluded.   Thus Japan represents
fourth place, out of 100 nations, with twenty-seven indigenous
societies.   A complete listing of these, plus those of the other
countries, is found in Appendix II.

Number of Missionary Personnel.   As we leave agencies and focus
upon individuals, the growth rates dramatically increase.   In 1972,
there were 3,404 estimated Third World missionaries.   In 1980, the
conservative estimate is 13,000.   This figure comes from three
sources.   First, from the 207 returned questionnaires were counted
10,841 missionaries.   Second, from personal correspondence, additional suggestions were given which helped to determine totals for

some of the remaining 161 confirmed active agencies. Third, where
no information was received, past trends of the same or similar
societies were studied in order to arrive at a conservative
estimate. The two previous studies (1972 and 1976) were used as
primary resource material in this. Therefore, this estimate of
13,000 Third World missionaries represents a 282.43% increase
since 1972!

Regionally, *Asia* increased 368.48%, from 1,063 to 4,980 missionaries; *Africa* increased 486.09%, from 1,007 to 5,884 missionaries;
Latin America increased 16.09%, from 820 to 952 missionaries; the
Third World peoples within the *United States* increased 6.69%, from
453 to 478 and *Oceania* beginning with its small base number increased
spectacularly by 1,057.37%, from 61 to 706 missionaries. Figure 7
visualizes this regional growth, and also presents the projections
of growth for missionaries in 1981.

Another important inquiry concerns the growth rates of missionary personnel for *each country* of the Third World. A few Western
oriented nations such as New Zealand and the United States are
included because of our psychological definition of the Third World.
There are many reported mission societies within the West which
identify more with non-Western peoples and are actively witnessing
to them. Figure 8 presents the missionary totals for each country,
including the West, which reported Third World missionary activity.
These totals are compared with the 1972 data and are listed in four
columns.

The first column within Figure 8 concerns the number of confirmed
missionary sending agencies. The second column relates the counted
missionaries which were reported primarily by means of the returned
questionnaires. Column three describes the total conservative
estimates for each country, which are the results of all three
sources mentioned above. Column four shows future recruitment projections although this represents only 56% of the active list of
368 agencies. Nevertheless, this last column is important because
it demonstrates the enormous potential for personnel growth among
non-Western missionary societies in 1981.

Figure 7: PERCENTAGES OF THIRD WORLD MISSIONARY GROWTH

The size of each diagram below represents the
average missionary growth rate for that region
since 1972.(10) The solid smaller image located
within each diagram represents the *projected*
missionary growth rate for 1981. It is easy to
visualize the good Oceanian increase since 1972,
and the African potential for 1981. Each square
within the diagrams represent a growth rate of
20%

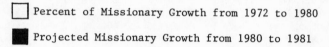

☐ Percent of Missionary Growth from 1972 to 1980

■ Projected Missionary Growth from 1980 to 1981

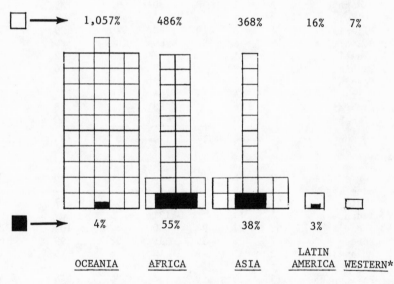

* – The projection of missionary growth for Western countries
  in 1981 was unavailable at the time of writing.

Figure 8:   MISSIONARY TOTALS FOR EACH COUNTRY

As compared with the 1972 Study.(11)   Numerically,
couples (husband and wife) equal two missionaries.

Country	Active Agencies		Reported Missionaries		Total Estimated Missionaries		Projected Additions
	1972	1980	1972	1980	1972	1980	For 1981
AFRICA:							
Angola	2				10		
Cameroon		2		23		28	
Chad	1		4		4		
Egypt (U.A.R.)	2	2		22	5	22	3
Ethiopia		1		50		50	15
Gabon		1		40		40	
Ghana		23		827		1,127	61
Kenya	2	16	10	827	15	1,002	281
Liberia	1	1			5	2	
Madagascar	2	2	30	30	35	30	2
Malawi	2	1		1	10	2	
Nigeria	4	16	810	2,350	820	2,500	353
So. Africa	6	6	59	569	84	579	11
Swaziland	1	1			5	2	
Tanzania		3		2		6	2
Uganda	1	1		22	5	22	400
Zaire	3	14	4	284	9	334	82
Zambia		6		88		88	4
Zimbabwe		8		40		50	25
Sub-Total	27	104	917	5,175	1,007	5,884	1,239
ASIA:							
Burma	2	5		988	10	988	33
Hong Kong	6	9	26	57	31	57	6
India	26	66	543	1,667*	598	2,277	504
Indonesia	1	13		131	5	201	96
Japan	32	27	97	130	137	184	21
Korea	7	22	33	319**	38	499	68
Malaysia	2	3	2	10	5	15	10
Nepal	1				5		
Philippines	13	30	155	364	170	544	49
Singapore	4	7	10	127	10	172	52
So. Vietnam	1		2		2		
Sri Lanka	2	8			13		
Taiwan	3	7	26	29	31	43	5
Thailand	3	3	3		8		
Sub-Total	103	192	905	3,832	1,063	4,980	844

Figure 8: Continued

Country	Active Agencies		Reported Missionaries		Total Estimated Missionaries		Projected Additions
	1972	1980	1972	1980	1972	1980	For 1981
LATIN AMERICA:							
Argentina	7	3	30	4	30	24	
Bolivia		1		4		4	
Brazil	26	29	495	649	595	693	37
Chile	2			2	10	8	
Columbia	2	5	2	12	7	30	7
Costa Rica	3		1	2	11	2	
Dom. Republic		1				2	
Ecuador	1	3	11	12	11	18	2
El Salvador				4		4	
Guatemala	3	7	3	28	8	43	2
Jamaica	3	2	4	26	14	30	14
Mexico	5	2	64	16	69	26	6
Panama				10		10	
Peru	2	2	3	41	8	46	
Puerto Rico	3		20		30	2	
Trinidad	1		5		5	4	
Uruguay	1		15		15	2	
Venezuela	2	1	2		7	4	
Sub-Total	61	56	655	810	820	952	68
OCEANIA:							
Amer. Samoa	1	2		35	5	35	20
Fiji	2	3	22	38	22	48	
Guam		3		2		2	
P. New Guinea		5		486		491	68
Solomon Is.	1	2	22	130	22	130	10
Tonga Is.	1	1	12		12		
Sub-Total	5	16	56	691	61	706	98
WESTERN COUNTRY:							
New Zealand	1				5	10	
U.S.A.	6	—	438	333	448	468	—
Sub-Total	7		438	333	453	478	
WORLD TOTALS:	203	368	2,971	10,841	3,404	13,000	2,249

* – Indian missiologist George Samuel has reported counting 2,084
cross-cultural missionaries. This is a 19.5% increase over our
total of 1,677 reported workers. This larger report further con-
firms our Total Estimated Missionaries for India of 2,277.

**– The reported number of 319 Korean missionaries is in error.
The accurate tabulated total is 112. However, the old reported
number remains in the graph because of difficulties involved in
text alteration. If the first note above concerning George Samuel's estimate is true, his additional 407 reported Indian missionaries would at least supplement the 207 Korean difference.
Thus neither the Asian Total nor the World Total for Third World
reported missionaries would be necessity be altered.

A brief study of the above information provides several pleasant surprises. In Asia, *Burma* has been the focus of many church planting and evangelistic activities, beginning with Adoniram Judson in 1813. But since 1966, when all Protestant and most Roman Catholic missionaries were expelled, many Christians worldwide have wondered about the missionary zeal of the Burmese Church. This report presents 988 Burmese workers! Many of them remain working in their country in diverse cross-cultural contexts; however, some have traveled to China and to surrounding areas. *India* is significant not only for its large national missionary force, but also because the number of missionaries have increased while foreign workers have declined 40% in the last fifteen years.(12) *Japan* lists few missionaries, proportionally, for having 27 active agencies. Several other countries with similar numbers of agencies record at least twice the number of missionaries. Upon further study, it is discovered that one of the unique features of Japan is the "one-missionary" agencies. There are several societies whose sole purpose is to support only one worker, usually a single lady. *Papua New Guinea* is the world's second largest island and the main reason why the data record Oceania increasing 1,057% in eight years. From no tabulated report in 1972 to 491 estimated missionaries in 1980, the growth is significant for world evangelization. Also assisting in Oceania's advance are *The Solomon's*, a diverse grouping of islands consisting of 78 distinct languages.

In Africa, *Uganda* is an encouragement particularly due to the Eastern Orthodox Church and their 1981 missionary recruitment projections. All missionary activity stopped during the years of Amin's regime. Since his defeat, the church reported twenty-two workers for 1980, with a prayerful goal of at least 400 by the end of 1981! *Ethiopia* also faces an erosion of religious freedom, yet reported fifty missionaries for 1980, and an additional 15 for 1981. *Nigeria* represents the leading missionary sending country in the non-Western world. The principle reason for this, however, is that perhaps the largest Third World mission agency is Nigerian, The Church of the Lord, 'Aladura', with 1,250 reported missionaries. Although some Christian leaders question the validity of including this group in the report (it is separatistic and includes aberrative practices in their normal ritual) nevertheless personal correspondence and counsel indicated their identification with basic Biblical doctrines. Also, it is recognized that a portion of their reported missionary force could be part-time evangelists; however, the data recorded here is the information received from the Primate himself, Dr. Emman O. Ade Adejobi. For 1980, he listed 250 missionary couples, 500 single men missionaries and 250 single women missionaries. By counting couples as one, he stated that there are 560 missionaries working among various tribes in Ghana (involving three language groups), 300 in Liberia (also involving three language groups), 150 in Sierra Leone (three language groups) and three in the United Kingdom.

Zaire, a country reportedly experiencing "many restricting laws on Christian activities"(13) demonstrated an impressive 3,611% increase of estimated missionaries over 1972. Because of Zaire's low base number of nine missionaries for 1972, and of its total estimate of 334 for 1980, Zaire received one of the greatest gains of any country during the last eight year period. One larger increase (again due to a low base number) was seen in Kenya with a 6,580% growth rate since 1972. It grew from 15 to 1,002 missionaries in eight years.

One of the reasons why both Kenya and Zaire reported great gain in sending out missionaries is perhaps the term "missionary" is more flexible and open to additional interpretations. Several Independent Churches reported large numbers of missionaries (i.e., Musanda Holy Ghost Church and The Holy Spirit Church of East Africa reported over 200 missionaries each) and one even suggested that our term "missionary" was inapplicable. Evidently, the differences between "missionary," "evangelist" and even "church planting pastor" were not clear. However, the important factor for us in this study is not the label one uses to describe a task, but the function he performs. Based upon responses to our questionnaire, the totals for these countries evidenced a dramatic increase in cross-cultural activity. These totals might have been altered, however, had field research been a viable option.

In Latin America, the general surprise is that the missionary force did *not* increase as expected. While Asia, as a region, grew 368% in missionary personnel, Africa 486%, and Oceania 1,057%, Latin America increased only 16%. And 73% of those missionaries reported in Latin America are Brazilian. Nevertheless, *Guatemala* along with the reports of good church growth also evidenced a 438% increase since 1972, and ranks third in missionary personnel from Latin America. *Chile* should have evidenced more due to its good church growth rates during the seventies, but for lack of sufficient information it was conservatively listed with eight cross-cultural workers. Although *Mexico* has received much Western influence and encouragement in missions, it evidenced very few structured societies. Therefore, a conservative, low total was given based on personal correspondence from that area. Mexico, like *Argentina*, perhaps represents many individual missionaries; evangelists who work effectively yet who are not accountable to any society because they are structurally unaligned with any specific missionary organization. Thus, the data for these Latin countries could represent lower totals than actually exist because the basis for this information primarily rests upon the responses from structured societies, not independent missionaries.

On the basis of the data, the 1980 list of leading missionary sending countries is considerably different from that of 1972. The lists in Figure 9 show this comparison. All the countries in

Oceania are grouped together as one unit because this was the policy
in 1972 when listing countries. It will be continued for compar-
ability.

Figure 9: LEADING TEN MISSIONARY SENDING COUNTRIES

By number of Estimated and Reported Missionaries
in comparison with the 1972 Study.(14)

	1972			1980	
Country	Reported Mis.	Total Estimated Mis.	Country	Reported Mis.	Total Estimated Mis.
1. Nigeria	810	820	1. Nigeria	2,350	2,500
2. India	543	598	2. India	1,677	2,277
3. Brazil	495	595	3. Ghana	827	1,127
4. U.S.A. (Third World)	438	448	4. Kenya	827	1,002
5. Philippines	155	170	5. Burma	988	988
6. Japan	95	137	6. Oceania*	691	706
7. Mexico	64	69	7. Brazil	649	693
8. So. Africa	59	84	8. So. Africa	569	579
9. Oceania*	56	61	9. Philippines	364	544
10. Korea	33	38	10. Korea	319	499

* - All the countries representing *Oceania* were placed
together as one group for the 1972 data. Therefore,
the same was done in 1980, providing the sixth largest
missionary sending "country" in the Third World.

Personnel and Agencies. By combining personnel and agencies, new
data are formed. One of the most popular questions in this area
concerns the largest missionary sending agencies in the non-Western
world. Again, Nigeria is prominent. India, although it has the
most agencies does not have the most missionaries; Nigeria does
with 2,500. India would have represented the most had it not been
for the Church of the Lord 'Aladura.' This one agency accounts
for almost half of Nigeria's mission sending force. Although some
question its inclusion, personal correspondence (even though
limited) indicated its missionary value, so it is included in
the list of the largest sending agencies which appear in Figure 10.

Figure 10: TOP TEN MISSIONARY SENDING AGENCIES

Based upon Reported Missionaries and
Compared with the 1972 Study.(15)

	1972				1980		
	Agency	Country	Mis.		Agency	Country	Mis.
1.	Christ Apostolic Church	Nigeria	616	1.	Church of The Lord 'Aladura'*	Nigeria	1,250
2.	Evangelize China Fellowship, Inc.	U.S.A.	350	2.	Burmese Baptist Convention	Burma	887
3.	Malabar Mar Thoma Syrian Evangelistic Association	India	250	3.	Apostles Revelation Society*	Ghana	569
4.	Brazilian Bapt. Convention	Brazil	250	4.	Evangelical Lutheran Church	Papua New Guinea	450
5.	New Tribes Mis.	Brazil	200	5.	Evangelical Mis. Society	Nigeria	440
6.	Evangelical Mis. Society	Nigeria	194	6.	Reformed Independent Churches Association	So. Africa	407
7.	All India Prayer Fellowship	India	142	7.	Brazilian Baptist Convention	Brazil	370
8.	No. Philippines Union Mis. of Seventh-Day Adventists	Philippines	72	8.	Musanda Holy Ghost Church*	Kenya	350
9.	Chinese Foreign Missionary Union	U.S.A.	66	9.	Evangelize China Fellowship	U.S.A.	308
10.	The Apostolic Faith Mission of South Africa	So. Africa	59	10.	The Brotherhood of the Cross	Nigeria	290
11.	Iglesia Evangelica de Los Peregrinos	Mexico	59				

* - These are African Independent Churches. Had field research
been a viable option, the results as reported here might have
been altered. However, this information comes from questionnaire
returns and personal correspondence with each group.

It is difficult to form a list such as the one above on the basis of equals, for great variation exists within the Third World. A tremendous difference in definition and structure - even within the same country (i.e., Nigeria) - is illustrated by two mission sending groups: The Church of the Lord 'Aladura' and The Evangelical Missionary Society. The first group fully identifies itself as part of the African Independent Church movement. The participants within 'Aladura' adhere to several questionable doctrines, maintain a limited missionary sending structure and practice an inclusive definition of "missionary." The Evangelical Missionary Society, on the other hand, is more identifiable with Western mission sending structures. This group is very evangelical in doctrine, well organized in structure (directed under the able leadership of Panya Baba) and practices an exclusive definition of "missionary." This last point explains why the Evangelical Missionary Society reported perhaps one-third the missionaries of 'Aladura.'

This variation in the definition of "missionary" is observed elsewhere. It is probable that the Malabar Mar Thoma Syrian Evangelistic Association (number three, 1972) (16) and the Evangelical Lutheran Church of Papua New Guinea (number four, 1980) equate mono-cultural pastoral activities with cross-cultural missionary endeavors, because both ministries are performed by church leadership. This is *not* abnormal among Third World missionary societies. A few other societies in the non-Western world are accustomed to lump together both local evangelists and resident foreign missionaries. To compare all societies on equal standards is very difficult. Certainly field research would have helped to sift through the many differences by measuring the diverse practices against one common definition. Nevertheless, those listed in Figure 10 represent the best possible deciphering of definitions and the best attempt at placing those who appear to be involved in cross-cultural endeavors together in one list. The vast majority of those included in these charts are involved in cross-cultural activities, working in evangelistic and church planting endeavors as funds and their society permit.

Perhaps the important inquiry into the emerging Third World missions scene concerns an analysis between the population of each region and the corresponding non-Western missionary force represented in that same region. It is important because from these data, much mission strategy and deployment can be made for world evangelization. If *Africa*, for example, represents 13.5% of the non-Western world, but records 28.26% of all the Third World agencies and 45% of all estimated Third World missionaries, what does this signify for the accomplishment of the Great Commission? Furthermore, if most of these African missionaries remain in cross-cultural endeavors *within* Africa, what does this imply to the great unevangelized areas *outside* of Africa? Should African leaders begin to encourage their missionaries to consider even more seri-

Figure 11: A REGIONAL ANALYSIS BETWEEN POPULATION,
MISSIONARIES, AND AGENCIES

P - Percent of Total Third World *Population*.(17)
A - Percent of Total Number of *Active* Third World Missionary
Agencies.
M - Percent of Total Number of Estimated Third World *Missionaries*.*

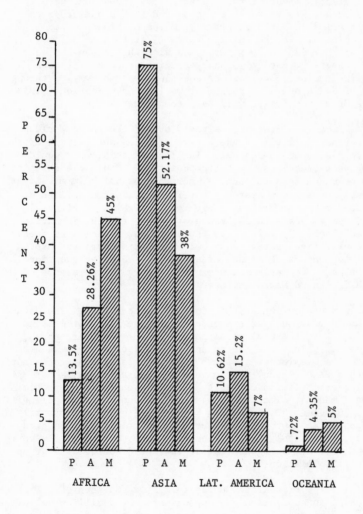

ously the work in other less represented portions of the Third
World? Or, because Africa is so diverse and because the estimated
5,884 African missionaries are significantly small in comparison
with their large continent, should their leaders encourage them
to continue working cross-culturally within Africa - without
attempting to give balance worldwide to frontier missions? Obviously, the answer is partly financial. Yet another part concerns
priorities. The list of values which each African society accepts
must be studied in light of these statistics. Questions need to
be asked such as, "Is it worth it to us and to God's Kingdom to
send missionaries to Northern Brazil, to the Carribean or to
certain peoples within the United States (just to name a few
places)?" or "How can we *best* serve God with what resources we
presently possess?" Each missionary sending group has its own
contextualized values; but also these values must be viewed through
the prism of God's overall program of world evangelization. This
is how the Great Commission will be accomplished.

   Latin America is different. With 10.69% of the Third World population, it reports 15.22% of the active agencies but only 7% of the
non-Western missionary personnel. In light of this, what would be
a few pertinent questions for Latin societies? Could the existing
societies be encouraged towards new horizons of faith in missionary
recruitment? Does Latin America itself possess unevangelized or
even "hidden" peoples which necessitate cross-cultural witness?
And if so, how many are there, where are they, and who is attempting to reach them? By faith, can the seven percent grow to twelve
during the next five years? And would the Latin American church
be willing to support these new missionaries? Similar questions
can also be asked for Asia and Oceania. Figure 11 represents
these data for Third World Regions.

   Another way of looking at this inquiry is to use the same data
on Third World missions (as presented in Figure 11), but instead
of comparing it to the biological population of the Third World,
to contrast it against the Protestant population. This will
demonstrate the missionary strength and weakness of the Protestant
Church within each region. The emphasis here, however, is not
upon the larger Christian community of nearly one billion people
(including Roman Catholics, Orthodox, Independent and Evangelical
Churches), but upon the Protestant Community (including primarily
the Independent and Evangelical Churches). Worldwide, this group
represents approximately 420 million believers, or 10% of the world
population.(18) Or, being limited to the Third World, this group
represents 155.5 million.

   Regionally, the Protestant Church in *Africa* consists of 27% of
the total African population and approximates 84.5 million believers
(or 54.35% of the total Third World Protestant population).(19) In
Asia the Protestant Church represents 2.75% of the total Asian popu-

Figure 12: A REGIONAL ANALYSIS BETWEEN THE PROTESTANT
POPULATION, MISSIONARIES AND AGENCIES*

P - Percent of Total Third World *Protestant* Population,
R - Percent of Protestant Church in *Regional* Population.
A - Percent of Total Number of *Active* Third World Missionary
    Agencies.
M - Percent of Total Number of Estimated Third World *Missionaries*.

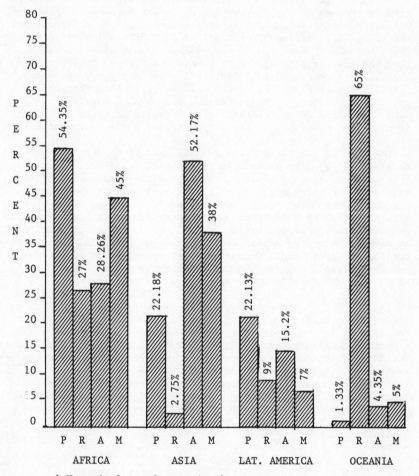

* Numerical totals are in the text.

lation with 34.5 million believers (or 22.18% of the total Third
World Protestant population).(20)   In *Latin America* the Protestant
Church represents approximately 9% of the total Latin region with
over 34.4 million believers (or 22.13% of the total Third World
Protestant population).(21)   In *Oceania* the Protestant Church represents 65% of the whole Pacific region, listing over 2.1 million
believers (or 1.33% of the total Third World Protestant population).
(22)

Obviously statistics for Third World Protestant populations vary
greatly because not only are there different bases upon which the
various denominations count members and not only do different governmental agencies define "Protestant" and/or "Christian" in diverse
ways, but also "every day of the year there are an estimated sixty
thousand new Christians. Every week about sixteen hundred new
churches are started."(23)   The statistics used above are dated
(1978) and therefore, represent smaller totals than that which
probably exist today.   Nevertheless, Figure 12 visualizes these
data, resulting in an interesting chart which presents a comparison between mission agencies and their own Protestant Church.

The Lord of the Harvest has taught us to count the cost, to
measure our days, to pursue His priorities, Scripture indicates
that wise stewardship of our total resources is essential to the
task of world evangelization.   Thus it is important to analyze
our activity and to present recent missionary data.   For with this
data in hand, the ability to be wise stewards and to promote sound
mission strategy become easier for all world Christians.   Critical
questions concerning missionary activity and personnel deployment
are better understood.   Comparisons between the size of populations
and the strength of missions are further clarified.   World Christians must ask tough questions and study recent data.

Yet it is not *only* necessary to study recent data, but *also* to
study the futuristic trends of missions.   Simply put, the recent
data reveal the size of missions whereas the trends reveal their
direction.   Therefore, it is to this subject of Third World Mission
trends that we now turn.   For there are several significant characteristics, inherent within the development of Third World mission
activity today, which will determine the course of missions for
years to come.

6

EMERGING TRENDS IN
THIRD WORLD MISSIONS

At the turn of the century, mission strategists Henry Venn (General Secretary of the Church Missionary Society in England) and the American Congregationalist Rufus Anderson independently came to the same conclusion. A Christian body which remains dependent on outside help and looks to some other outside body for support and guidance will never grow beyond the state of infancy. If a mission agency is dependent upon foreign assistance, it remains subordinate and limited. If an agency becomes autonomous, indigenous in structure and contextualized in content, different patterns of ministry emerge because of its freed nature. The 1980 Study on Third World mission agencies concerns itself primarily with such freed and autonomous groups.

Within Africa, Asia and Latin America today, there are at least 368 of these cross-cultural, autonomous agencies. These 368 agencies are sending out an estimated 13,000 national missionaries who work in every region of the world. Because they are supported and directed by non-Western personnel, interesting trends emerge. Some of these trends are similar to Western characteristics; others are significantly different. It is important for world Christians to understand these trends since much of the responsibility for global evangelization will be in the hands of Third World peoples.

For example, one significant characteristic of Third World missions is that 77% of these non-Western missionaries can be theologically labeled *evangelical*. The word evengelical comes from the Greek EVANGELION, and means the evangel or good news. It describes anyone who is devoted to the good news of Christ's redemption. Recently, within the United States, this term has been used to

include several diverse yet conservative beliefs (see Robert E.
Webber's COMMON ROOTS); the same diversity exists within the Third
World. For interpretive purposes, our study places "evangelical"
in counter-distinction to other theological persuasions such as
"Ecumenical/Conciliar" (the approach of dialogue towards unity),
"Liberation" (the pursuit of freedom from oppression) and "Separa-
tist" (spiritual purity through withdrawal). This resulted in the
assumption that within non-Western missions today, there appears
to be a direct relationship between those who are evangelicals and
those who are involved in cross-cultural evangelistic endeavors.

During February 1980, a special effort was made to discover new
ecumenically oriented missionary endeavors within the Third World.
Seventy-two personal letters were sent to specially chosen ecumenical leaders throughout the world in hopes of finding additional
groups which might not be discovered by the standard questionnaire.
Four responses were received and no new endeavors were discovered.
Among those listed and personally confirmed, only 7% were found to
be ecumenical.

This indicates that among the various possible theological persuasions evangelical beliefs significantly affect the development
of cross-cultural missionary endeavors. To believe in the Bible
as God's authoritative Word, to accept man as basically sinful and
to be convinced that one must accept Christ's vicarious death on
the cross in order to receive salvation are a few of the evangelical positions which seem to motivate believers towards involvement in missions. Normally, one does not accept the lostness of
man and the free offer of salvation by Christ without thinking of
missions. The regional data concerning these diverse persuasions
of those agencies who responded to our questionnaire is presented
in Figure 13.

Figure 13: THEOLOGICAL PERSUASIONS OF
MISSIONARY AGENCIES

Based upon data from the returned
Questionnaires, both the estimated
number of missionaries and the
regional *percentages* are reported
for each theological persuasion.

	Evangelical		Fundamental		Charismatic		Liberation		Ecumenical	
Afria	3,707	63%	412	7%	941	16%	177	3%	647	11%
Asia	4,183	84%	150	3%	448	9%			199	4%
Latin America	704	74%	48	5%	200	21%				
Oceania	621	88%							85	12%
Percentage of Total	9,215 miss.	77%	610 miss.	4%	1,589 miss.	12%	177 miss.	.01%	931 miss.	7%

Another significant characteristic of these missionary agencies
concerns their history as indigenous groups and their present church
affiliation. For example, throughout the non-Western world, it is
calculated that 45% of these agencies are closely connected with
or sponsored by their own denominations. But in addition, the
interesting fact is that almost an equal number of cross-cultural
missionary societies (44%) are oriented interdenominationally.
What the United States experienced after the Second World War, by
seeing dozens of interdenominational "Faith Missions" develop, is
similar to what the Third World is experiencing. For every denominational group, there is almost one interdenominational agency.

Seventy-five percent of all Third World agencies were originally
started as indigenous groups, without foreign or Western administrative direction. Although all claim indigenity now, the vast majority
began as contextualized as possible, thus demonstrating God's hand
in producing this apparent balance between denominational and interdenominational groups. A regional analysis of these data is found
in Figure 14.

There are many trends, such as those mentioned above which surface through the questionnaires and correspondence. Each one
describes an important aspect of Third World missions. Together
they not only portray the differences between Western and non-Western

Figure 14: REGIONAL PERCENTAGES OF INITIAL INDIGENEITY
AND DENOMINATIONAL AFFILIATION

A. INITIAL INDIGENEITY - Percentage of agencies which were founded as indigenous societies.

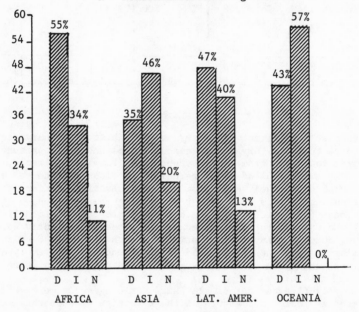

Africa   - 82%

Asia   - 89%   equals

Lat. Amer. - 71%

Oceania - 57%

25%

75%

75% of the total
reported Third
World Societies
were founded as
indigenous agencies.

B. DENOMINATIONAL AFFILIATION

D - Denominational Agencies
I - Interdenominational Agencies
N - Nondenominational Agencies

TOTAL PERCENTAGES

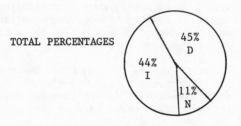

45%
D

44%
I

11%
N

agencies, but also the changes (or lack of) within the Third World itself.

Some of these missionary trends are difficult to measure. For example, Marlin Nelson, in 1976, mentioned the problem of "diaspora" missionaries - "those working among their own nationality in another country."(1) What Nelson cited continues. However, it is difficult to gather precise data concerning the degree of "foreignness" which each missionary confronts as he or she is sent out to witness. The 1980 study indicates that the majority of Korean, Japanese and Ghanian missionaries work with very familiar cultures, similar to their own. Yet as one researches the specific endeavor, significant differences still emerge. Even though Korean believers work with Koreans in other countries, many of them face cultural dissimilarities. There is the dissimilarity of *context* (i.e., a rural Korean working among urban Koreans in Los Angeles, U.S.A.) or the dissimilarity of *content* (i.e., a first generation Korean-born missionary working among second generation "Brazilianized" Koreans in San Paulo, Brazil). Subtle linguistic and conceptual differences remain. In India, over 90% of the 2,277 Indian missionaries never leave their own country. They work with one or more of the 800 different linguistic Indian groups. Perhaps some are involved in pure "diaspora" missions. Yet to what extent can this be measured? Can there be any missionary endeavor without some cultural dissimilarity? Can different linguistic entonations and regionalized expressions, even with the same known language, be considered elements of cross-cultural exposure? Although the tendency to prefer involvement with one's *own* people exists (i.e., Brazilian *Paulistas* working with Brazilian New Yorkers), it remains a trend which is difficult to measure unless one visits all workers and standardizes judgments.

There are other trends, however, which facilitate documentation. Three specific ones were included in the questionnaire, which more fully describe these Third World agencies. They concern missionary training, missionary finances and missionary partnership. A brief report of each is given.

Missionary Training. One of the most significant emerging trends within Third World Missions is indigenous missionary training. Instead of depending upon foreign instruction, the general thrust is for agencies to create their own pre-service candidate training.

Rev. P.K. Amponsah, senior pastor of the Church of Salvation, writes, describing this church's private training institute:

> Aspiring missionaries are trained at our headquarters at Techiman, Nkwaeso (Ghana). They fast and pray for several days and become spiritually developed. After some time, when they are found and considered to be competent, they are sent out to one of our sub-stations in the Ashanti regions where they carry out their missionary work.(2)

Another example of indigenous candidate training comes from the Independent Lutheran Church of Kenya. Before departing for the field, each missionary studies "missiology, arts and crafts, music and literature."(3) Notice the involvement with both spiritual (missiology) and practical aspects (arts, crafts, music, etc.) of candidate training. This is normal for non-Western pre-service preparation. Not only is there a desire to coordinate their own candidate training programs, but also to provide balanced training.

Additional indications of Third World training surfaced as completed questionnaires were returned. Question D6 (see Appendix I) refers to several areas of training which might be considered "basic training or preparation...for missionaries *before* they depart for the field." Among the possibilities are Bible Institute, Language Learning, Seminary, Practical Experience and Mission-Related Orientation. The significance of this question is that every agency which responded, indicated personal involvement in missionary candidate training. The average number of requirements by Third World mission agencies everywhere is 2.61. Bible Institute, Practical Experience and Mission-Related Orientation appeared on 70% of the returns. Again, the balance between spiritual (Bible Institute) and practical aspects (Practical Experience) is evident.

Regionally, *Asia* averages 2.65 training requirements in pre-service orientation, *Oceania* responds with 2.25 training areas, *Africa* indicates 2.61 items while *Latin America* lists a high 2.92 preparatory stages. Obviously, not every missionary receives such complete training; and not every agency within the same region requires the same pre-service preparation. However, all responding agencies seem to support the assumption that pre-service candidate training is an integral element within Third World missions today.

Furthermore, from our questionnaire, an interesting relationship between the number of designated requirements for pre-service training and the length of time required by the mission for a missionary's normal term of service on the field was noted. By viewing this regionally, Latin America expressed the general desire to train each

candidate in nearly three separate pre-service stages. This is
the highest expressed level of regional training anywhere in the
Third World. Directly related to this is the fact that *Latin
America* prefers the longest term of service, being an average of
3.95 years. *Oceania*, on the other hand, represents the lowest
level of training requirements (2.25) and also reports the shortest
expected term of service (3.06 years). Thus, there could be a
direct relationship between training and term of service: the
more extensive the pre-service candidate training becomes, the
longer the term of service is required for a missionary on the
field. And although this is difficult to prove definitely, nevertheless Figure 15 visualizes this possible relationship and further
illustrates the trend that Third World mission agencies are exten-
sively involved in pre-service candidate training.

Figure 15: REGIONAL RELATIONSHIPS BETWEEN TRAINING
            REQUIREMENTS AND TERM OF SERVICE

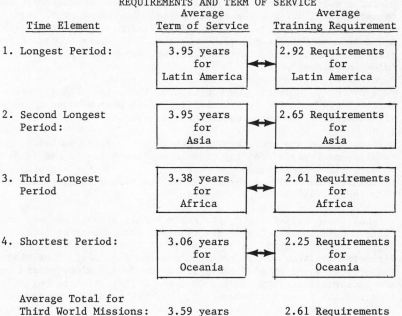

Time Element	Average Term of Service	Average Training Requirement
1. Longest Period:	3.95 years for Latin America	2.92 Requirements for Latin America
2. Second Longest Period:	3.95 years for Asia	2.65 Requirements for Asia
3. Third Longest Period	3.38 years for Africa	2.61 Requirements for Africa
4. Shortest Period:	3.06 years for Oceania	2.25 Requirements for Oceania
Average Total for Third World Missions:	3.59 years	2.61 Requirements

One significant factor important to any successful program of candidate training and mission outreach is lay interest. And the fact that most every agency reported an increasing interest in missions on the part of their lay people is important to Third World missionary education.

Statistically, this report on lay interest can be observed in two stages. The first concerns the present reality. On a scale where 2.0 represents "little interest," 3.0 equals "some interest" and 4.0 is "much interest," the average rating of lay members by Third World agencies is 3.4 (or "Significant Interest"). *Asia's* agencies responded with a 3.5, indicating that her lay people demonstrate considerable interest toward missionary outreach. *Oceania* rated 3.25, Africa scored 3.65, and *Latin America* received the low 3.19. The second stage concerns future projections of missionary interest by lay people. Virtually every agency that completed a questionnaire agreed with the fact that the interest level is increasing. If 2.0 represents perfect agreement by *all* agencies, *Asia* scored 1.99, *Oceania* tabulated 1.88, *Africa* represented 1.95 and *Latin America* rated 1.95. With such lay interest, candidate preparation can do no other than become even more adept in its purposes and plans.

Missionary Finances. On February 2, 1980, His Holiness Dr. Angali-I of "H.H. The Angali Loyalist Missionary Sending Agency" of Kenya, wrote me saing that they are hoping:

> ...to send her Black Missionaries to foreign countries. Ways and means of sending them is our problem. We can send more Black Missionaries to various places but you can pray for us. Our major problem lies at the side of *finance* and *material*.(4)

What Dr. Angali-I wrote has been repeated often. No less than fifteen additional letters were received from countries like Nigeria, India, Burma and Guatemala, all stating the same need for financial assistance. It became clear that in order to maintain the present level of missionary involvement, let alone expand into new endeavors, further funding is needed. Inflation is beginning to drain the financial accounts of many Third World agencies.

Statistically 91% of all funding for non-Western missions comes from the Third World. Ten of the responding fifty six-countries reported 100% indigenous funding. Yet in spite of this good news, many missionaries do *not* receive their full salary. Approximately 24% of the Asian missionaries, 40% of Oceania's workers, 49% of the African laborers and 27% of the Latin American personnel do not receive their full salary. At times this forces the missionary into extra agricultural pursuits as partial substitutes. Tent

making in secular jobs is another alternative. It also explains
why many agencies have openly requested additional funding.

Some might think that part of this problem is caused by the
high percentage of indigenous funding. Africa, for example,
representes the highest level of unpaid salaries (49%) and also
receives the highest level of indigenous funding (95.27%). However, Asia has the second highest level of indigenous funding
(91.7%) and represents the highest percentage of paid salaries
(76%). Therefore, indigenous funding cannot always be the direct
cause of unpaid salaries.

Others might blame unorthodox payment schedules as part of the
problem. It is true that some non-Western societies have the
policy of paying the missionary's salary only once to twice a year.
But, similar to the West, 92.5% of the non-Western societies prefer
to pay salaries on a monthly basis. Africa represents the one major
digression with 17% of the reported agencies paying yearly, bi-
yearly or quarterly. Yet in Asia, with the lowest percentage of
unpaid full salaries (24%), 9% of her agencies prefer long extended
periods for paying salaries. Thus, unorthodox payment schedules
have little contributing influence towards causing 35% of the Third
World missionaries to work on less than full salary.

There are other possible reasons for partial payments, such as
insufficient lay support, poor priorities or international governmental restrictions. But with the present increase in lay interest,
and the additional opportunities for mission partnership (even with
the West), some of this deficit will be removed. Figure 16 relates
the tabulated financial information.

Figure 16: THIRD WORLD AGENCY FINANCIAL INFORMATION

A. Sources: What percentage of total received funds come *from* the
              Third World?

                    Africa   - 95.27%
                    Asia   - 91.7%
                    La. America - 88.17%
                    Oceania   - 88.75%

B. Payment:

    1. When - How often is the salary paid?

                    Africa   - 81% Monthly; 2% Weekly; 17% Yearly,
                                   Bi-yearly or Quarterly
                    Asia   - 89% Monthly; 2% Weekly; 9% Quarterly
                                   or other
                    La. America - 100% Monthly
                    Oceania   - 100% Monthly

Figure 16: Continued

B. Payment:

2. How Much - What percentage receives a full promised salary?

              Africa   - 51%
              Asia   - 76%
              La. America - 73%
              Oceania   - *60%*

                 Average   65% (or 35% do *not* receive their
                           full promised salary)

Missionary Partnership. In the September 1980 issue of World
Vision's MARC Newsletter, the following commanded front page.

World vision and the Asia Evangelistic Commission (AEC)
are pioneering a new concept in mission-church relations.
Called the Korea-Indonesian Church Planting project, Korean
Churches and World Vision are assisting Indonesian Churches
to plant 100 new congregations over a two-year period.
Thirty-five have already been planted.

This partnership grew out of the vision of Dr. Han Chul-
Ha, associate director of the Asian Center for Theological
Studies and Mission in Seoul, Korea. Christianity has
grown rapidly in Korea. Some reports indicate up to six
new churches are planted daily. Dr. Han wanted to see the
zeal to evangelize Korea broadened to view Asia as a whole.
He felt that Indonesia was an ideal place to begin.(5)

Recently, similar ideas were expressed in a book entitled
Chinese and Western Leadership Cooperation Seminar Compendium.
Within it, various leaders of active Third World agencies ex-
pressed their opinions concerning missionary partnership. Philip
Teng, says:

The missionary cry among the Chinese churches today may
be the first sign of the touch off of the release of the
expansive power that will generate a doubling or a tripl-
ing growth of the Chinese churches around the world....
(This can be seen) if western missions open up their
fellowship to Chinese missionaries who meet their standard
of training and spiritual calibre and who will serve under
the direction of their field chairman or conference.(6)

Thomas Wang, continues,

We would like Western churches to know: this is the best
time for Chinese and Western cooperation. We strongly believe that under such cooperation, the Gospel will be preached
unto all parts of the world.(7)

Missionary literature from various parts of the globe is full of
ideas concerning partnership. Primarily these ideas are not organizational but associational in nature. They are cooperative working agreements between agencies; they will assist to form international teams of missionary specialists for evangelistic purposes.
And what is expressed in books and magazines was also indicated in
the questionnaire responses. It is a third major emerging theme.
Figure 17 presents the data.

Figure 17: MISSIONARY PARTNERSHIP

Reading: 1.40 to 1.50 is hesitant to participate

1.50 to 1.75 is acceptive to participate

1.75 to 2.0 is very willing to participate

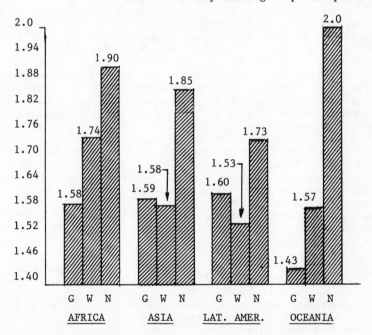

Note: G - General willingness to participate
W - Willingness to participate with Westerners
N - Willingness to participate with non-Westerners

According to the above data, *Asia* is very willing to cooperate
with other agencies but also expresses the highest number of reservations (fifteen). It is important to note that almost three-
fourths of these reservations concern difficulties with theological
differences. Partnership is permitted when theological persuasions
are compatible. *Oceania* rated the lowest in willingness to cooperate with other agencies. Part of the reason, perhaps, is because
almost half the agencies are strong denominational groups, and that
43% of the agencies were *not* founded as indigenous groups and already experienced some form of foreign influence. *Africa* is willing
to cooperate, but as with Asia, records many reservations (twelve).
Latin America seems to be the most open towards missionary participation. With the highest rating (1.6) and one of the lowest number
of expressed reservations (two), Latin America, particularly Brazil,
is ready for certain types of associative activity, principally if
the other partner is equal in both status and responsibility.

Regarding partner preference, all regions are more willing to
cooperate with non-Westerners than with Westerners. With any rating over 1.50 being acceptive of cooperation, the toal results for
all of the Third World missionary agencies showed a 1.61 towards
Westerners and a 1.87 towards non-Westerners. The difference (.26)
represents a favorable increase in willingness to cooperate with
those "from below" rather than with those "from above."

This never implys that Third World agencies are exclusively
interested in developing cooperative endeavors only among themselves. The above cited illustrations show this. It does mean,
however, that if choices are available, some will prefer those
who, like themselves, identify with the Third World.

One good description of the non-Westerner's relationship with
the West is indicated by Figure 18. *Asia* reports an interdependent spirit with the West, whereas *Oceania* reveals a tendency
towards independence. *Africa* and *Latin America* are equal in rat-
ings and demonstrate almost half and half - half independent and
half interdependent. Obviously, the self-image of Third World
missionary agencies has greatly matured, involving a good level
of self-confidence.

WHAT DOES ALL THIS MEAN TO ME?

Summarizing simply, we are all members of Christ's body. We are
all commissioned to "make disciples" (Matthew 28:19). We need to
learn about each other in order to work together in world evangelization.

Statistically, by the year 2000, Mexico City will swell to more
than 31 million people.(8) If we are all under orders to "make

disciples," we need to know which groups will work together in
Mexico City and win the yet unreached people to Christ?   In India
by the year 2000, "Calcutta will teem with nearly 20 million, and
more than 15 million will jam Bombay and Cairo, Jakarta and
Seoul."(9)   Who will strategize and reach those yet unreached
peoples?   Sao Paulo will join hands with Rio de Janeiro and from
one giant "megalopolis of 50 million habitants with tragic conditions of life, lack of services, pollution and violence."(10)   Who
will be partners for this near-impossible conquest?

No longer is missions dressed only in North American clothes
and speaking English.   There are hundreds of additional tongues,
dressed in simple garbs which God is using mightily.   Third World
missions is part of God's plan.   To be a world Christian is to
live in this dimension.

Figure 18:   REPORTED RELATIONSHIP OF THIRD WORLD
AGENCIES WITH WESTERN CHURCHES

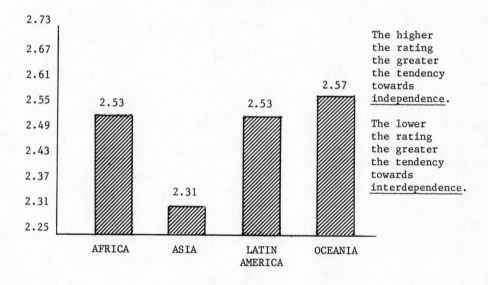

The higher
the rating
the greater
the tendency
towards
independence.

The lower
the rating
the greater
the tendency
towards
interdependence.

7

OF PEOPLE AND PLACES

In September of 1977 the Lord called my family and me
to serve Him at the Tuba City Presbyterian Church and
Mission in Arizona. The Tuba City Presbyterian Mission
is located at the Western End of the Navajo Indian Reservation in Northern Arizona, about 80 miles north of the
City of Flagstaff. We feel excited, yet somewhat appre-
hensive, for we have never worked in an American Indian
Mission before. Moreover, all our experience in the past
was either in cities or large towns. This is our first
experience working and living in an isolated rural area.
But, trusting in the all-sufficient power of Christ as
promised in the Scripture, 'I can do all things through
Christ who strengthens me' (Philippians 4:13), we set
out for Tuba City.(1)

One of the significant facts about the above diary is that the
author is not a North American from New York but a Chinese from
Asia. Upon arriving at the Navajo Indian Reservation, Paul and
Polly Wong experienced all the dimensions of culture shock which
westerners normally experience during their first months overseas.
Yet with their heart set to the task, the Wongs began to evangelize
Indian youths through Bible classes on weekdays and worship services on weekends. Apparently, the Indians and the Wongs mutually
benefited from these efforts.

The missionary structure which coordinated their efforts and
supported their financial needs also provided the Wongs with a
simple yet adequate home, weekly transportation and the necessary
complex of church buildings from which to minister. Although Paul

and Polly were willing to work cross-culturally among the Navajo
Indians, they probably never would have done so had it not been
for the already existing missionary organization. They not only
received help from their missionary colleagues, but experienced
greater gains in the ministry due to the agency's established
rapport with the people. Thus, the second fact, although only
implied in the above diary, is that a missionary agency structure (which provided the Wong's with a platform for ministry) is
a key for continual and expanding cross-cultural evangelistic
activity within the Third World.

It is important to note that today Third World missionary agencies average an expected personnel increase of 21% for 1981. If
we use the data of 13,000 estimated missionaries as our 1980 base,
this means that by the end of 1981, there could be at least 15,730
cross-cultural workers. This is impressive! Yet due to the regional enormity and explosive growth of the Third World church, these
facts will only represent a portion of the true picture. There
will be additional missionaries sent out by the many as yet un-
established agencies; and it is virtually impossible to project
this growth. For example, in Asia, the 1980 study listed forty-
three newly formed agencies involving at least 755 missionaries
who were not even included in the projections of 1972. Similar
data are seen from both the African independent churches and Latin
American renewal movements. Thus, with today's increasing interest
and high recruitment rates could it be that the next decade would
see even more activity than before.

One principle for missionary recruitment worldwide is that there
must be *a sufficient number of financially sound agencies located
within physical, psychological and doctrinal proximity to enable a
constantly increasing number of potential missionaries to serve
cross-culturally in evangelistic and/or church planting endeavors.*
This principle implys such a vast diversity of international agencies and boards that our present picture is only a shadow of a more
extensive and fully developed age of newer agencies to come.

But how will these agencies begin? How can they be established
and grow? Some Western evangelical agencies are studying this subject in order to stimulate the creation of newer agencies. One
worthy mention is the International Missionary Advance, located in
Pasadena, California. Another within the Third World is the
Brazilian arm of O.C. Ministries, Inc. (SEPAL). Both are helping
in the formation of yet newer societies so that more missionaries
will assist in the task of world evangelization.

One way of learning how *we* might be involved in developing new
Third World mission structures is to study *older* agencies. How
were they formed? What do they indicate to us regarding the future?

Is it possible for foreigners to initiate an indigenous missionary
structure? Is it possible for a smaller church to establish a missionary agency by cooperating with a larger, more established group?
It is profitable for cross-cultural ministers, to work independently,
separate from any church or denomination? What are the basic signs
indicating the readiness of some Third World people to organize
themselves into a mission sending agency? Certainly a study of the
past can help us understand how we can become efficient "agency
initiators."

Study reveals that Third World missionary activity was initiated
in at least four ways: 1) Foreign Influence; 2) Indigenous Influence; 3) Cooperative Agreements; and 4) Individual Service. Each
one represents a means by which God forms new missionary sending
agencies. Could it be, if we reflect upon these four historical
patterns, that we will be encouraged not only to support the well-
known, already existing Third World agencies, but also to pray for
the formation of others, even to assist in their formation if the
opportunity and ability exist? For this purpose, examples or para-
digms of each method are here presented.

FOREIGN INFLUENCE

The Aymaras of Bolivia

High in Bolivia's Andes Mountains is a large tribe of Aymara
Indians. Numbering over one million, the Aymaras had been traditionally resistant to the Gospel, until small community-wide people
movements began during the second decade of this century. Since
1972, the Gospel has been widely received, causing church growth
among all the existing denominations. The evangelistic activity
was done primarily by the Aymara's themselves producing an indigenous Christianity. Yet, while they worked "to save" their brothers, there existed virtually no *foreign* missionary vision among
them at all. Their effective evangelistic activity began and
ended with themselves.

Bruno Frigoli was an Assembly of God missionary among the
Aymaras during the seventies, the period of their greatest receptivity. One of his accomplishments was to develop an evangelistic
program called "Each-Church-One-Church-In-One-Year" which helped
20 Aymaran churches become 400 in five years.(2) But his greatest
contribution to the Aymaras began for him on September 9, 1977.
While representing Latin America at the Montreal Executive Meeting
of the Lausanne Congress on Evangelization, Frigoli received a
further challenge from C. Peter Wagner concerning the Aymaras and
their potential missionary involvement.

It was five years earlier, in 1972, when Wagner himself began to consider the Aymaras, praying that they would send missionaries to the culturally similar Navaho peoples in the United States. Thus, at Montreal, Bruno listened to Wagner's counsel and enthusiastically accepted the challenge to instill the missionary vision among Aymaran leadership. The goal during the next three years was to encourage the Aymara Indians to evangelize cross-culturally the Navaho Indians, a tribe little known and very distant from Bolivia.

Traditionally, the Navahos were hostile to any foreigners; and any potential Aymara missionary needed to learn the difficult and very complex Navaho language. Furthermore, the large Aymara church was untaught in matters concerning the need for missionary training and constant financial support. To provide proper information and adequate training was a significant task in itself. But, in spite of these difficulties, Bruno proceeded to influence the Aymaran Christian leadership towards world missions. Evidently the advantages far outweighed the difficulties.

For example, both the Aymara and Navaho Indians are similar in their physical features, life style, religious idolatry and historical Spanish denomination, acceptance of an imposed language and bilingual ability, tolerance for oppressive overlords, dry lands, high mountains, ponchos and polleras, and youthful culture (50% under 20 years of age).(3) The cultural similarities were so abundant that upon leaving Montreal, Bruno made contact with "some of the most knowledgeable missionaries to the Navahos on the reservation, David Skates and Tom Dolaghan."(4) With them, at Farmington, Mexico, a plan was born. The short range goal to:

> ...prepare a group of Aymara Christian singing evangelists to send along with their regional director to visit the Navaho churches.... After the visit, they will return and inform the Aymaras in Bolivia and the Navahos will or will not invite them.(5)

Once the returned evangelistic team challenged the Aymara churches and after the Navaho invitation was received, the long-range program would begin. This would include the sending of:

> ...two families from Bolivia to live with a family (hogan) in Red Mesa or some (similar) location on a permanent basis. Five years is the missionary term of duty. A third family may be invited to come, after the first two years.(6)

The task is to plant new churches, provide leadership training for Navaho Pastors in the art of planting new churches and to do this on a monthly salary of $400 per month, per family. Language study

is to begin in Bolivia before departure. Also, the plan revealed
that "it would be good to receive a visit of Navaho leaders in
Bolivia during the preparation of the two missionary couples"(7)
in order to assist them in their language study *and* to assist the
Aymaras in their understanding of the Navaho peoples.

In 1979, the first two couples readied themselves to leave
Bolivia for the Navaho Mission field. One of the Aymara church
leaders commented, saying that for us "to send missionaries to the
Navaho Indians is the equivalent of the Americans sending a man to
the moon!"(8) Indeed the concept of missionary sending was foreign
to the Aymaras. Yet with encouragement, the "impossible" became a
reality; the unknown was crossed with confidence. As a foreign
missionary, Bruno Frigoli was used by God to initiate a loosely
structured Third World mission sending agency. Although it began
with him, it has now become a contextualized cross-cultural effort.
It is hoped that the first Aymara missionaries will be sent off to
the U.S.A. soon.

Early Karen Mission
Societies, Burma

One of the more exciting stories from Asia begins with Ko-Thah-
byu, the first Burmese to become a Christian from the Karen tribe.
The Karens were predominantly animistic in their religion and inhabited the mountains and valleys of interior Burma.

In 1828, through the influence of Adoniram Judson, unbelieving
Ko-Thah-byu found employment with and lived within the famous
Burmese Mission compound. Mrs. Wade, one of the original members
of the Mission, writes concerning his time as an employee:

> It was not long after he came to live in our compound,
> that we began to perceive the influence of religion on his
> outward character, and that, by slow degrees, light dawned
> upon his dark mind, and the work of the Holy Spirit became
> perceptible on his hard heart.(9)

Soon after his conversion, missionary George Boardman started to
spend time with him, influencing his life through personalized Bible
study. Eventually Boardman and Ko-Thah-byu moved to the city of
Tavoy, in order to live together in the place then described as "one
of the strongholds of Buddhism."(10) Under close supervision, Ko-
Thah-byu matured in his understanding of the Great Commission, and
developed an evangelistic message. Notice what Mrs. Macleod Wylie,
a friend of Ko-Thah-byu's said about his maturing missionary vision:

> This remarkable man had been a robber and a murderer and
> possessed such an ungovernable temper, that even after his
> conversion he had often to spend many hours in prayer for

strength to overcome it, but he had been "forgiven much and
he had loved much." One who knew him well wrote: "The
preaching of Christ crucified was to his mind a work of
paramount importance to all others. He was not only not
ashamed of the gospel of Christ, but he gloried in being
its humble messenger to guilty men. It has been said if
ever a man hated idolatry it was Ko-Thah-byu. And I would
add if ever a man loved the gospel, Ko-Thah-byu was that
man. It was his love for the gospel that kindled that un-
conquerable desire to proclaim its precious truths to his
fellow men."(11)

Ko-Thah-byu began to travel preaching the gospel to his Karen
people. He gained experience and grew in spiritual authority,
and "as the result of Ko-Thah-byu's indefatigable labours, many
of the Karens from the villages scattered over the mountains of
Tavoy, flocked in from the distant jungles with curious interest."(12) Scores of Karens streamed into the church confessing
Jesus to be the Christ and reflecting the importance which Ko-
Thah-byu placed upon the cross. Additional evangelists were
trained and new regions were reached with the gospel. By 1833,
just five years after Ko-Thah-byu began his training under George
Boardman, several Burmese home missionary societies were formed
by the Karens in both the Tavoy and Moulmein areas. By 1850,
the cross-cultural Bassein Home Mission Society began by appoint-
ing three men to go to a hill tribe several hundred miles away,(13)
an endeavor fully supported and directed by the Karen people! What
God started in Ko-Thah-byu's life, through the influence of George
Boardman, became multiplied a thousand fold in the lives of count-
less other Burmese.

Thus foreign influence towards missionary endeavor cannot only
be directly given to national leaders (as in the case of the
Bolivian Aymaras), but also indirectly channeled to a nation
through the testimony of just one life. It can be instilled in
one potential leader who multiplies the vision in his own contextualized ways.

INDIGENOUS INFLUENCE

The Melanesian Brotherhood, Oceania

    As early as 1830, while Alexander Duff, a renowned mis-
sionary of the Church of Scotland, was beginning to preach
Christ among the young intellectuals in Calcutta, India,
eight Tahitian missionaries were preaching the same Christ
among heathen villagers on the Samoa Islands. Five years
later the first European missionary arrived to find 2,000
native Christians meeting in small groups in sixty-five

villages. It is rather surprising to realize that those
Islanders were missionaries ten years before David Living-
stone landed in Africa; before Hudson Taylor was even born.

Since then, over 1,000 Pacific Islanders have gone out
as missionaries to add a remarkable record to the history
of Christian expansion. One of the most significant of all
the missions in the South Pacific is a dynamic missionary
sodality called the Melanesian Brotherhood. It was born
out of the missionary vision and passion of a young Melanesian; backed up by both Western missionaries and Island
Christians. It has been mightily used of God to win
Thousands of Islanders to Christ.(14)

Geographically, the region under discussion is labeled Oceania.
Little known to most world Christians, Oceania consists of some
1,500 vastly diverse islands which are often divided into three
major groupings:

1. *Polynesia* (Many Islands) including the Marquesa,
   Paumotou, Austral, Society, Cook, Phoenix, Union,
   Samoa and Tonga Islands.

2. *Micronesia* (Little Islands) including such regions
   as the Gilberts, Marshalls, Marianas and Caroline
   Islands.

3. *Melanesia* (Black Islands) including such islands as
   Ellice, Fiji, Santa Cruz, Banks, Loyality, New
   Hebrides, New Caledonia, Solomon, Bismark and Papua
   New Guinea.(15)

The unique history of Melanesian Brotherhood involves all of
Oceania, but focuses its beginning upon the Island of Guadalcanal,
which is part of the Central Solomons within Melanesia.

At the start of our century, Ini Kopuria was born in a small
village of Moravovo, Guadalcanal. Named after a famous Anglo-Saxon
Christian King of Dorset, Ini began to study, receiving the best
possible education through missionary organized schools. Upon
graduation, he joined the armed constabulary, however, after two
years of service, he had an accident which left him permanently
lame. During his convalescense, Ini received a vision from God
saying: "All this I gave to you; what have you given to me?"(16)

Ini could not neglect this vision. He began to dedicate his life
to the Christian ministry. At first he shared the vision with
several nearby Anglican leaders of the Western oriented Malanesian
Mission. "Arthur Hopkins, then in charge of the Mission College at

Maravovo...helped him to shape his dream of spreading the gospel
to every village where he (previously in the armed constabulary)
had sought after prisoners."(17)

Then he shared his idea with Bishop John M. Steward who once
himself dreamed of organizing a brotherhood of active Christian
workers. Now, Ini received encouragement from the Bishop to be
that missionary initiator. Together they structured the basic
rules for Melanesian Brotherhood. The primary thrust, according
to Ini's desire, was "to proclaim the teaching of Jesus Christ
among the heathen, not to work among Christians."(18)

Philip Tsuchiya writes in his historical report:

> Each Brother was to take a vow not to marry for a year,
> nor to take any pay nor disobey their superiors. He could
> choose to renew his vow at the end of each year. Ini, who
> had been deeply impressed with the life of St. Francis of
> Assisi, took a life-long vow in the presence of three dis-
> tinguished witnesses, Bishop John Steward, Bishop F.
> Merivale Molyneux, and Bishop Rev. A.I. Hopkins.

> He was joined by six others who took a similar vow for
> one year. They banded together to go and preach the Gospel
> first to their fellow Islanders and then to the region be-
> yond.(19)

Stuart Artless, another missionary who knew the initial year
writes:

> The year 1925 will be marked in the annuals of the Mission
> as having been the year of the formation of a native Evangel-
> istic Brotherhood, consisting of a small "hand of young men
> whose hearts the Lord hath touched."(20)

The rest is famous missionary history. The Brotherhood eventually divided themselves into households of eight to twelve people
throughout the islands. Bareheaded and simply dressed (black loin-
cloth and white sash), they traveled barefoot while making contacts
with heathen peoples. As they grew in numbers, the Brotherhood
began to reach out to additional islands: Mala, Santa Cruz, New
Britain and even Papua New Guinea. Over one hundred missionaries
were sent out in the fifteen years of existence before the dis-
ruptive Second World War. It took bombing and massive foreign
occupation to stifle their growth but not their evangelistic
spirit. Although Ini died, soon after the war the Melanesian
Brotherhood continued in effective evangelism. "It is reported
that between 1955 and 1975, they were successful in winning forty-
five heathen villages to Christ in New Britain and New Guinea,
involving 9,500 people."(21)

But now the personnel involved is much smaller due to a lack
of evangelistic fervor. With the entrance of many economic pressures and Western modernization, as well as the growth of several
attractive religious sects, Christian nurture has taken the place
of evangelistic endeavors. Preservation of the saints through
pastoral care is now priority.

Nevertheless, Ini Kopuria and his contextualized missionary
movement stand as one of the Third World's success stories. Although assisted by Western counsel, the Melanesian Brotherhood
developed by itself within the thought forms and structural
patterns of Melanesia. Perhaps this is why the national believers supported it so widely. In expression of their support they
developed the Company of Companions, which was a group of active
lay supporters who committed themselves to pray for and contribute
to the Brotherhood while remaining identified with their own local
churches. Also, they developed the Copra Brothers, various groups
of dedicated youths who worked at gathering coconuts and in making
copra in order to help support the missionaries. In short, the
Melanesian Brotherhood became the heroes of the national church.

Their inner strength came from their communal life. They
mutually accepted strict vows, pledging to live together in small
groups, to voice openly their personal criticisms (but *only* among
group members themselves), and to worship and enter into personal
rededication collectively. This created an inner bond of spiritual strength. The guiding star was Ini Kopuria. As he prayed
during the founding of the Brotherhood:

> Myself and my land; my portion with thy servants. I will
> receive no pay from the Mission for work to which Thou shalt
> send me, or which I shall do for Thee. I will remain Thy
> celibate all my days till I die.

> Strengthen me to remain steadfast, quiet, faithful in
> this all the days of my life, on Thee who lives and reign-
> est One, in the truly one Being of God forever. Amen.(22)

The Kingmi Mission of Kalimantan

One of the largest islands within Indonesia's vast possessions
is Kalimantan, known mostly to Westerners as Borneo. A rugged
island with sporadic mountain chains and many coastal swamps,
Kalimantan has been the recipient of much Western missionary
activity. One principal group has been The Christian and Missionary Alliance, which established work among the Dyaks and initiated
the Kingmi Church. Nearly fifty years ago, in response to Western
efforts, national evangelists began taking the gospel to additional

Dyak tribes, sometimes traveling great distances. It was evident
that the Great Commission mandate was an integral part of church
life in Kalimantan.

Recently, however, a much bolder yet indigenous cross-cultural
missionary movement developed through the offer of air transportation. Peter N. Nanfelt, director of Pacific Islands and Hong Kong
for the Christian and Missionary Alliance, shares the exciting
story. The map is given to help locate the significant geographical regions of missionary outreach by the newly established
Kingmi Mission (April, 1973 of the Kingmi church).

The Kerayan Valley in north-east Kalimantan has a population of 8,000-9,000 people. All are professing Christians. The Bible school there usually has about 250
students and every church has 4-5 pastors. A few years
ago the Kerayan Christians finally got the opportunity to
reach out beyond the confines of their very isolated valley
when MAF (Mission Aviation Fellowship) received permission
to launch a flying program in the area.

Between 1973-1976 the Kerayan church sent approximately
40 missionaries to the Berau area (2 hours flying time) to
the south. The missionaries went for a minimum of two
years and ministered to a different tribe in an entirely
different language. They planted about 25 churches in the
area during that period.

More recently, Kerayan workers have gone further south
to the church districts in the Mahakam River Basin to help
pastor churches that were leaderless. At least 15 people
have ministered in this way.

About two years ago, the church in West Kalimantan was
concerned about the unreached villages in the Upper Melawi
River area and asked for workers from Kerayan District.
(Except for MAF flights, there is no transportation or
communication between interior East Kalimantan and interior West Kalimantan). The West Kalimantan churches raised
funds to fly four workers over from the Kerayan. Now there
are six families presently ministering in the Melawi area
of West Kalimantan.

To this point, I have spoken only of the missionary
efforts of the Kerayan District which is one of the nine
districts of the Kingmi Church in East Kalimantan. At
the present time, the East Kalimantan regional leadership
is in the process of launching an even more ambitious program. The island of Java is the most densely populated in

the Indonesian chain. The Kingmi Church is making Java
church planting a top priority, and mission and church
hope to establish 500 churches and church groups in Java
by 1990. The church districts located in the outer islands
have been challenged to send missionaries to Java to participate in this effort. East Kalimantan will probably be
the first region of the church to do so. At the recent
East Kalimantan regional church conference, the church
leaders set a goal to send three families to Java in
1980.(23)

Similar to the Dani missionary movement in nearby Irian Jaya,
the Kalimantan Kingmi Mission has become a model of indigenous
involvement. Through national funding, localized recruit training,
and personalized goal-setting, an indigenous structure emerged for
world evangelization. Because Western missionaries included a
missionary vision as part of their total evangelistic endeavor,
the Kingmi church is now actively involved in Third World Missions.
And this is only the beginning of their enormous potential for
church planting outreach.

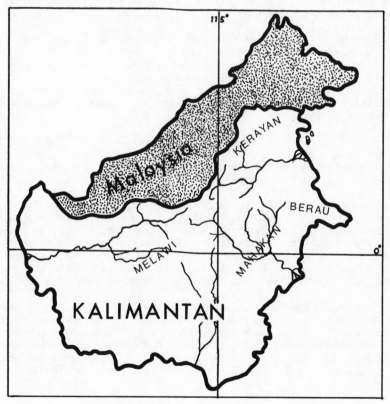

COOPERATIVE AGREEMENTS

Immanuel Gospel Mission, Japan

In July 1938, Pastor David T. Tsutada experienced a revival in his downtown Tokyo church. Being an eminent pastor and teacher-dean of a denominational Bible School (Seikyokai - an indigenous church of the Wesleyan tradition), David Tsutada saw develop during the next four years a loosely structured fellowship called "Revival League." Young ministers from many denominations were attracted to him because of his powerful preaching. As a result, this inter-denominational group grew stronger and began to evangelize Tokyo.

As with the Melanesian Brotherhood, the Second World War totally disrupted the Revival League. In 1941, the Japanese government created one nationally united church (the Kyodan) which David and approximately 140 additional pastors from the Holiness persuasion refused to join. So on June 26, 1942, Tsutada with many others was placed in prison. "The apparent reason for the arrests was that the doctrine of the second coming of Christ...represented Christ as superior to the emperor."(24)

For two years he quietly reflected upon his past life, the state of the Japanese national church and upon Christ's biblical teachings concerning church life and evangelistic outreach. He became convinced in his mind that he needed to launch a "venture of faith"; to start a new denomination apart from the one united church, to proclaim "the biblical faith by the early Methodists" and to be involved in world missions.(25)

As the war ended in August, 1945, Tsutada was released from prison. After recovering his health, he began, in October, 1945, a work based on his newly found convictions. Several former friends from the old Revival League joined him in this venture.

God began to bless his efforts. By 1949, the Immanuel Bible Training College began, and by 1960, with over 5,000 members in his Immanuel Gospel Church, three "missionary-students" went to the Union Biblical Seminary in India. The idea behind this project was to train future missionaries within the culture of the host church, and to allow them to learn the language, customs and thought patterns at a well established Bible Seminary within the host country.

For awhile the idea was a great success, and the students received adequate contextualized training until applications were made for permanent visas. After a few years of study, the Indian government prohibited their stay. Nevertheless, God allowed this experience to solidify into policy the church's desire for inter-denominational missionary cooperation. Like remnants from the older "Revival

45938

League", Immanuel Gospel Mission began with the concept of participating together with older institutions possessing similar theological persuasions. Thus, one of the original three "missionary-
students," now married, returned to India as a teacher in the South
India Bible Seminary. Another couple went to Jamaica as teachers
in the Wesleyan Bible School, while a third began work in Kenya,
teaching at the Kenya Highland Bible College.

A few years later, Taiwan, Papua New Guinea and the Philippines
were added to their list of engaged fields. Except for Taiwan,
where it became the only church planting work independent of additional organizational cooperation, all the engaged fields under
the Immanuel Gospel Mission purposely involve associational partnerships with other (often Western) mission agencies. In the words
of Paul Aihara, one of I.G.M.'s Missionaries to Papua New Guinea:

> We *must* cooperate with some older mission agencies. We
> think it is far better to practice foreign missions work
> now in a capacity possible for us than not practicing it at
> all. The reasons for it are as follows:
>
> 1 - The denomination is still too small to send several
>   families to one place, both financially and in the
>   number of personnel.
>
> 2 - The young (or infantile) mission board is inexper-
>   ienced to totally do independent work from the older
>   mission organizations. We have to learn from them.
>
> 3 - In reality, all the governments request that we
>   have some sponsoring agencies in the countries where
>   we want to work.
>
> 4 - Why should we create another tiny denomination in a
>   country where a number of churches of the same doc-
>   trine with ours already exists?(26)

According to Paul Aihara, Immanuel Gospel Mission's policy on
missionary cooperation is well defined. *Financially*, all support
should come from Japan. "Missions work is really mission work only
when the vision of missions is firmly held (financially) by the
national Christian workers and believers themselves of the respec-
tive countries."(27)

Information gathering must be a cooperative venture for each
agency is too small to do an adequate job itself; and the tendency
towards duplication in field research is too great in any country
containing various groups. Thus "I.G.M.'s Missionaries to Jamaica,
Kenya and Papua New Guinea were sent on the information we obtained

from either the Wesleyan Mission (USA) or the World Gospel Mission
(USA)."(28)

   Candidate training likewise needs to be a cooperative endeavor,
"not only in linguistic training but in general cross-cultural and
missiological training, missionary-professors from the older agencies would find a potential role to play."(29)   A prime example of
this type of cooperative agreement is I.G.M.'s Union Biblical
Seminary experiment in India.

   Lastly, *Joint-field activity*, where several agencies cooperate
together "in institutions like seminars or Bible Schools...(or) in
evangelistic work (where) there should not be any major hindrances
because of the diversified nationalities of missionaries."(30)

   The idea of organizational or associational cooperation is significant to Third World missions, particularly from a large denomination of over 11,000 members like Immanuel Gospel Church. More
cross-cultural evangelistic activity can be generated by such cooperative agreements. Like the united Body of Christ, it is good
when diverse peoples join hands for strength in world evangelization and for counsel in daily difficulties.

International Missionary
Fellowship, Jamaica

   One of the most unique missionary organizations in the non-
Western world began from a prayer meeting involving three concerned Christian leaders in November 1961. Their desire to direct
interested young people into world missions led Richard Bell, Tom
Northern and Dave Ho to form the International Missionary Fellowship in April 1962. Their purpose statement declares why.

      Challenging Christians to accept world missionary respon-
   sibility is the main job of I.M.F., from which stems a program to offer practical guidance, help and other fellowship,
   for those who have a burning desire for missionary work.(31)

   The element that makes I.M.F. unique is not that it was formed
by Jamaicans as an indigenous missionary organization; this is
important. However, it is special because it is an assistive
agency which provides basic missionary training to Bible School
graduates *and* which also enlists them for cross-cultural service
with *other* existing missionary groups. The financial support is
Jamaican while the ministry is performed in partnership. As Billy
Hall, the voice of missions for Back to the Bible in the West
Indies writes:

      In many respects, I.M.F. is unique. It is not a mis-
   sionary society or a mission board which sponsors candidates

and controls their many activities in any way. Rather
I.M.F. seeks to work in cooperation with existing
churches and mission boards on each field. I.M.F. does
not start churches in its own name, but does assist missionaries in being placed with the local churches or
missions needing their assistance.(32)

Through such cooperative ventures, the I.M.F. has seen over
thirty-five missionaries complete their training and be sent out
to work as partners with various mission societies worldwide.
India, Indonesia, Papua New Guinea, Nigeria, Bolivia and Surinam
are a few of the target countries where their church planting
efforts are now used. The funding and prayer correspondence like
Immanuel Gospel Mission of Japan is home based. Thus, an international fellowship of I.M.F. trainees exists and continues to be
encouraged through their eight-page mini-magazine *Outreach*. Every
three months this report is published to share missionary news of
the international I.M.F. family and their current church growth.
But it is made clear through this fellowship that I.M.F. is not
to become an autonomous missionary sending agency itself but to
assist other existing agencies in their evangelistic outreach.
Because the field is the world, I.M.F. encourages the fellowship
to establish these cooperative structures in order to maximize
evangelistic outreach while minimizing their own organizational
overhead. So far it has proven highly successful.

INDIVIDUAL SERVICE

Tsai Lin, Brazil

There are hundreds of fervent Christians, throughout the Third
World, who maintain the status of independent missionaries. Usually connected only associationally with some specific group or
denomination, these "individualists" desire to remain organizationally unattached. While on the one hand, they live unencumbered
with church traditions and authoritative structures, on the other
hand, they are burdened with the need to provide for their daily
sustenance. Tsai Lin is such a missionary.

Born September 9, 1931, in Tainan County, Taiwan, Tsai Lin was
soon converted and, at 18 years of age, began his long course of
theological studies. It took him nearly thirty years, from August
1949 to January 19, 1979 to complete all requirements for the
Master of Divinity degree from Taiwan Theological College. The
basic reason why his course took so long lies in the fact that,
during this period, Tsai Lin planted eight new churches, pastored
three additional churches, built two parsonages and one Christian
education complex, served as Chairman or Secretary in five regional

Presbyteries and learned six different languages. Tsai Lin has
been greatly used of the Lord.

But even beyond this, from June 1966 to November 1979, Tsai Lin
independently volunteered to be a self-sent missionary to Brazil,
serving for thirteen years in the megalopolis of Sao Paulo. Although officially part of the Taiwanese Presbyterian Church, his
Brazilian experience gave him new liberties and difficulties.
Tsai Lin was "on his own."

After paying for his own passage to Brazil, Lin began to earn a
living for his family of six by accepting various odd jobs, particularly in domestic gardening. He located his family in the international neighborhood of Vila Formosa where he met other transplanted
Taiwanese immigrants. Immediately, evangelism became his primary
task.

His church planting philosophy was three fold: 1) with his wife,
visit as many people as possible; 2) read the Bible and show how
God's World is not a parable but the truth, and 3) clearly express
that each man or woman needs to believe in God. As in T̶a̶i̶w̶a̶y̶, so
in Sao Paulo. Tsai Lin won people to the Lord and planted a church.

During the following ten years, the church grew to its present
200 church membership and formalized relationships with the United
Presbyterian Church, U.S.A. They called their church, "The Presbyterian Church of the Heavenly People of Formosa in Sao Paulo," the
first Taiwanese Presbyterian congregation in the city.

But this was not enough for Lin. Because of his constant desire
to evangelize unreached peoples, in 1978, he took three faithful
Taiwanese Brazilians on a trip to Buenos Aires where he has eventually planted another church among the Taiwanese there. Soon
thereafter, he made several trips to Asuncion, Paraguay planting
his eighth church, now a growing group of over forty active
members.

The significance of Tsai Lin to Third World Missions is that he
is only one example of *many* independent non-Western missionaries.
Most are highly productive, accomplishing significant tasks. They
are extremely sensitive to their "Macedonian calls" and respond
unhesitatingly. Their own possessions are sold in the process and
the harvest greatly multiplies God's kingdom.

CONCLUSION

From August 12 to 15, 1980, perhaps the largest gathering in the
history of Christendom occurred in Seoul, Korea. An estimated count
of the crowd for just one night was 2.7 million people! The "'80

Evangelization Crusade", sponsored by Campus Crusade of Korea, under the direction of Dr. Joon Gon Kim, demonstrated the vitality of the Korean Protestant church. The great climax of the Crusade was the response by Korean young people volunteering for cross-cultural missionary service. "Over 10,000 indicated their willingness to serve for at least a year. Mr. Kim and others predict that thousands more will volunteer before 1984, which is the centenary of Protestant missions in Korea."(33)

"Christ Jesus came into the world to save sinners" (I Timothy 1:15). The unprecedented numbers of young people volunteering for missionary service, whether in Korea, or elsewhere, is part of God's plan "to save sinners." But *how* can this tremendous influx of new workers be received and commissioned for service?

Some will join existing agencies and thereby form international teams. One example of this comes from the Sudan Interior Mission which last year accepted Dr. Andrew Ng and his wife Belinda, a Singaporean couple, to work at S.I.M.'s Galmi Hospital in Niger Republic. They will work alongside African and North American believers in medical evangelism. Furthermore, S.I.M. announces that because of the increased "inquiries from Hong Kong, the Philippines, Korea and Taiwan,"(34) S.I.M. recently has formed a committee to handle further applications in Singapore. Tony Lee, chairman of the committee says, "Why wouldn't God send Asian Christians to serve as missionaries in Africa?"(35) Many of younger Asian missionaries who go to Africa will participate in international teams, and work with existing structures such as S.I.M.

But additional missionaries will organize their *own* structures. Tom Chandler of O.C. Ministries, Inc. writes from Singapore describing many local believers who feel overwhelmed by large Western-oriented missionary "machines." "They'd much prefer to form their own sending bodies" if they could maintain contact with the historic mission agencies.(36) This sentiment is repeated often. New groups are being formed within the Third World in order to obey Christ's Great Commission.

Some will begin through foreign influence, others by indigenous influence. A few will become cooperative agreements; however, many will be simplified and involve only one's individual service. Our concern here is that the full missionary potential inherent within the diverse Third World regions be used to build God's Kingdom. To encourage this, is our responsibility!

PART THREE
THE MUTUAL COOPERATION
WITH THE THIRD WORLD

8

THE LAST AGE OF MISSIONS

The task of "making disciples" is facing its greatest challenges today. With over three-fourths of the world's billions yet un-reached, one great need in missions is a vast new cooperative ef-fort, prioritized in accordance with God's mandate, in order to maximize resources and minimize field duplication. Perhaps the reported explosive growth among Third World mission sending agen-cies in the seventies is a sign for the eighties, indicating that the hour has arrived for substantial missionary partnership. Since over 95% of all reported agencies stated a willingness to join meaningful and reciprocal missionary relationships, perhaps the decisive hour for such ventures is now.

In Scripture, God informs us concerning the normalcy of these special and strategic periods of life. One example comes from Second Corinthians 6:2 where the Apostle Paul describes his evan-gelistic message and points to a period of decision for all his hearers. "Behold, now is the acceptable time, behold now is the day of salvation." The word he uses for time is KAIROS suggest-ing a definite situation in life which demands a verdict. This is a critical point in one's history where decisions must be made. This "decisive moment" for salvation is now, for there is no other "day."

Elsewhere in his epistles, Paul presents further KAIROS situa-tions. He lists additional points in time which involve activi-ties of great importance. Like Moses in the Exodus (Deuteronomy 1:9, 16, 18), or David building his altar (I Chronicles 2:28) or Solomon building the temple (II Chronicles 7:8), Paul focuses

attention upon specific events which are extremely significant.
There is the person of Christ, "born at the proper time" (II
Timothy 4:6), the work of righteousness, redeeming the present
time (Colossians 4:5) and the future time of rewards, "...if we
do not grow weary" (Galatians 6:9). Even Jesus, in His evangelistic preaching pointed to a specific period of decision when he
said, "The time is fulfilled, and the kingdom of God is at hand;
repent and believe in the gospel" (Mark 1:15). As revealed in
Scripture, KAIROS is part of life. It is a special period of time
which forces us to focus upon priorities and challenges us to make
decisions.

THE "KAIROS" OF WORLD EVANGELIZATION

One of the most demanding KAIROS - type activities mentioned
in the New Testament is the phase of world evangelization. Although the word KAIROS is not specifically used, Matthew 24:14
presents an equal situation in all its fullness. This is a specially designated time period when decisions are made - decisions
concerning both those who will be sent and those who will respond
to the gospel. And when this period of world witness reaches its
climax, "...then the end shall come."

Tension for believers within this specific KAIROS is found not
so much upon the opportunity to witness as it is upon its scope.
Christ is directing us towards a collective witness to *all peoples*
(PASIN TOIS ETHNESIN, Matt. 24:14; also Matt. 28:19). This may
mean every distinct ethnic group worldwide. Some of these groups
are very small (i.e., the Lati of China with 450 people, or the
Sanuma of Brazil with 326(1)). Other ethnic groups are significantly large (i.e., the Quechua of Peru with 3,000,000 members or
the Ibibio of Nigeria with 2,000,000(2)). Based upon 1982 research,
there are at least 3,265 distinct ethnic people groups which have
not yet been reached with the gospel.(3) Many more are bound to be
discovered in the years to come.

We know that our KAIROS situation has an ending. And that
before our Lord returns, the "gospel of the Kingdom shall be
preached in the whole world for a witness to all peoples." As
Christians, in light of this, our faithfulness to Christ's will
stirs up an inner tension. For this special phase of history now
demands of us a personal verdict: "How are we going to be involved?" It also demands sincere decision: "Am I contributing
my best towards reaching the yet unreached peoples?"

Historically, many from Western-oriented countries have effectively reached out and witnessed to a myriad of subcultures. Yet
for the West to continue reaching as many *new* peoples as before

with the same ability is extremely doubtful. Ninety-six percent
of Western missionary personnel, it is estimated, are found presently in perfecting ministries. Only four percent are involved
primarily in pioneer or frontier missions.(4)

God has raised up at least 13,000 Third World missionaries, and
they are reaching additional "unreached peoples." But difficulties likewise exist. Primary needs range from financial to technical, with few solutions in sight. One illustration comes from the
Sierra Madre mountains in the Philippines where up to 20,000 non-
Christian nomadic peoples live and the only evangelical agency
operating in the area is one, financially-limited Third World
society.(5) Another illustration comes from the administrative
zone of Copacabana, Rio de Janeiro, Brazil, where 600,000 upper-
middle class sun-worshippers live within five square miles! Although there are six evangelical churches within this region, only
one is growing slightly. Thus Osmar Ludovico da Silva, Lausanne
participant and pastor of a growing independent work has chosen
this distinct fun-loving group as his "target people." Yet he
continually requests additional personnel; he is working within
one of the most densely populated areas of the world.

What would it be like if we could supply these needs? What
would happen if half our missionary monies, internationally, were
invested specifically in pioneer or frontier missions? How would
the Great Commission be altered if several well-trained international teams were strategically placed in the areas ripe for
harvest? Serious consideration needs to be given to these questions. An honest analysis of our *own* efforts merits consideration
as we enter our KAIROS. And a solid inquiry concerning our cooperative spirit, even with other Third World agencies, is necessary.

THE NEW AGE OF COOPERATION

Neither the West nor the Third World is equipped to reach the
yet unreached peoples by themselves. Modern missions is beginning
to involve feet and faces of all colors. The West is noted for
its mission history and surplus funds. The non-West is indis-
pensable for its valuable mentality "from below" and increased
vision. Together, with cooperative relationships, we cannot
only "give witness to the resurrection of the Lord Jesus" (Acts
4:33), but also increase our effectiveness in world evangelization.

On the basis of my personal correspondence with Third World
mission leaders, at least four areas stand out as strategic for
international agency cooperation. They are education, information, finances and technics. Each demands equal participation
from *both* Western and non-Western alike, and is based primarily

upon purpose or task, rather than specific theologies or experience.

Educational Cooperation

One of the first strategic areas of international cooperation
must be educational. This includes both advanced courses in missions for career workers and assistance in lay education for those
who have pastoral influence, whether foreign missionary or national
pastor. As Solomon wrote in Proverbs, "a wise man will hear and
increase in learning, and a man of understanding will acquire wise
counsel.... For by wise guidance you will wage war, and in abundance of counselors there is victory" (1:5 with 24:6). The victory
comes when there is an abundance of counselors; and by necessity,
this "abundance of counselors" often comes from specialists of
other countries.

One example of needed educational cooperation is found within
the missionary's Bible School training. Stephen J. Akangbe,
president of the Evangelical Churches of West Africa begins by
saying:

> National churches need more sound Biblical graduate and
> post-graduate institutions and the general level training
> to meet the need of everybody of this generation. Seminaries,
> Bible Colleges, Crash programs, Theological Education by
> Extension, leadership courses of evangelism, Seminars and
> management courses, workshop and Bible study conferences
> are all needed. These have their places in our national
> churches today, for effective witnessing of the Gospel.(6)

However, it is not just any kind of theological training that is
referred to here. It is biblical education which graduates students
successful in church planting. Relevant contextualized courses are
needed which are marked by flexibility and commitment to world evangelism. Practical training must be given so that not only does one
understand God's mandate and experience the "how," but also com-
prehends his own gifted area, and his God-designed position in light
of the task. As reported, the Third World, has developed their own
training programs. But much more *could* be done.

Met Castillo, of the Philippine Christian and Missionary Alliance
Church writes:

> I don't want to close my eyes to the numerous theological
> schools all over Asia. In fact, I am of the opinion that
> theological schools have been over-planted in many places
> such as the Philippines where denominational Bible Schools
> abound. Almost every denomination has its own...(yet) the

nature of the curricula of existing theological schools in Asia explains their inadequacy in preparing cross-cultural missionaries. One cannot, however, condemn them for being what they are, because they have been established to meet a particular need in the churches. Designed to train pastors and deaconesses, they have kept their trust faithfully. And to a large extent they have been crowned with success.

This type of school, however, is far from being equipped to train missionary candidates. These schools are not "cut out" for such a purpose. Missions courses, if any, are very few. Missiology as an academic discipline is generally a kind of "tack-in" department in one solitary corner of the entire program.(7)

The principal point of Castillo's statement is that there still exists a large need within parts of the Third World for adequate missionary education. But to offer such exposure, it is important to receive assistance from one who understands the problems and frustrations of cross-cultural work. From his own experience, a veteran missionary from any country, or trained missiologist of any nationality can communicate the difficulties of international witnessing, the temptations in world evangelization, the challenges of Bible translation, the barriers of ethnic differences, the tensions from personal adjustment and the thrill of foreign church development. A national pastor or church leader can communicate factual knowledge in these areas; whereas a veteran missionary goes beyond and shares reality - his own experiences. And because of actual situations within many Third World regions, such assistance must come from outside.

This cooperation can be either short or long term, in seminars or mission departments. It can assist in establishing new mission courses or help to glean material from other already existing courses (i.e., the Missionary Training Course at the Institut Indjil Indonesia, Batu, Malang, Indonesia). This cooperation can work through residency or extension centers, teaching in person or by tape, through translator or in translated publications. The variations are *many*. The thrust here is that hundreds of missionaries, and perhaps many more lay believers throughout the missionary world could benefit from additional missiological education. And it is important to recognize, as the 1980 study indicated, that this assistance can come from non-Western sources. Assistance is *not* exclusively Western.

Many agencies within the Third World are nearly as old as the oldest Western societies and have gained much experience. Some are as large as the largest Western agencies and fully identify with deployment problems. Some have grown faster than their Western counterparts and are involved with very diverse and

culturally distinct peoples. They experience difficulties with
government policies and in matters concerning international financial exchange. They all sense the need for further education and
welcome assistance, especially from other "emerging agencies."
Because the involvement in cross-cultural missions is virtually
no easier for non-Western workers than for Western, educational
updating, participating in refresher courses, perfecting one's
skills and developing further one's spiritual gifts are important
tasks for all missionaries and interested believers everywhere.
The fulfillment of this, necessitates educational cooperation from
Christ's international body.

Informational Cooperation

    A second strategic area of international cooperation involves
providing important researched information to active missionary
sending agencies. Information such as new governmental openings,
the location of as yet unreached peoples, newly discovered population trends and societal interests, available support ministries
and church growth insights, etc., is a valuable contribution to
any frontier endeavor. There are several specialized information
gathering groups which contribute such pertinent trend analysis
to cross-cultural societies. A general listing of these organizations appears in Appendix III.

    Unintentionally, many research centers find their analysis
gaining only limited exposure, usually assisting those agencies
who lie in the same region as the researching group. To this
extent the expensive research is helpful and valuable. Yet there
are hundreds of additional agencies, both in the Third and Western
worlds which are located outside this limited region, who are also
desirous of receiving new relevant information. Could not their
studied insights assist them as well? Could not a losely structured, international research network be established whereby, no
matter where the agency is located or what denomination it represents those interested could receive pertinent insights, helpful
for making future assignments and policies? Research is too
painstaking a science and too expensive an art to limit its
results to just a region or geographical area. The new age of
missions implys international cooperation with research information.

    Furthermore, our KAIROS demands *new* researched areas. One
example concerns tentmaking - those cross-cultural missionaries
who earn their salary in the marketplace, while planting churches
in evenings and on weekends. Waldron Scott, past General Secretary of the World Evangelical Fellowship states that tentmaking
ministries are to be "the next great creative movement that God's
Spirit is going to bring into existence in missionary effort."(8)
Because of the increasing financial difficulties in missionary

support, many co-laborers are choosing this alternative method.
Like the Apostle Paul (Acts 18:1-3; I Thessalonians 2:9), they
support themselves in the ministry.

Since all indications point to the continued interest in missionary tentmaking worldwide(9), why could not these study and
research centers assist in providing reliable "tentmaking information?" As with other subjects, many centers could divulge key
potential jobs to agency headquarters, provide information concerning the most harvestable peoples within the host country,
compile lists of existing agencies so that the tentmaker could
cooperate with one or more of them while working in the country.
A few research centers are doing this. Others need to begin.
This related information not only helps agencies organizationally,
but spiritually could help stimulate many potential tentmakers
towards missionary service. International cooperation in research
is crucial.

Financial Cooperation

A third strategic area for international cooperation in world
evangelization involves financial assistance. As the 1980 Study
reveals, an average 35% of Third World missionaries do *not* receive
their promised full salary. One African analyzed the situation and
expressed that the problems of wealth in missions "is not one of
quantity but of distribution."(10) Proof of this comes from any
United Nations economically-oriented world map because it demonstrates definite lines separating the "haves" from the "have nots."

Part of this problem might be resolved if lessons from the past
were studied seriously, discovering how "the Karens, the Koreans,
those from Oceania were able to solve this problem when wealth was
not as easy to obtain as it is today."(11)

Another part of this problem could be resolved if sound financial
policies were instituted within certain Third World agencies.
Samuel Kim, a Korean missionary who was in Thailand for over seven-
teen years gives a personal testimony concerning this reality.

There is a Korean saying, "Cha-Muc-Ku-Ku", which means
"counting the fingers." Modern missionary works cannot be
carried out by rough finger counting but it must be precise
and scientific.

Since 1956, my wife and I were sent out...to Thailand.
We have suffered and become victims of these rough calculat-
ing mentalities' abstract missionary maneuvering. Nothing
is really specified, including missionary housing, work
budget, medical cares, transportations, children's education, etc. But the General Secretary of the board

always emphasized the saying that "the Lord provides
everything, just pray for the needs." We also needed the
Lord's power and needed to pray in our missionary works,
but administrational practice and missionary functions
are certainly more precise and scientific than prayers.

I know these kinds of mentalities of rough finger
counting sort of figuring is quite common throughout the
Third World missions and organizations. We have to correct
these out of date methods in order to avoid jeopardy or
catastrophy of the Third World mission.(12)

A third way of partially resolving the problem of unpaid salaries and deficit project spending is if additional international
financial cooperation was achieved. But to spend money freely
without direction or purpose is financial malpractice. Therefore,
guidelines must be established for the sake of biblical stewardship.

For example, one guideline could be that of frontier missions;
the "haves" (whoever they might be" primarily would invest their
additional funds in cross-cultural church planting or evangelistic endeavors. This by no means diminishes the importance of
perfecting ministries. It merely attempts to balance missionary
work by encouraging more interest in Christ's imperative.

Another guideline could be that of project accounts. Within
the Third World, there is a debate over the viability of foreign
monies paying national salaries. Missionary statesmen like Andrew
Furuyama are against it. Others like Stephen J. Akangbe support
it. Good points are expressed by both sides. Perhaps the best
general policy, in light of world nationalization and missionary
indigenization, is to support special missionary projects, but
allow the national churches to pay personal salaries. The basic
purpose for suggesting this, of course, is to avoid the depressing
problem of foreign dependence. It is demeaning for many missionaries to know that their basic existence is being influenced and
determined by foreigners, not by one's own friends and Christian
family. It stifles spiritual growth among national believers for
there is little "stretch," little faith involved when basic mission salaries are assured from the outside and not dependent from
within. To take care of one's own is not only a scriptural principle (i.e., Acts 20:35; Gal. 6:10), but also a sociological
axiom and a missiological basis for indigenous activity. The
national church must be responsible to support those whom they
send as missionaries and to send out no more than what they can
adequately support.

At times, however, it is not easy to abide by this second principle of project support. For example, on February 18, 1980, a dear
brother from The Christ Church Mission in Nigeria wrote me stating:

> Since 1971, when we erected our theological school, many
> evangelists, Pastors and Christian workers have been trained
> and sent out to plant indigenous churches within nineteen
> states of Nigeria. Some even went to serve in the Cameroons
> and Ghana. The Lord Jesus is using these workers to win many
> souls for himself. Many of them are working to win Muslim
> believers in Northern Nigeria for Christ.... However, some of
> them have returned home before completing their work and
> signed contract, before completing their three years. The
> fact is clear that lack of funds in the ministry to support
> these workers does not allow them to stay in the field and
> do a successful service to the end.(13)

What do you do in a situation like this? If you had extra funds
available, the immediate tendency would be to invest in this very
worthy group and help pay salaries. After all, these national missionaries are planting churches, even evangelizing Muslims in a
difficult cross-cultural experience. But what would such assistance eventually do to the indigeneity of the national church? To
the spirituality of those believers who's responsibility is to pray
for and help support their own missionaries? Would such cooperation enhance their self image and produce greater Christian maturity? These are some of the difficult questions which must be
answered before foreign *salary* support becomes credible. However,
foreign funds applied towards special time-bounded projects can
enhance our KAIROS task and compliment national indigeneity, as
missionary history reveals.

One specific example of a valid project was offered to various
Western agencies in 1973 by Byang H. Kato, then General Secretary
of the Association of Evangelicals of Africa and Madagascar. He
explained:

> Last February the A.E.A.M. (Association of Evangelicals
> of Africa and Madagascar) Assembly called for the sending
> churches to consider the training of an African to the level
> of each missionary sent to Africa, if the concept of partner-
> ship is truly to be adhered. In an average situation it
> would take only about 10% of the support of a (Western) mis-
> sionary to put a young African through seminary in Africa.
> If that program had been envisaged and followed, the evangel-
> ical church would have at least 4,000 adequately trained men
> in Africa today. Contrary to that, probably less than a
> quarter of African workers have training equal to that of the
> average missionary. Let me illustrate with one of the more
> progressive missions. For more than 30 years, the Sudan

Interior Mission probably had between 300 and 400 missionaries at any given year in Nigeria. If a nominal 1% African
leadership were developed to the level of missionary training,
in 30 years there should be at least 90 leaders. But looking
at the trained leadership in the Evangelical churches of West
Africa's 1,500 churches, only about 12 out of some 1,000
pastors and evangelists have a recognized B.Th., or above in
1973. The situation is much worse in other missions. It is
not too much to ask mission boards to work out this per quota
system to accelerate the training of leadership to meet the
demands of the day. The best of structures will be successful
only if there are capable people to make it work both at the
grassroot and on the highest leadership levels.(14)

A third financial guideline can be that of specific agreements;
to be clear as to how much money, for how long, to whom, via which
process. Many missionaries can validate the fact that bitter feel-
ings and harsh disagreements arise faster between Christian brothers
over financial matters than with almost any other area, including
theology or politics. It is crucial to be specific lest diverse
cultural backgrounds produce false expectations and result in sinful
division.

With these three simple assistive guidelines, international
cooperation in financial areas becomes a significant supportive
force in world evangelization. Instead of exercising control over
recipients, funds are used with equals towards the accomplishment
of one task: the making of disciples in all ethnic peoples. Instead of being a sign of power, money becomes a symbol of cooperative trust. Generosity is expressed because of function and goal,
not tradition or denomination. And although such cooperative
efforts are difficult, this radical departure from past patterns
is needed. While maintaining a conservative theological stance,
the need now is to become financially liberal, cooperating regu-
larly with the many rapidly developing missionary agencies "from
below."

Technical Assistance

The fourth strategic area of international cooperation involves
technical assistance. This implys ministry from many "support
groups" such as Missionary Aviation Fellowship, Medical Assistance
Programs, or Missionary Services, Inc. But it goes beyond this.
Many of the larger "non-support groups" can render a form of
technical aid by assisting in the formation of conferences, missionary consultations or conventions. This is what occurred with
the First All Asia Mission Consultation as the Korea International
Mission provided time and technical support. David Cho, president
of K.I.M. helped plan and promote the consultation.

Also, technical assistance includes loaning office personnel
(treasurer, president, founder, etc.) to other agencies in need of
ideas or functional models. CLAME (Community of Latin American
Evangelical Ministries), the contextualized parent organization
for Latin America Mission, has shared their key personnel several
times whenever other missionary agencies desire input on agency
nationalization. There are *many* ways missionaries can share with
one another the diversity of talents and gifts that exist in
Christ's body. Each part is a significant contributory function
to the whole; without which the body suffers. Thus, in the new
age of missions, increased technical assistance must be part of
our cooperate stance.

                            CONCLUSION

The world is a global village. Missions strategy must adapt to
this trend. Edward C Pentecost, professor of Missions at Dallas
Theological Seminary writes:

   The period of internationalization of missions is a period
   into which we are stepping. The world is shrinking. The
   world is becoming a world where there is exchange in spite of
   nationalization. The recognition of internationalization....
   Missions must move in this direction. Both sides, those from
   the North American agencies, and those from the Third World
   must take steps to build relationships. Relationships that
   will be built in a spirit of cooperation and demonstration
   of confidence and mutual recognition.(15)

By successfully cooperating together in these four suggested
areas, new endeavors will be established for world mission. One
example of this might be new associational organizations, such
as the international network for missionary research. Emilio
Castro, director of the Commission on World Mission and Evangelism
in Geneva suggests even another idea: "a multiple traffic system"(16) whereby the exchange of missionary personnel could be
coordinated in all possible directions, dependent upon need,
willingness and ability.

Another result of our international associative partnership
might be the planting of new missionary *agencies*. Whether by
encouraging an already known gifted visionary to form a new work
(the historical pattern) or by sensing a need and planning an
effort to meet that need (the systems pattern), with counsel and
cooperation from many sources, new pioneer movements can be
established.

Cooperation will also produce freshly restructured agencies as
Western and non-Western societies and churches join hands in

missionary partnership. On June 25, 1965, for example, after four-
teen years of "wandering in the wilderness" and trying to discern
how to identify with Asia's millions, the century-old China Inland
Mission became Overseas Missionary Fellowship, with headquarters,
activity and personnel resident in Asia.(17) Similarily Latin
America Mission spawned CLAME (Community of Latin American Evangelical Ministries) with residency in Costa Rica, and the Sudan
Interior Mission's African Missionary Society became part of the
Association of Evangelical Churches of West Africa.(18) Because
Third World agencies often prefer non-Western structures, meaning-
ful, long-term cooperation can produce valuable restructured societies.

Whatever develops, we must be wise and cautious concerning the
duplication of efforts. Just as cooperative endeavors assist world
evangelization, too many defeat biblical stewardship. At this
point, the words of missionary anthropologist Charles Tabor have
much value.

> It is important to avoid *both* the proliferating of ad
> hoc agencies competing for the same resources to reach the
> same people, and a rigidly orchestrated effort under a
> single monolithic organization. The first leads to the
> present chaos, with its inexcusable overlappings and
> omissions, as well as a caricature of the church which
> can only hurt its witness. The second leads to paralysis
> through excessive size and complexity, because too great
> a proportion of the resources are consumed by a top-heavy,
> unresponsive, and unimaginative bureaucracy; there would
> also be a tendency in this situation to try to devise
> those universal methods which we have seen to be a chimera.
> It would be much better to mobilize existing organizations,
> merging some when genuine gain can be foreseen, and estab-
> lishing pragmatic links between them based on a minimum of
> machinery and a maximum of shared information and experi-
> ence.(19)

What do you visualize for the future? What do you foresee as
the task of world evangelization grows and becomes more mature?
With a sizeable missionary force both in the Third World and in
the West, with needs and difficulties faced on both sides, with both
parts of the one body under the same commander and involved in the
same decision - making KAIROS, the new age of missions must be one
of task - oriented cooperation. Both the Western and non-Western
agencies are experienced in mission. Both are maturing and interested in preaching the Gospel of the Kingdom to the whole world.
Both desire to be an effective witness to *all the nations* (peoples)
before God's appointed end comes (Matt. 24:14). Therefore, let us
join friendly hands and purpose in our hearts that everyone may
hear before He returns. Let us accept each other as equals, and

cooperate together as partners. It is foolishness to think we can do the job alone. As the Apostle Paul exhorts the Romans to "be devoted to one another in brotherly love" and to "give preference to one another in honor" (12:10), so we must be exhorted to do the same in missions. By accepting God's Word as our authorative guide, by depending upon the Holy Spirit as our energizing dynamic, and by joining hands internationally as partners we can effectively disciple the nations before He returns.

APPENDIX I

Research Questionnaires

Three questionnaires were used in the 1980 Study of Third World
Mission Agencies. One went to 143 mission leaders worldwide in an
attempt to update the list of Third World Mission Agencies. A
second questionnaire was mailed to the listed 462 agencies, of
which 368 were confirmed as active mission sending agencies. The
third questionnaire was a Portuguese version of the second. This
was the only translation made of the MISSION AGENCY QUESTIONNAIRE.
The author's Brazilian residency facilitated this translation.
Samples of the first two questionnaires follow.

Questionnaire One: MISSION AGENCY LIST UP-Date

Please Return To: Lawrence E. Keyes

A. NAMES AND ADDRESSES OF INDIGENOUS MISSIONARY SOCIETIES

1. _____

2. _____

3. _____

4. _____

5. _____

6. _____

(Please use the back if more space is needed)

B. CURRENT TRENDS WITHIN THE THIRD WORLD MISSIONARY MOVEMENT

1. _____

2. _____

3. _____

C. SUGGESTED QUESTIONS FOR THE SURVEY QUESTIONNAIRE

1. _____

2. _____

3. _____

4. _____

THANK YOU!

This is your official Questionnaire. Please fill in the name of your mission and answer as much as possible. This important questionnaire concerns THE INDIGENOUS MISSIONARY SENDING AGENCIES which are *located* in Africa, Asia and Latin America, and who *send* missionaries from their own country, state or "people" to another. In order to be included in the results, it is important to return this questionnaire as soon as possible, or by April 1, 1980 at the very latest. In appreciation for your assistance, and if requested, a free copy of the results will be sent to you upon publication.

THANK YOU VERY MUCH FOR YOUR HELP!

Rev. Lawrence E. Keyes
Research Coordinator

A. NAME AND ADDRESS OF YOUR MISSION, ORGANIZATION OR AGENCY

1. Official Name:_____

2. Name in English:_____

3. Postal Address:_____

4. Street Address:_____

5. Country:_____ 6. Telephone:_____

7. Name and title of the chief executive officer of your Mission:
_____Title:_____

B. HISTORY OF YOUR MISSION, ORGANIZATION OR AGENCY

1. When was the mission ORGANIZED? (date)_____ 19_____

2. WHERE was the mission organized?_____

3. What is the name of the person and/or group who FOUNDED the mission?
_____

4. Was your mission initially founded as an INDIGENOUS MISSION []Yes[]No

5. Do you consider your mission to be an Indigeous Mission NOW? []Yes[]No

6. Choose one term which BEST DESCRIBES your mission now.

[ ] Denominational [ ] interdenominational [ ] nondenominational

7. Among the activities listed below, which are the two PRIMARY TASKS of your mission? (Please use number 1 for the primary task and number 2 for the secondary task)

___Church planting   ___Translation   ___Speciality (radio,
                                              medicine, etc.)
___Evangelism   ___Literature
                                           ___Other:_____
___Pastoring local   ___Teaching/training
   churches   _____

8. How many missionaries are INVOLVED in these two tasks?_____

9. Choose one THEOLOGICAL ORIENTATION which best describes the position of your mission.

___Evangelical   ___Charismatic   ___Ecumenical/Conciliar

___Fundamentalist/   ___Liberation   ___Other:_____
    Separatist   _____

C. AFFILIATION OF THE MISSION, ORGANIZATION OR AGENCY

1. Does your mission allow missionaries TO COOPERATE with other existing churches or groups while serving on the field?

[ ] Yes   [ ] No   [ ] DEPENDS on the group
                                       Explain:_____

2. Does your mission accept "westerners" as missionaries, TO SERVE AS PARTNERS on the mission field?

[ ] Yes   [ ] No   [ ] I Don't Know

3. Would your mission permit working with other NON-WESTERN NATIONALITIES of like faith if given the chance on the field?

[ ] Yes   [ ] No

D. INFORMATION ABOUT MISSIONARIES

1. How many ACTIVE missionaries with the mission, organization or agency? (Include those on temporary leave)

YEAR	COUPLES	SINGLE MEN	SINGLE WOMEN	TOTAL
1980				
1978				
1975				
1972				

2, What percent of all received funds for missionary outreach come from NON WESTERN SOURCES_____

3. Among the following categories, which best describes THE SOURCE of financial support for your missionaries? (Check as many as possible and please give percentages of support if YES)

| | NO | YES | ...IF YES, does the finan- support come | | |
			from the WEST	from your OWN COUNTRY	from another THIRD WORLD COUNTRY
a. a denomination					
b. several denominations					
c. another mission society					
d. a local church or congregation					
3. small groups or "prayer bands"					
f. various separate individuals					
g. missionary self-support					

4. How often do your missionaries RECEIVE financial support?

___MONTHLY ___BI-WEEKLY ___WEEKLY ___OTHER:_____

5. Do your missionaries normally receive their FULL SALARY?

[ ] Yes   [ ] No

6. What basic training or preparation is required for missionaries BEFORE they depart for the field?

___Bible Institute ___Language Learning ___Seminary ___University

___Practical Experience (please explain):_____

___Mission related orientation (What length of time is involved in training_____)

7. Is it required by the mission that an active missionary REPORT HIS or HER PROGRESS to someone?

[ ] Yes   [ ] No [If NO, proceed to question number 8]

a. If YES, to whom does the missionary report his or her progress?

___Mission Society   ___Own Denomination   ___Local Church

___Other: _____

b. If Yes, how often is this reporting expected?

___Weekly   ___Bi-weekly   ___Monthly

___Bi-monthly   ___Other: _____

8. Now long is an average TERM OF SERVICE in your mission?_____years.

9. What percentage of missionaries return home BEFORE COMPLETING one term of service? _____%

10. What percentage of missionaries REMAIN HOME after completing one term of service? _____%

11. In which countries are your missionaries NOW SERVING?
(Please complete as much as possible)

NAME OF COUNTRY	PROVINCE OR STATE	PEOPLE AMONG WHOM MISSIONARIES ARE WORKING	LANGUAGE SPOKEN BY THESE PEOPLE	IS THERE AN ESTABLISHED CHURCH?	NUMBER OF MISSION-ARIES	LANGUAGE USED BY THE MISSIONARIES	THE PRIMARY TASK OF THE MISSIONARIES

12. What do you believe to be the MOST CHALLENGING PROBLEM which your mission has faced?

13. How difficult has it been to SEND FINANCIAL SUPPORT <u>Internationally</u> to missionaries?

___Major Difficulty ___Average Difficulty ___Little Difficulty ___No Difficulty

14. How difficult has it been to offer ADEQUATE TRAINING to new recruits?

___Major Difficulty ___Average Difficulty ___Little Difficulty ___No Difficulty

15. How difficult is it to raise support for NEW MISSIONARIES?

___Major Difficulty ___Average Difficulty ___Little Difficulty ___No Difficulty

E. THIS YEAR'S PROJECTIONS

1. If you plan to send out more missionaries in 1980-1981, please give the approximate number:_____.

2. If you plan to send out more missionaries in 1980-1981, please list the countries, states or "peoples" within the country where you plan to go.

a._____ b._____ c._____

d._____ e._____ f._____

3. Are there "PEOPLES" in your country which, in so far as you know, have <u>no</u> evangelistic influence amont them?

[ ] Yes [ ] No

F. INFORMATION ABOUT YOUR NATIONAL CHURCH

1. The church in your country represents which RELATIONSHIP with the West?

___DEPENDENT ___INTERDEPENDENT ___INDEPENDENT

2. What degree of interest do laypeople demonstrate toward your missionary outreach?

___No interest ___Little interest ___Some interest ___Much interest

3. Is missionary interest among laypeople INCREASING [ ] Yes [ ] No

G. NAMES OF NEW THIRD WORLD INDIGENOUS MISSIONARY SOCIETIES OR AGENCIES

1. Please list the NAMES and ADDRESSES of other missionary societies which you consider to be indigenous to your area. Also please write the name of the chief executive officer if possible. THANK YOU!

NAME OF MISSION	MAILING ADDRESS	NAME OF CHIEF OFFICER

Thank you for filling out this questionnaire. If you would like to receive a free copy of the results from this survey, please answer the following:

COMPLETE NAME of individual filling out questionnaire:_____

COMPLETE MAILING ADDRESS:_____

TITLE:_____DATE:_____19_____

APPENDIX II

Third World
Mission Agency Directory

The following listings include Active Missionary sending agencies only. They do *not* include the thirty-one specialized support-oriented organizations which also responded to the 1980 questionnaire, nor the ninety-eight older agencies which were originally listed but presently unconfirmed as being active, nor the additional eight responses from active agencies which were received too late for inclusion into this directory. But this listing is the basis for the report found in Chapter 5 with a few additional reported agencies from Western countries and with several newer updates for a few already listed agencies. This directory is subdivided into five regional sections:

African Respondents (no survey information)

African Protestant Church
P.B. 26
Lolodorf-Kribi, CAMEROON
   Rev. Salinzo Ver

All Christian Spiritual Church
Box A 123
Labadi, GHANA
   Rev. E. A. Kodi

Apostolic Church of Ghana
P.O. Box 633
Accra, GHANA
   Pr. Ernest H. Williams
    Evangelism

Apostolic Reformed Church
P.O. Box 13965
Accra, GHANA
   Rev. M.D. Afful

Christ the King Church
P.O. Box 4263
Accra, GHANA

Christians United in Action
P.O. Box 319
Akim Oda, GHANA
   Rev. E.A. Yeboah

Divine Healing Church of Christ
P.O. Box A 136
Labadi, GHANA
   Rev. Herbert K. Amoah
   Founded October 1975
   Nondenominational

F'Eden Revival Church
P.O. Box 6757
Accra, GHANA
   Rev. Bro. Yeboah-Korie

Jehova's Peace Church
P.O. Box 68
Offinso, Ahanh Region, GHANA
   Emmanuel Mwadno Nkrumah

Redemption Church of Christ
P.O. Box 124, Offenso
Mpehin, Ashanti, GHANA
   Rev. George Darko Nkansah

Supreme Nazareth Church
Nkenkaasu-offinso,
Ahanh Region via Techninan
B.A., GHANA
   Rev. Cesei Dickson

Episcopal Church of Christ
P.O. Ahero
via Kisumu, KENYA
   Bishop Benson Otieno

AIC Rift Valley Region Mission
   Committee
P.O. Box 382
Eldoret, KENYA
   Pr. Samuel Kisang

Bible Alliance Mission
P.O. Box 15566
Mbagathi, Nairobi, KENYA
   Mr. Vic Paul

I.B.P.
P.O. Box 21633
Nairobi, KENYA
   Rev. Daniel Kyanda

Peace and Mercy Church
c/o P.O. Box 18
Kipilelyon, KENYA
   Joshua A. Chumo

E.N.I. Mission
P.O. Box 167
Sinoe County, LIBERIA
   Bishop Augustus Marwieh

Missionary Work Among the Islams
P.O. Nkhoma
c/o Nkhoma Synod Offices
MALAWI
   Rev. C. Human

AFRICAN RESPONDENTS (Continued)

Apostolic Church of God
P.O. Box 95
Ikot Ekpene, NIGERIA
Elder U.O. Imeh

Chinese Christian Africa Fellow-
ship
P.O. Box 219
Ikeja, Lagos, NIGERIA
Mr. William Id

Universal Missions, Inc.
EKA NTO-OBO
P.M. B.43
Abak, S.E. State NIGERIA
Rev. Joseph Sam

The Leprosy Mission
30, Seventh Ave.
Highlands North,
Johannesburg, SOUTH AFRICA
Walter O. Maasch

The Evangelical Church
P.O. Box 868
Mbabane, SWAZILAND
Dr. A.B. Gamedze

Moravian Church
P.O. Box 29
Tabora, TANZANIA
Rev. Thoophil Kisansi

Swedish Free Mission
P.O. Box 222
Taborah, TANZANIA

Kimbanquist Church
B.P. 7069
Kinshasa 1, ZAIRE
S. Em. Diangenda

Lutheran Evangelical Church of
Western Zaire
B.P. 12575
Kinshasa 1, ZAIRE
Rev. Mayemba Mosesi

Mambasa Church
B.P. 24
Mambasa, Haute-Zaire, ZAIRE
Rev. Kumbowo Babili

African Reformed Church
P.O. Box 670
Fort Victoria, ZIMBABWE-RODESIA
Rev. G. Murry

D.R.C.
Rm. No. 1983
Highfield, ZIMBABWE-RODESIA
Rev. Gift Mabaudi

Presbyterian Church in Cameroon   Rt. Rev. J.C. Kangsen, Chief Officer
P.C.C. Box 19 Buea   Organized 1958
S.W. Province, U.R. CAMEROON   Denominational

PERSONNEL: 1980, 23
MISSIONARY PREPARATION: Bible Institute, Practical Experience,
Mission Related orientation (6 months)
FIELDS OF SERVICE:
Cameroon, the Ngolo and Batanga people and language, Church Planting
Cameroon, The Mbenbe people and language, Church Planting
Cameroon, the Eximbi people and language, Church Planting

Apostolic Church of Christ
Shoubra
Cairo, EGYPT

PERSONNEL: 1980, 1; 1981, 4 (projection)
MISSIONARY PREPARATION: Practical Experience, Mission Related
Orientation (2-3 years)
FIELDS OF SERVICE:
U.S.A., Arabic people, English and Arabic languages, evangelism,
   teaching

Souls Salvation Society   Moussa Girgis, Chief Officer
12 Kotta Street   Organized 1927
Shoubra, Cairo, EGYPT   Interdenominational

PERSONNEL: 1972, 12; 1975, 13; 1978, 13; 1980, 21 (75% growth)
MISSIONARY PREPARATION: Bible Institute

FIELDS OF SERVICE:
Egypt, "Egyptian" people, Arabic language, Preaching

Word of Life Church   Ato Berhanu Deressa, Chief Officer
Box 5829
Addis Ababa, ETHIOPIA   Denominational

PERSONNEL: 1972, 100; 1975, 100; 1978, 70; 1980, 50 (-50% growth)
MISSIONARY PREPARATION:

FIELDS OF SERVICE:
Ethiopia, Oromo and Shenasha people, Oromo language, Evangelism
Ethiopia, Wolleyta, Ari and Mali people and language, Evangelism
Ethiopia, the Oromo and Amharac people and language, Evangelism
Ethiopia, the Kamgatta, Hadiya and Gurage people, Evangelism

Psalm David   Prophet Ekang-Ngwa, Chief Officer
B.P.   4000   Organized 1956
Libreville, GABON

PERSONNEL: 1978,41; 1980, 29 (-29% growth)
MISSIONARY PREPARATION: Language Learning, Mission Related Orientation
(4 years)
FIELDS OF SERVICE:
Gabon, various peoples and languages, Evangelism

African Orthodox Church   Archpriest Michael, Chief Officer
P.O. Box 12   Organized March 25, 1955 / Abradu Amoah
Kofi Pare, GHANA

PERSONNEL: 1980, 7; 1981, 14 (projected)
MISSIONARY PREPARATION: Bible Institute, Seminary, University,
Mission Related Orientation (3 years)
FIELDS OF SERVICE:
Ghana, the Ghanian people, Twii and Ewe languages, Church Planting

---

Apostles Revelation Society   Charles Kobla Nutornutsi, Chief Officer
P.O. Box 1   Organized November 2, 1939 / Wovenu
New Tadzewu, GHANA

PERSONNEL: 1972, 48; 1975, 60; 1978, 80; 1980, 569 (1085% growth)
MISSIONARY PREPARATION: Seminary

FIELDS OF SERVICE:
Ghana, various people, vernacular and English languages, Evangelism
Togo, Togolese people, Ewe and French languages, Evangelism

Christ Apostolic Reformed Church Rev. D.K. Saforo, Chief Officer
P.O. Box 6298   Organized January 28, 1978
Accra, GHANA   Interdenominational

PERSONNEL: 1981, 1 (projected)
MISSIONARY PREPARATION:

FIELDS OF SERVICE:
U.S.A., English language, Evangelism

Christian Outreach Fellowship
c/o Christian Service College
P.O. Box 3110
Kumasi, GHANA

Mr. Ransford Senavoe, Chief Officer
Organized 1979
Nondenominational

PERSONNEL: *1980, ±3*
MISSIONARY PREPARATION:

FIELDS OF SERVICE:

Church of Jesus
P.O. Box 11
Tamatoku-Ada, GHANA

Brother John Sewu, Chief Officer
Organized March 10, 1960
Denominational

PERSONNEL: *1972, 3; 1975, 10; 1978, 15; 1980, 20 (567% growth)*
MISSIONARY PREPARATION: *Practical Experience*

FIELDS OF SERVICE:
Ghana, various peoples, Church Planting

Church of the Lord (Ghana)
P.O. Box M113
Accra, GHANA

Bishop Albert Yamoah, Chief Officer
Organized April 7, 1957
Denominational

PERSONNEL: *1980, 16; 1981, 21 (projected)*
MISSIONARY PREPARATION: *Bible Institute, Practical Experience,*
Mission Related Orientation
FIELDS OF SERVICE:

Church of Melchizedek
P.O. Box 13141
Accra, GHANA

Bishop Isaac Wontumi, Chief Officer
Organized February 26, 1965
Interdenominational

PERSONNEL: *1972, 18; 1975, 20; 1978, 21; 1980, 24 (33% growth)*
MISSIONARY PREPARATION: *Bible Institute, Practical Experience,*
Mission Related Orientation (3 years)
FIELDS OF SERVICE:
Ghana, local people and language, Evangelism

The Church of Pentecost   Rev. James McKeown, Chief Officer
P.O. Box 2194   Organized 1937
Accra, GHANA   Interdenominational

PERSONNEL: 1972, 24; 1975, 6; 1978, 8; 1980, 8; 1981, 14 (projected)
MISSIONARY PREPARATION: Bible Institute, Practical Experience
Mission Related Orientation (36 months)
FIELDS OF SERVICE:
Togo, Ewe people, French language, Evangelism and Church Planting
Benin, Ewe people, French language, Evangelism and Church Planting
Upper Volta, the Moshies and Bobos people, French language, Evang. and Ch. Pl.
Ivory Coast, the Fantis, Aowins and Sanwins people, French language,
      Evangelism and Church Planting
Liberia, the Bassas and Krus people, English language, Evangelism, Ch. Planting

Church of Salvation   Rev. P.K. Anpinsah, Chief Officer
P.O. Box 27   Organized June 4, 1978
Techinan, B.A. GHANA   Nondenominational
PERSONNEL: 1978, 9; 1980, 14; 1981, 39 (projected)
MISSIONARY PREPARATION: Practical Experience

FIELDS OF SERVICE:
Ghana, Ashanti people, Akan language, Evangelism Healing
Ghana, Brongakefo people, Akan language, Evangelism, Healing

Crusaders Universal Mission   Dr. J.B. Kwofie, Chief Officer
P.O. Box 44   Organized March 25, 1959
Sekondi, GHANA   Interdenominational

PERSONNEL: 1981, 5 (projected)
MISSIONARY PREPARATION: Seminary

FIELDS OF SERVICE:
Nigeria, Togo, Ivory Coast, Sierra Leone and U.S.A.; Evangelism

---

Divine Healers' Church   Brother Lawson, Chief Officer
P.O. Box 3017   Organized February 24, 1954
Accra, GHANA

PERSONNEL: 1972, 83; 1975, 102; 1978, 129; 1980, 125 (51% growth)
MISSIONARY PREPARATION: Bible Institute, Practical Experience

FIELDS OF SERVICE:

136

Divine Redeemers Society
P.O. Box 243
Accra, GHANA

Brother Emml Kwao, Chief Officer
Organized 1966
Denominational

PERSONNEL: *1980, 6; 1981, 126 (projected)*
MISSIONARY PREPARATION: *Bible Institute*

FIELDS OF SERVICE:
Ghana, Evangelism

Episcopal Holy Temple and
*   Tabernacle Mission*
P.O. Box 209
Kumasi, GHANA

Rev. J.A. Coffie, Chief Officer
Organized 1953
Denominational

PERSONNEL: *1980, 5*
MISSIONARY PREPARATION:

FIELDS OF SERVICE:
Ghana, tribal people, Church Planting

Sacred Cherubim and Seraphim
Church of Ghana
P.O. Box 2840
Accra, GHANA

Rt. Rev. Isaiah Adegoke, Chief Officer
Organized December 13, 1954
Denominational

PERSONNEL: *1972, 15; 1975, 16; 1978, 8; 1980, 50 (233% growth)*
MISSIONARY PREPARATION: *Practical Experience*

FIELDS OF SERVICE:
Ghana, Ghanian people, Church Planting

African Gospel Unity Church
Box 33
Bomet, KENYA

Rev. Dishion A. Kesembe, Chief Officer
Organized December 9, 1964
Denominational

PERSONNEL: *1972, 52; 1975, 86; 1978, 112; 1980, 130 (150% growth)*
MISSIONARY PREPARATION: *Bible Institute, Practical Experience*
Mission Related Orientation (3-4 years)
FIELDS OF SERVICE:
Kenya, the Masai and Kalenjin people, English, Swahili and Masa languages,
*   Evangelism*

Africa Inland Church
    Missionary Board
P.O. Box 45019
Nairobi, KENYA

Pr. Peter Mualuko Kisulu, Chief Officer
Organized 1960
Denominational

PERSONNEL: *1980, 28; 1981, 30 (projected)*
MISSIONARY PREPARATION:

FIELDS OF SERVICE:
S. Sudan, the Taposa and other people, Arabic and English language, Evang.
Kenya, the Somali, Turkana, Giriama, Pokomo, Duruma, Kisii, Pokot, Embu and
    mixed peoples, Swahili language, Evangelism and Church Planting.

Covenant Baptist
P.O. Box 13
Sondu, Kisumu, KENYA

Rev. Paul O. Obange, Chief Officer
Organized January 13, 1978
Denominational

PERSONNEL: *1978, 4; 1980, 4; 1981, 7 (projected)*
MISSIONARY PREPARATION: *Bible Institute, Practical Experience,
Mission Related Orientation (5 years in service)*
FIELDS OF SERVICE:
Kenya, Kiswahili and Shozno languages, Evangelism

The *Ethiopian* Orthodox Holy Spirit
    & United Churches of East Africa
P.O. Box 47909
Nairobi, KENYA

Nathan Bullemi, Chief Officer
Organized March 18, 1959
Nondemoninational

PERSONNEL: *1980, 100; 1981, 112 (projected)*
MISSIONARY PREPARATION: *Bible Institute, Language Learning, Mission
Related Orientation (1 month)*
FIELDS OF SERVICE:
Kenya, the Swahili, Luhya, Kikuyu, Kamba and Luo languages, Church Planting

---

Fellowship of Spreading Good News
    (A.I.C.)
P.O. Box 1208
Kangundo, KENYA

Aaron Kivuva Kitusa, Chief Officer
Organized February, 1963
Interdenominational

PERSONNEL: *1972, 3; 1975, 6; 1978, 8; 1980, 8 (167% growth)*
MISSIONARY PREPARATION: *Bible Institute, Language Learning, Practical
Experience, Mission Related Orientation (2 weeks)*
FIELDS OF SERVICE:
Kenya, Meru people and language, Church Planting
Kenya, Tharaka people and language, Church Planting
Kenya, Kamba people, Swahili and Kekaiba language, Church Planting
Kenya, Boran people, Swahili language, Church Planting

Free Baptist Church of Kenya   Bishop Richard Muumbi, Chief Officer
P.O. Kambu   Organized August 24, 1975
Makinou, _KENYA_   Interdenominational

PERSONNEL: *1981, 4 (projected)*
MISSIONARY PREPARATION: *Bible Institute, Language Learning, Seminary,*
Practical Experience
FIELDS OF SERVICE:
Kenya, various peoples, Evangelism
Tanzania, Chagga people, Evangelism

Holy Spirit Church of East Africa   Japhet Z. Ambula, Chief Officer
P.O. Box 78   Organized 1927 / Archbishop
Maragoli, _KENYA_

PERSONNEL: *1980, 200*
MISSIONARY PREPARATION: *Bible Institute, Language Learning, Practical*
Experience, Mission Related Orientation
FIELDS OF SERVICE:
Kenya, Evangelism and Pastoring

Holy Trinity Church in Africa   Rt. Rev. Joshua Alvoch Gawo, Chief Off.
P.O. Box 160   Organized June 22, 1927
Kisumu, _KENYA_   Denominational

PERSONNEL: *1980, 3; 1981, 13 (projected)*
MISSIONARY PREPARATION: *Bible Institute*

FIELDS OF SERVICE:
Kenya, the English and Swahili languages, Evangelism
Uganda, the English and Swahili languages, Evangelism
Tanzania, the English and Swahili languages, Evangelism

Independent Lutheran Church   Dr. Angali - I, Chief Officer
c/o "H.H. Angali Loyalist Mission- Organized March 6, 1961
   ary Sending Agency"   Denominational
P.O. Box 142, Lumbatania Castle, Maragoli, _KENYA_

PERSONNEL: *1975, 4; 1978, 4; 1980, 2 (-50% growth)*
MISSIONARY PREPARATION: *Seminary, Mission Related Orientation (2 years)*

FIELDS OF SERVICE:
Kenya, the Maragoli, Baluhia, Namdi and Gusii people, the Luragoli, Luhia,
*   Namdi and Ekegusii languages, Evangelism*
Uganda, the Banyoro people, Evangelism
Australia, the English language, Evangelism

Lost Israelites of Kenya   William Misiko Waswa, Chief Officer
P.O. Box 699   Organized June 30, 1960
Kitale, _KENYA_   Denominational

PERSONNEL: *1980, 28; 1981, 54 (projected)*
MISSIONARY PREPARATION: *Bible Institute*

FIELDS OF SERVICE:
Uganda, the Bagishu people, the Swahili language, Literature, Evangelism
Uganda, the Suk people, the Swahili language, Literature, Evangelism

---

Musanda Holy Ghost Church   Rev. John Mark Odera, Chief Officer
P.O. Box 13111   Organized May, 1931
Nairobi, _KENYA_   Interdenominational

PERSONNEL: *1972, 235; 1975, 315; 1978, 346; 1980, 350 (49% growth)*
MISSIONARY PREPARATION: *Practical Experience*

FIELDS OF SERVICE:
Kenya, various peoples, Swahili, English, other mother languages, Church Plant.

Malagasy Protestant Church   Rev. Dr. Ratovonarivo, Chief Officer
  Tranozozoro Antranobiriky   Organized 1894
V. B-48 Ialana Ratsimilaho   Nondenominational
Antananarivo, _MADAGASCAR_

PERSONNEL: *1980, 9*
MISSIONARY PREPARATION: *Bible Institute, Practical Experience*

FIELDS OF SERVICE:
Madagascar, Malagasy people and language, Evangelism

Renewed Malagasy Lutheran Church   Rev. Pr. Ernest Rakotondratsimba, Chief
P.O. Box 1006   Officer
Antananarivo, _MADAGASCAR_   Organized August 24, 1970 / Denominational

PERSONNEL: *1972, 24; 1975, 20; 1978, 19; 1980, 21 (-13% growth)*
MISSIONARY PREPARATION: *Bible Institute, Language Learning, Seminary*
Practical Experience, Mission Related Orientation (6 months)
FIELDS OF SERVICE:
Madagascar, the Merina, Sakalave, Antandroy, Bara and Betsileo people,
*   the Malagasy language, Evangelism, Language Learning*

The Brotherhood of Cross and Star *O.O. Obu, Chief Officer*
34 Ambo, P.O. Box 49, Calabar *Organized January, 1955*
C.R.S., NIGERIA *Nondenominational*

PERSONNEL: *1978, 290; 1980, 290; 1981, 490 (projected)*
MISSIONARY PREPARATION: *Bible Institute, Language Learning, Seminary,*
University, Practical Experience, Mission Related Orientation (3 years)
FIELDS OF SERVICE:
Nigeria, England, U.S.A., Ghana, Cameroon, Liberia, the English language,
      Evangelism

Christ Army Church *Rev. O. Ekanem, Chief Officer*
c/o Nung Ukim P.A. *Organized June 16, 1946*
Ikot Ekpene *Denominational*
C.R.S. NIGERIA

PERSONNEL: *1972, 26; 1975, 26; 1978, 24; 1980, 56 (115% growth)*
MISSIONARY PREPARATION: *Bible Institute, Pracitcal Experience*
Mission Related Orientation (2 years)
FIELDS OF SERVICE:
Nigeria, the Ibibios people, the English and Ifik language, Evangelism,
      Church Planting

The Christ Church Mission *Rev. O. M. Akpan, Chief Officer*
P.O. Box 162
Uyo, C.R.S., NIGERIA *Interdenominational*

PERSONNEL: *1980, 88*
MISSIONARY PREPARATION:

FIELDS OF SERVICE:
Nigeria, various peoples, Evangelism

Christ Temple Church, Inc. *Rev. Imeh J. Akpan, Chief Officer*
P.O. Box 32 *Organized March 23, 1967*
Abak, C.R.S., NIGERIA *Nondenominational*

PERSONNEL: *1972, 14; 1975, 11; 1978, 11; 1980, 18 (29% growth)*
MISSIONARY PREPARATION: *Seminary, Mission Related Orientation (6 months)*

FIELDS OF SERVICE:
Nigeria, the Efik people, the English and Efik language, Evangelism, Preaching

Church of Christ in the Sudan Among   Dr. S. Yakobu, Chief Officer
  the Tiv. Mission Board   Organized November, 1975
P.A. MKAR, P.O. Gboko   Denominational
Benue State, *NIGERIA*

PERSONNEL: *1978, 20; 1980, 18 (-10% growth)*
MISSIONARY PREPARATION: *Bible Institute, Seminary, Practical Experience*
FIELDS OF SERVICE:
Nigeria, the Ibibio people, the English language, Pastor, Evangelism
Nigeria, the Fulani people, the Hausa language, Evangelism
Nigeria, the Tiv people and language, Church Planting
Nigeria, the Tiv people, the Tiv and English languages, Church Planting

---

Church of the Lord 'Aladura'   Dr. Emman O. Ade Adejobi, Chief Officer
P.O. Box 308, Ikeja   Organized July 27, 1930
Lagos, *NIGERIA*   Interdenominational

PERSONNEL: *1972, 670; 1975, 720;1978,1000;1980, 1250 (87% growth)*
MISSIONARY PREPARATION:

FIELDS OF SERVICE:
Sierra Leone, Creole, Menote, Temene, English people, Mende, Temene, English
   language, Evangelism, Teaching
Liberia, Krooi, Bassi people and language, Evangelism, Teaching
Ghana, Twi, Fanti and English people and language, Evangelism and Teaching
Togoland, Ewe, Awunah, French and English people, Evangelism, Teaching
United Kingdom, African, West Indian, English people, Eng. lang., Evang.

Evangelical Missionary Society   Rev Panya Baba, Chief Officer
P.O. Box 63   Organized 1948
Jos. *NIGERIA*   Denominational
PERSONNEL:*1972, 190;1975, 240; 1978,260; 1980, 440 (132% growth)*
MISSIONARY PREPARATION:

FIELDS OF SERVICE:
Nigeria, app. 50 various tribes, Hausa language, Evangelism, Church Planting
Niger, 5-6 different tribes, Hausa language, Evangelism, Church Planting
Ghana, Hausawa people, Hausa language, Evangelism, Church Planting

---

The Fellowship of Churches of   Rev. Dr. Bishop Akila Todi, Chief Officer
  Christ in Nigeria   Organized February 16-20, 1955
P.O. Box 475   Denominational
Jos, *NIGERIA*

PERSONNEL: *1981,5 (projected)*
MISSIONARY PREPARATION: *Bible Institue, Language Learning, Seminary,*
University, Practical Experience, **Mission Related Orientation (3 months)**
FIELDS OF SERVICE:
Republic of Sudan, Evangelism

Life and Light Apostolic Mission
P.O. Box 90
Ikot Ekpene, NIGERIA

Bro. N.A. Umoh, **Chief Officer**
Organized February 27, 1960
Nondenominational

PERSONNEL: *1972, 40; 1975, 40; 1978, 90; 1980, 90 (125% growth)*
MISSIONARY PREPARATION: *Bible Institute, Language Learning,*
Practical Experience, Mission Related Orientation (3 years)
FIELDS OF SERVICE:
Nigeria, Cameroon and Ghana, the English language, Church Planting

---

Nigerian Advent Christian
Mission, Inc.
c/o Use Ikot Egio P.A. Uyo
C.R.S., NIGERIA

Pastor E.P. Etuk, Chief Officer
Organized April 12, 1966
Denominational

PERSONNEL: *1980,5; 1981, 10 (projected)*
MISSIONARY PREPARATION: *Bible Institute, University, Practical*
Experience, Mission Related Orientation (4 years total)
FIELDS OF SERVICE:
Malaysia, India, Philippines, Japan and Nigeria, Evangelism

Nigerian Baptist Convention
Baptist Bldg., P.M.B. 5113
Ibada, NIGERIA

Rev. Dt. S.T. Ola, Chief Officer
Organized March 11, 1914 / Akande
Denominational

PERSONNEL: *1972, 10; 1975, 16; 1978, 10; 1980, 14 (40% growth)*
MISSIONARY PREPARATION: *Seminary, Practical Experience*

FIELDS OF SERVICE:
Nigeria, the Yorubas people and language, Evangelism
Nigeria the Afenmai and Ohuri people, Edo langauge, Church Planting
Nigeria, Southern Ijaw people, Ijaw and English languages, Church Planting
Nigeria,Hausas people and language, Evangelism
Nigeria, Batonu people, Bariba language, Evangelism
Sierra Leone, the Tondolili people, the English language, Evangelism
Sierra Leone, the Bombali people, the English language, Evangelism
Sierra Leone, the Korauku people, the English language, Church Planting

West African Episcopal Church Patriarch Daniel Olarimiwa, Chief Off.
  Mission   Organized May 24, 1903 / Epega
St. Stephen's Cathedral   Denominational
76 Adeniji Adele Road, Lagos, NIGERIA

PERSONNEL: *1972, 72; 1975, 76; 1978, 80; 1980, 84 (17% growth)*
MISSIONARY PREPARATION: *Practical Experience, Mission Related Orientation*
(2-3 years)
FIELDS OF SERVICE:

African Enterprise   Michael Cassidy, Chief Officer
P.O. Box 647   Organized 1964
Pietemanitzburg, 3200 SOUTH AFRICA Interdenominational

PERSONNEL: *1972, 8; 1975, 15; 1978, 22; 1980, 30 (275% growth)*
MISSIONARY PREPARATION: *Bible Insitute, Seminary, University,*
Practical Experience, Mission Related Orientation (varies)
FIELDS OF SERVICE:
Uganda, various peoples and languages, Evangelism and Teaching
Kenya, various peoples, the English language, Evangelism
Tanzania, various peoples, the Swahili language, Evangelism
Zimbabwe, various peoples, the English language, Evangelism
South Africa, various peoples, the English language, Evangelism

African Evangelical Fellowship   Rev. L.E. Glass, Chief Officer
Rowland House   Organized 1947
Montrose Ave.   Interdenominational
Claremont, 7700, SOUTH AFRICA
PERSONNEL: *1980, 22; 1981, 27 (projected)*
MISSIONARY PREPARATION: *Bible Institute, Practical Experience*

FIELDS OF SERVICE:
Malawi, the Malawian people, the Chichewa language, Teaching
Zambia, the Zambian people, the Kaonde and English languages, Teaching
Zimbabwe, the African people, the English language, Teaching
Botswana, the African people, the Setswana language, Teaching
Nambia, various peoples, the Afrikaans language, Teaching
Swaziland, the Swazis people, the Siswati and English language, Teaching
South Africa, the Zulus and other peoples, the Zulu and English language,
*   Teaching, Med., Evangelism*

The Apostolic Faith Mission of   Dr. F.P. Moller, Chief Officer
   South Africa   Organized 1908
P.O. Box 89187   Denominational
Lyndhurst, 2106, TVL. SOUTH AFRICA

PERSONNEL: 1972, 60; 1975, 72; 1978, 80; 1980, 83 (38% growth)
MISSIONARY PREPARATION: Seminary, Practical Experience

FIELDS OF SERVICE:
South Africa, Swaziland, Lesotho, Botswana, Bophuthatswnana,Venda, Zimbabwe,
   Malawi, Zambia and Kenya, Training and Church Growth

Full Gospel Church of God in   M.L. Badenhorst, Chief Officer
   South Africa   Organized May 31, 1910
P.O. Box 40   Denominational
Irene, 1675, SOUTH AFRICA

PERSONNEL: 1972, 21; 1975, 29; 1978, 29; 1980, 29 (38% growth)
MISSIONARY PREPARATION: Bible Institute, Seminary, Practical
Experience
FIELDS OF SERVICE:
Rhodesia, Malawi, Lesotho, Zululand, Transkei; the English language, Evangel.
Republic of South Africa, the English and Afrikaans languages, Evangelism

---

Reformed Independent Churches   The Rt. Rev. Isaac P.B. Mokoena, Chief Off.
   Association   Organized July 4, 1970
P.O. Box 32309   Interdenominational
Braamfontein 2017 SOUTH AFRICA

PERSONNEL: 1980, 407
MISSIONARY PREPARATION: Seminary, Practical Experience, Mission Related
Orientation (4 years total)
FIELDS OF SERVICE:
South Africa, Lesotho, Botswana, Bophuthatswana, Swaziland, Transkei
and Ciskei, Evangelism and Training

Evangelical Lutheran Church of   Rev. Uswege Mwakalinga, Chief Officer
   Tanzania, Department of Missions
   and Evangelism   Interdenominational
P.O. Box 3033, Arusho, TANZANIA

PERSONNEL: 1980, 2; 1981, 4 (projected)
MISSIONARY PREPARATION: Bible Institute, Seminary, Practical Experience,
Mission Related Orientation (5 years total)
FIELDS OF SERVICE:
Kenya, the Kenyani people, the Swahili language, Evangelism
Zaire, the Zairian people, the Swahili language, Evangelism

Eastern Orthodox Church
P.O. Box 1487
Kampala, UGANDA

Rev. S.K. Kasasa, Chief Officer
Organized January 6, 1929
Interdenominational

PERSONNEL: *1972, 86; 1975, 135;1978, 0; 1980, 22 (-74% growth)*
MISSIONARY PREPARATION: *Bible Institute, Language Learning,*
Practical Experience, Mission Related Orientation (1-3 years)
FIELDS OF SERVICE:

African Baptist Episcopal Church
  (CEBA)
B.P. 3866
Lubumbashi, Shaba, ZAIRE

Bishop Kabwe-Ka-Leza, Chief Officer
Organized December 1, 1956
Interdenominational

PERSONNEL: *1980, 4*
MISSIONARY PREPARATION: *Bible Institute, Language Learning, Seminary,*
University, Practical Experience
FIELDS OF SERVICE:
West Germany, the Swahili, English, French and other languages, Evangelism,
    Medicine
Denmark, the Swahili, English, French and other languages, Evangelism

---

Churches of Christ of Zaire
  Sankuru Region
B.P. 24
Kole via Lodja, ZAIRE

Rev. Elembe Iwuwd, Chief Officer
Organized January 13, 1936
Denominational

PERSONNEL: *1980, 5; 1981, 10 (projected)*
MISSIONARY PREPARATION: *Bible Institute, Language Learning, Seminary,*
University
FIELDS OF SERVICE:
 Zaire, the Bakutshu people, the English language, Evangelism

---

Church Union of the Zairean
  Baptist Churches (CUEBZ)
B.P. 78 - Kikwit II
Bandundu, ZAIRE

Rev. Wai-Wai Dibudi
Organized May 6, 1960
Denominational

PERSONNEL: *1980, 2*
MISSIONARY PREPARATION: *Bible Institute*

FIELDS OF SERVICE:

Evangelical Church of the Deuvres   Nzolele Nluengisi Nkuka, Chief Officer
  Saints (CEDS)   Organized March 3, 1963
B.P. 10963   Denominational
Kinshasa, ZAIRE

PERSONNEL: 1980, 10
MISSIONARY PREPARATION: Bible Institute, Seminary, University

FIELDS OF SERVICE:

Evangelical Church of Sacrificers   Kadima Bakenge Musangilayi, Chief Off.
  (CES)   Organized November 22, 1963
B.P. 12232   Denominational
Kinshasa, ZAIRE

PERSONNEL: 1972, 4; 1975, 16; 1978, 78; 1980, 72 (1700% growth)
MISSIONARY PREPARATION: Seminary, Practical Experience

FIELDS OF SERVICE:
Zaire, U.S.A. Tanzania, Isreal, Belgium and France, Evangelism

---

Evangelical Church of Zaire   Rev. Luyindu Iwa Marambu, Chief Off.
  (CEZ)   Organized 1881
c/o B.P. 68 I.M.E.   Denominational
Kimpese via Kinshasa, ZAIRE

PERSONNEL: 1972, 44; 1975, 37; 1978, 24; 1980, 109 (147% growth)
MISSIONARY PREPARATION: Language Learning Seminary or University

FIELDS OF SERVICE:
Congo, Ecuador, Japan and Zaire

Evangelical Episcopal Church of Zaire Bishop Assani Baraka Koy, Chief Off.
B.P. 216   Organized November 21, 1932
Kisangai, ZAIRE   Denominational

PERSONNEL: 1980, 8; 1981, 25 (projected)
MISSIONARY PREPARATION: Seminary, University

FIELDS OF SERVICE:

Free Baptist Church
B.P.39
Equateur, Bikorl, ZAIRE

Rev. Nzee Luemb'Engambi, Chief Officer
Organized November 23, 1965
Denominational

PERSONNEL: *1980, 4*
MISSIONARY PREPARATION: *Bible Institute Language Learning, Seminary,*
University, Practical Experience, Mission Related Orientaiton
FIELDS OF SERVICE:
Zaire

Free Evangelical Church of Zaire
  (CEIZ)
B.P.3020
Kinshasa/Gombe, ZAIRE

Muhung Ndumba Tembo, Chief Officer
Organized May 9, 1969
Denomnational

PERSONNEL: *1980, 12*
MISSIONARY PREPARATION: *BIble Institute, Language Learning, Practical*
Experience
FIELDS OF SERVICE:

Free Reformed Church of Zaire
B.P. 879
Kinshasa/Limere, ZAIRE

Eveque Mwamba Mukishi, Chief Officer
Organized June 6, 1969
Denominational

PERSONNEL: *1981, 7 (projection)*
MISSIONARY PREPARATION: *Bible Institute*

FIELDS OF SERVICE:

Holy Spirit Church in Africa
  (CSEA)
B.P. 10172 ZAIRE

Rev. Mangitukwa Lukombo, Chief Officer
Organized February 12, 1961
Denominational

PERSONNEL:*1972, 20; 1975, 22; 1978, 22; 1980, 28 (40% growth)*
MISSIONARY PREPARATION: *Practical Experience*

FIELDS OF SERVICE:
Zaire, the Bakongo people, the Kikongo language, Evangelism
Zaire, the Zairian people, the Lingala language, Evangelism
Zaire, the Baluba people, the Tshiluga language, Evangelism
Zaire, the Baluba people, the Swahili language, Evangelism

Pentecost Christian Church of Zaire Rev. Tsassa Dinasa D., Chief Officer
  (CCPZ)   Organized 1977
B.P. 10679   Denominational
Kinshasa 1, ZAIRE

PERSONNEL: *1980, 278; 1981, 280 (projection)*
MISSIONARY PREPARATION: *Bible Institute, Seminary*

FIELDS OF SERVICE:
Zaire, the Lingala language, Church Planting
Zaire, the Kokongo language, Evangelism
Zaire, the Shiluba language, Evangelism
Zaire, the Swahili language, Evangelism

Shaba Pentecost Evangelistic Church Rev. Mwepu Bondapa Wa Lunda, Chief Off.
B.P. 1517   Organized August 15, 1965
Likasi, Shaba, ZAIRE   Denominational

PERSONNEL:*1981, 5 (projected)*
MISSIONARY PREPARATION: *Bible Institute, University*

FIELDS OF SERVICE:
France, Evangelism
U.S.A., Evangelism

United Church of the Holy Spirit   Rev. M'Panya Mamba, Chief Officer
B.P. 11. 763   Organized June 15, 1965
Kinshasa 1, ZAIRE

PERSONNEL:*1981, 3 (projected)*
MISSIONARY PREPARATION: *Practical Experience, Mission Related*
Orientation (varies)
FIELDS OF SERVICE:
Zambia, Angola and Bujumbura, Evangelism

The Apostolic Church in Zambia   Hans Peter Pedersen, Chief Officer
P.O. Box KJ92   Organized 1958
Ndola, ZAMBIA   Interdenominational

PERSONNEL: *1972, 4; 1975, 6; 1978, 9; 1980, 8 (100% growth)*
MISSIONARY PREPARATION: *Bible Institute, Seminary, Practical*
Experience, Mission Related Orientation (203 years)
FIELDS OF SERVICE:
Republic of South Africa, the Indian tribal peoples, the Zulu and other
    languages, Evangelism, Teaching

```
ARONI                              Rev. Z. Limbango, Chief Officer
PO Box 71339                       Organized 1947
Ndola, ZAMBIA                      Interdenominational
```

PERSONNEL: *1980, 12*
MISSIONARY PREPARATION: *Bible Institute*

FIELDS OF SERVICE:
Zaire, the Zairean people, the Lingala language, Evangelism
Zambia, the Zambian people, the Zambian Language, Evangelism
Zimbabwe Rhodesia, the Zimbabwen people and language, Evangelism

---

```
Churches of Christ                 Rev. Chester Woodhall, Chief Officer
P.O. Box 2297                      Organized 1910
Kitwe, ZAMBIA                      Nondenominational
```

PERSONNEL: *1972, 32; 1975, 30; 1978, 48; 1980, 55 (72% growth)*
MISSIONARY PREPARATION: *Bible Institute, Practical Experience*

FIELDS OF SERVICE:
Zaire, the Bemba people and language, Church Planting
Angola, the Lunda people and language, Church Planting
Zambia, the Tonga people, the Tonga and English languages, Evangelism
Zambia, the Nyanja people, the Nyanja and English languages, Training
Zambia, the Bemba people and language, Church Planting

```
Dorthea Mission                    Mr. H. Von Staden, Chief Officer
P.O. Box 32696                     Organized September, 1942
Lusaka, ZAMBIA                     Interdenominational
```

PERSONNEL: *1980, 5*
MISSIONARY PREPARATION: *Bible Institute, University, Mission*
Related Orientation (3 years)
FIELDS OF SERVICE:
Zambia, the English language, Evangelism, Teaching
Zambia, the Bemba language, Evangelism, Teaching
Zambia, the Nyanja language, Evangelism, Teaching

```
Lusaka Baptist Church              Joe Simfukwe, Chief Officer
P.O. Box 30636                     Organized 1960
Lusaka, ZAMBIA                     Interdenominational
```

PERSONNEL: *1978, 4; 1980, 4 (400% growth)*
MISSIONARY PREPARATION: *Bible Institute, Practical Experience*

FIELDS OF SERVICE:
Zambia, the Urban people, the English and Cinyanja languages, Church Plant.
Zambia, the Urban people, the English language, Counselling, Evangelism

```
Pentecostal Holiness Church          Bishop J. Wilhan, Chief Officer
P.O. Box 1751                        Organized 1956
Kitine, Lusaka, ZAMBIA               Denominational
```

PERSONNEL: *1975, 4; 1978, 4; 1980, 4*
MISSIONARY PREPARATION: *Bible Insittute, Seminary or University,*
Practical Experience, Mission Related Orientation
FIELDS OF SERVICE:

```
African Apostolic Church of Johane  Abel John Momberume, Chief Officer
  Maranke                           Organized June 17, 1932
Plot No. 52, Crete Rd.              Denominational
Waterfalls, ZIMBABWE-RHODESIA
```

PERSONNEL: *1980, 3; 1981, 3 (projected)*
MISSIONARY PREPARATION:

FIELDS OF SERVICE:
Zimbabwe, the Shona language; Zaire, the Swahili language; Zambia, the
Bemba language; Malawi, the Chewa language; Mozambique, the Sena
language; and Angola, the Kalunda language; Church Planting

```
Christian Marching Church           Bishop Petros Katsande, Chief Officer
P.O. Box 10016, Mabvuku             Organized July 1, 1956
Salisbury, ZIMBABWE-RHODESIA        Interdenominational
```

PERSONNEL: *1972, 2; 1975, 3; 1978, 4; 1980, 9 (350% growth)*
MISSIONARY PREPARATION:*Bible Institute, Practical Experience, Missions*
Related Orientation (1 year)
FIELDS OF SERVICE:
Zimbabwe, the English, Shona people, the Shona, Ndebele, English languages
    Evangelism
Zambia, the Bemba, Tonga people, the English language, Evangelism
Mozambique, Portuguese Sena people, the English language, Evangelism
Botswana, the Tswana people, the English language, Evangelism

```
Church of Central Africa,           Rev. A.J. Viljoen, Chief Officer
  Salisbury Synod                   Organized 1912
P.O. Box 533                        Denominational
Salisbury, ZIMBABWE-RHODESIA
```
PERSONNEL: *1972, 10; 1975, 10; 1978, 8; 1980, 6 (-40% growth)*
MISSIONARY PREPARATION: *Seminary, University*

FIELDS OF SERVICE:
Zimbabwe, the Malawian people, the Chichewa language, Evangelism

City of Jehova   Ishmael Jimiel Chiwara, Chief Officer
Rm. No. 2637, Jerusalem Highfield   Organized June 1954
Salisbury, ZIMBABWE-RHODESIA   Denominational

PERSONNEL: 1981, 6 (projected)
MISSIONARY PREPARATION: Practical Experience

FIELDS OF SERVICE:
U.S.A., Malawi, Ghana, Botswana, Mozambique and Zambia; Evangelism and
     Church Planting

Independent African Church   Rev. S.C. Machinguria
P.O. Box 9027   Organized January 6, 1946
Hararie, Salisbury, ZIMBABWE-RHODESIA Interdenominational

PERSONNEL: 1980, 24
MISSIONARY PREPARATION: Bible Institute, Practical Experience,
Mission Related Orientation (4 years total)
FIELDS OF SERVICE:

Zion Christian Church   Bishop Nehemiah Mutendi, Chief Officer
Stand 2705, Five Street   Organized November 1923
Mucheke Township
Fort Victoris, ZIMBABWE-RHODESIA

PERSONNEL: 1981, 4 (projection)
MISSIONARY PREPARATION: Practical Experience

FIELDS OF SERVICE:
Zambia, Malawi, Mozambique and Botswana, Evangelism

Asian Respondents (no survey information)

Ao Baptist Churches Association
Impur
Nagaland, 798 615 INDIA
Rev. K. Lanumeren

Bharat Evangelical Mission
41 Main Road, St. Thomas Mt.
Madras, 16 INDIA

Bible Church of India
Dayavihar Dhankote
Gurugaon, Haryana, INDIA
Rev. Joyel Kulakkada

Board of Missions of the Methodist Church in South India
15 Nehru Road, Kilkusha
Lucknow-2, U.P. INDIA

Christian and Missionary
Alliance of India
P.O. Box 5
Akola, Maharashtra 444 001 INDIA
Rev. Palaspagar

Christian Outreach Uplifting
New Tribes
P.O. Box 1720, 14-45 Yopalnagar
Colony, Malkajgin,
Hyderabed 500 047 INDIA

Church Missionary Movement
Bryantnagar P.O. Tuticorin
Tamil Nadu, 628 003, INDIA
Mr. Emil Jebasingh

Discipleship Centre
17 Darya Ganj, P.O. Box 7011
New Delhi, 110 002, INDIA
Dr. C. Rajkumar

Foreign Mission Board of
Maharashtra Synod
P.O. Box 5, Akola
Maharashtra 444 001, INDIA
Rev. D.L. Telgote

Full Gospel Fellowship
P.O. Bhagalpur, Deoria Dist.
U.P., INDIA
Rev. James S. Morar

Garo Baptist Convention
Tura, Garo Hills
West Meghalaya, INDIA
Mr. Elgin Momin

Gospel Missionary Association
P.O. Box 962
Madras, 600 012 INDIA
Mr. J. Palmer

High Range Missionary Society
c/o Joy Pampady
Korrayam, Kerala, INDIA

Hill Tribe Missionary Prayer Band
KK District
Tamil Nadu, INDIA

Home Missionary Society
Marlhandom and P.O.
K.K. District
C.S.I. Nagercoil, INDIA
Rev. A. Samuel

India Pentecostal Church
Mission Board
Hebron, Kumbanadu,
Kerala, INDIA

Jesus Lives Evangelistic Ministry
Usilampatti
Madurai Dt. T.N., India

Lotha B. Association Outreach
P.O. Wokha,
Nagaland, INDIA
Mr. K. Tsanglao

Makedonia
P.O. Lunglei
Mizoram, 196 106 INDIA
Pachuau C. Muanthanga

Marantha Full Gospel Association
68 Dr. Alagappa Chettiar Rd.
Vepery
Madras, 600 007, INDIA
Dr. D. Henry Joseph

Mulung Mission
Mulung via Kazipet Warangal Dist.
Andhra Pradesh, INDIA

Nagaland Baptist Missionary
Movement
Bayavii Hill, Kohima
Nagaland, 797 001   INDIA

National Missionary Society of
India
102 Peters Road, Royspettah
Madras, 600 014 INDIA
   Rev. K.G.S. Dorairat

North Bank Baptist Church Assoc-
iation
P.O. Charali, Dist. Darrang,
Assam, 784 176 INDIA
   C. Lal Rema

Partnership Mission Society
Sielmat, Churachandpur
P.O. Manipar, INDIA
   Dr. Rochunga Pudaite

Praise Him Ministries of India
163/3RT Vijayanayar Colony
Hyderbad 500 457 INDIA

Tanghjul Naga Baptist Convention
Mission to Maring
P.O. Ukhrul
Manipur, INDIA

Tribal Gospel Team
Pangottil House, Panamkuzhi
Kombanad, P.O.
Kerala, 683 546 INDIA

Upper Room Prayer and Evan-
gelistic Fellowship
Post Box No. 151
Visakhapatnam,
Andhra Pradesh 530 004 INDIA
   Rev. N. Krupa Rao

The Village Evangelism and
Revival Crusade
8/13 Bethel Society
Nandiad, Yujarat, INDIA

Zoram Evangelical Fellowship
P.O. Aizawi
Misoram State, INDIA
   Rev. Khuanghana

ABDIEL
Genuk, Ungaran
Semarang, INDONESIA

Gereja Beritakan Injil
Jalan Kemurnian 5/35
Jakarta Barat, INDONESIA

Asian Outreach
P.O. Box 36
Toyonaka
Osaka, 560 JAPAN
   Wm. Molenkamp, Rep.

Chinohate Senkyokai
1043 Kotake-cho
Nerima-ku
Tokyo, 176 JAPAN
   Rev. Nakaichi Ando

Indonesia Senkyo Kyoryokukai
4-78 Takami-cho
Yao-shi 581 JAPAN
   Rev. Yosuke Furuyama

Japan Alliance Foreign Mission
Board
Naka, P.O. Box 70
Hiroshima 732, JAPAN
   Rev. Elichi Fujika

Japan Baptist Renmei
7-26-24 Shinjuku
Shinjuku-ku
Tokyo 160 JAPAN

Japan Evangelical Free Church
33-4 Higasiono-cho
Koyama, Kita-ku
Kyoto-shi 603 JAPAN
   Rev. Shigeru Masaki

Japan Holiness Church
1-30-1 Megurita-Machi
Higashimurayama-shi
Tokyo 189 JAPAN

Japan Overseas Mission
2-27-11 Horinouchi
Suginami-ku
Tokyo 166 JAPAN

Japan Scripture Union
1-33-30 Sengawa-sho
Chofu-shi, Tokyo 182 JAPAN

ASIAN RESPONDENTS (Continued)

Kakudai Senkyokai (W.M.E.)
1817-33 Mizumachi
Hanagashima-sho
Miyazaki-shi, 880 JAPAN
   Rev. A. Nagai

Kanadka Eiko Shiensuru Kai
c/o Shirogane Christ Church
3-2-11 Shirogane-cho
Sakaide-shi 762 JAPAN

Karasawa Junko O Shiensuru Kai
c/o Horinouchi Kyokai
2-27-11 Horinouchi, Suginami-ku
Tokyo 166 JAPAN

Karuizawa Christian Center
2163 Karuizawa-machi
Nagano-ken 389-01 JAPAN
   Pr. Hideo Nakada

Nigon Iesu Kirisuto Kyodan
506-1 Taga-cho
Omihachiman-shi 523, JAPAN

Overseas Missionary Fellowship
3-18-10 Nukuikitamachi,
Koganeishi, Tokyo 184, JAPAN
   Rev. Tadashi Haga, 1965

South American Mission
2-29-19 Matsubara,
Setagaya-ku
Tokyo 156, JAPAN
   Rev. Sadaharo Ide Mangei

Taiheiyo Hoso Kyokai Kaigai
   Dempa O Sasaeru Kai
c/o P.B.A. 3010-8 Umegaoka
Setagaya-ku, Tokyo 154 JAPAN

Asian Gospel Mission
330-12 Mia 8 Dong, Do-Bong Ku,
Seoul, KOREA
   Rev. Lee Il

Association of Philippine
   Missionaries in Korea
P.O. Box 56, DaeGuji
KOREA 630-00
   Rev. Chang Ryum Kim

Church of Christ Mission
C.P.O. Box 2511
Seoul, 100 KOREA

Korea Baptist Mission
Yoi Do, P.O. Box 45
Seoul, KOREA
   Rev. Don Jones

Korea Methodist Mission Dept.
Kwangwhamoon, P.O. Box 740
1 Ka 64-8 Choong-ku, Tai Pyung Ro
Seoul, KOREA
   Rev. Kim Choon-Young

Korea Translation Mission
C.P.O. Box 3476
Seoul, KOREA 100
   David J. Cho

Korean Womans Evangelism Service
95-9 Shin kil Dong
Yungdeugpo-ku, Seoul, KOREA
   Mrs. Yang Seung-Tam

The Presbyterian Church in Korea
   (Haptong)
Tong Cha Dong 35-4, Yong San ku
Seoul, KOREA
   Rev. Chung Bong-cho

Presbyterian Church in Korea
   (Tonghap)
C.P.O. Box 1125, Chongno-ku
Seoul, KOREA
   Rev. Seung Kap-Shik

Sai Moonan Presbyterian Church
Sai Moon-Ro, Chong Ro-Ku
Seoul, KOREA
   Dr. Simeon Kang

Malaysia Home and World Missionary Fellowship
4, Jalan Utara,
Petaling, Jaya, Selangor,
MALAYSIA

Rev. Ronney Kon
P.O. Box 1031
Jalan Semangat, Petaling Jaya
Selangor, MALAYSIA

Association of Baptists for
   Philippine Evangelism
c/o Faith Baptist Church
Cagayan de Oro City, PHILIPPINES
   Rev. Ernesto Rivera

Christ for Greater Manila
761 P. Gomez St., Mandaluyong
Metro Manila, PHILIPPINES

Convention of Philippine Baptist
  Churches, Inc.
P.O. Box 263
Iloilo City, PHILIPPINES

Doane Baptist Bible Institute
Iloilo City, PHILIPPINES
  Rev. Roberto Geguillana

FIFCOP Missions, Inc.
P.O. Box 4546, Caloocan City
Metro Manila, PHILIPPINES

Grace Christian Church, Mission
  Board
Grace Village
Quezon City, PHILIPPINES

Grace Gospel Church, Mission
  Board
429 Pina Ave.
Manila, PHILIPPINES 2806

Karuhatan
Valenzuela, Metro Manila Office
P.O. Box 1467
Manila, PHILIPPINES

Korean Mission to the Philippines
89 Scout Delgado
Quezon City, PHILIPPINES
  Rev. Harold Kim

March of Faith
Cebu City, PHILIPPINES

Overseas Missionary Fellowship
P.O. Box 2217
Manila, PHILIPPINES

Philippine Association of
  Baptist Churches
Padre Faura,
Metro Manila, PHILIPPINES

Philippine Independent Church
1320 V. Concepcion, Santa Cruz
Manila, PHILIPPINES

Philippine Mission Churches of
  Christ
P.O. Box 2774
Manila, PHILIPPINES

Quezon City Evangelical Church
  Mision Board
P.O. Box SM 258
Manila, PHILIPPINES 2806

St. Stephen's Parish, Mission Board
1267 G. Masangkay Street
Santa Cruz
Manila, PHILIPPINES 2806

United Methodist Church
P.O. Box 756
Manila, PHILIPPINES

Board of Mission TRAC - Singapore
23-B Coleman Street
SINGAPORE 0617
  David Liow
  1/7/55, Denominational

Church of Christ of Malaya
54 Sophia Road
SINGAPORE 9

SCEM
14 Dolvey Estate
SINGAPORE

The Overseas Mission Commission
  of the Presbyterian Church
89-5 Chang Chun Rd.
Taipei, TAIWAN R.O.C.

Taipei Christian Church Mission
Nanking East Rd., Sec. 2 #110
Taipei, TAIWAN R.O.C.

True Jesus Church
TAIWAN, R.O.C.

Christian Missionary of Thailand
P.O. Box 1581
Bangkok 5, THAILAND
  Rev. Jacob Lim

South East Asia Evangelizing
  Mission
THAILAND

Burma Baptist Convention
143 St. John's Road
Rangoon, <u>BURMA</u>

Rev. Victor San Lone, Chief Officer
Organized 1865
Denominational

PERSONNEL: 1980, 887
MISSIONARY PREPARATION: Seminary, Mission Related Orientation (3-6 years)

FIELDS OF SERVICE:
Burma, the Burmese people and language, Evangelism

Churches of Christ
P.O. Box 299
Rangoon, <u>BURMA</u>

Joshua Fish, Chief Officer
Organized 1969
Nondenominational

PERSONNEL: 1972, 14; 1975, 16; 1978, 16; 1980, 30 (114% growth)
MISSIONARY PREPARATION: Bible Institute

FIELDS OF SERVICE:
Burma, the Lish and Rawang people, the Lisu, Rawan, Ngochang and Jinghpaw
    languages, Evangelism
Burma, the Naga people and language, Evangelism
Burma, the Lisas people and language, Church Planting
Burma, the Chins people and language, Evangelism
Burma, the Karens people, the Karen and Burmese language, Evangelism, Church
    Planting
Thailand, the Lisu and Lahu people, the Thai, Lahu and Lisu languages,
    Evangelism, Church Planting, Literature
<u>Thailand, the Ahka and Ngochang people and languages, Evang., Ch. Planting</u>

Evangelical Fellowship of Burma
P.O. Box 1301
Rangoon, <u>BURMA</u>

U. Robin H. Seia, Chief Officer
Organized June 15, 1978
Interdenominational

PERSONNEL: 1978, 4; 1980, 6. (50% growth)
MISSIONARY PREPARATION: Bible Institute, Mission Related Orientation (3 Years)

FIELDS OF SERVICE:
Burma, Arakanese people, Arakanese and Burmese languages, Evang., Ch. Plant.
Burma, the Dai Halka people and language, Evangelism
Burma, the Shan, Palaung and Pa U people, the Shan and Burmese languages
    Evangelism

Home Mission Board of the
  Presbyterian Church
Tahan, Kalemyo, *BURMA*

Rev. Kawl Thang Vuta, Chief Officer
Organized February 16, 1968
Denominational

PERSONNEL: *1972, 8; 1975, 23; 1978, 29; 1980, 33 (313% growth)*
MISSIONARY PREPARATION: *Practical Experience, Mission Related Orientation, (6-8 months)*
FIELDS OF SERVICE:
Burma, the Chin and Naga people, the Chin and Burmese languages, Evangelism
   Church Planting

Methodist Home Mission to the
  Southern Chin State
Taban, Kalemyo, *BURMA*

Rev. Chalhvuna, Chief Officer
Organized October 14, 1966
Denominational

PERSONNEL: *1972, 5; 1975, 14; 1978, 25; 1980, 32 (540% growth)*
MISSIONARY PREPARATION:

FIELDS OF SERVICE:
Burma, the Matu people, the Burmese and Matu languages, Evangelism
Burma, the Mon people, the Burmese and Mon languages, Evangelism
Burma, the Dhai people, the Dhai and Burmese languages, Evangelism
Burma, the M'Kang people, the Burmese and M'Kang languages, Evangelism
Burma, the Yindu people, the Burmese and Yindu languages, Evangelism

---

China Evangelistic Mission, Ltd.
138-140 Argyle St. G/F.,
Flat B
Kowloon, *HONG KONG*

Calvin C. L. Chu, Chief Officer
Organized April 28, 1975
Nondenominational

PERSONNEL: *1975, 1; 1978, 1; 1980, 1*
MISSIONARY PREPARATION: *Seminary*

FIELDS OF SERVICE:
Thailand, the Chinese and Lahus people, the Mandarin and Lahu languages,
   Church Planting

Evangelical Free Church of China   Reb. C. L. Lee, Chief Officer
46 Chi Kiang St., 1/F., "8"   Organized 1979
Tokwawan, Kowloon, HONG KONG   Denominational

PERSONNEL: 1980, 3
MISSIONARY PREPARATION:

FIELDS OF SERVICE:
Taiwan, the Chinese Hakka people and language, Evnagelism
Singapore, the Chinese and Malay people, the English and Malay languages,
    Church Planting

The Foreign Missionary Society of   Mr. Philip Lee, Chief Officer
  the Chinese Christian and Mis-   Organized 1962
  sionary Alliance Churches of   Denominational
Hong Kong, PO Box 34902, Kings Rd., HONG KONG

PERSONNEL: 1972, 11; 1975, 13; 1978, 13; 1980, 15 (36% growth)
MISSIONARY PREPARATION: Bible College, Practical Experience

FIELDS OF SERVICE:
Peru, local people of Lima, the Spanish language, Evangelism
Thailand, the Chinese people, the Swatow language, Evangelism
Indonesia, the Chinese people, the Hokin language, Evangelism
Indonesia, the Chinese people, the Hakka Indonesian langauge, Evangelism
Taiwan, the Chinese people, the Mandarin language, Evangelism
Macao, the Chinese people, the Cantonese language, Evangelism

Hebron Evangelical Association   Dr. Philemon Choi, Chief Officer
20 Austin Ave., 1/F   Organized 1972
Kowloon, HONG KONG
PERSONNEL: 1980, 14
MISSIONARY PREPARATION:

FIELDS OF SERVICE:
Taiwan, Evangelism, Church Planting
Thailand and Malaysia, Church Planting
Singapore, Teaching, Evangelism
Canada, Church Planting

Hong Kong Baptist Church   Rev. Timothy S. H. Lau, Chief Officer
  Board of Evangelism   Organized 1901
50 Caine Rd. HONG KONG   Denominational

PERSONNEL: 1975, 1; 1978, 4; 1980, 8 (700% growth)
MISSIONARY PREPARATION: Bible Institute, Language Learning

FIELDS OF SERVICE:
Japan, the Japanese people and language, Church Planting
Taiwan, the students, the Chinese language, Student Work
Hong Kong, the students, the Chinese language, Student Work

159

Hong Kong Swatow Christian Church Rev. David Chu, Chief Officer
  Mission   Organized 1972
23 Prat Ave.   Denominational
Tsimslatsui, HONG KONG

PERSONNEL: 1980, 4
MISSIONARY PREPARATION:

FIELDS OF SERVICE:
Malaysia, the Chinese Hakka people and language, Church Planting
Malaysia, the Chinese people and language, Church Planting
Taiwan, the Chinese people, the Mandarin language, Church Planting

---

Kowloon City Evangelical Church   Samuel Chan, Chief Officer
71, Fuk Lo Tsuen Road., 3/F   Organized March, 1978
Kowloon City, Kowloon   Nondenominational
HONG KONG

PERSONNEL: 1978, 1; 1980, 4 (300% growth)
MISSIONARY PREPARATION: Bible Institute

FIELDS OF SERVICE:
South Korea, the Korean people, the Mandarin language, Radio Evangelism
Thailand, the Chinese people, the Thai and Chinese languages, Evangelism,
    Training
Hong Kong, the Chinese people and language, Teaching

Mission Board of the Church of   Mr. Chik Kam Yuen,Chief Officer
  Christ in China   Organized 1968
Chuk Kui Terrace, Spring Garden   Nondenominational
  Lane, Wanchi, HONG KONG

PERSONNEL: 1980, 6
MISSIONARY PREPARATION: Bible Institute, Language Learning, Seminary
University, Mission Related Orientation
FIELDS OF SERVICE:
China, the Mandarin and Cantonese languages, Evangelism
Thailand, the Thai people and language, Evnagelism
Japan, the Japanese people and language, Evangelism
S.E. Asia, the students, the English language, Church Planting

---

Overseas Missionary Fellowship   Mr. Ted Hsueh, Chief Officer
  Hong Kong Council   Organized 1966
PO Box 95019, Tsimshatsui, Kowloon Interdenominational
          HONG KONG
PERSONNEL:1972, 1; 1975, 2; 1978, 3; 1980, 3 (200% growth)
MISSIONARY PREPARATION: Mission Related Orientation (10 weeks)

FIELDS OF SERVICE:
Japan, the Japanese people and language, Church Planting
Thailand, the Thai people, the Malaysian language, Evangelism

The Hong Kong Overseas Mission
G.P.O. 3976
HONG KONG

Prof. S.Y. King, Chief Officer
Organized October 20, 1962
Nondenominational

PERSONNEL: 1972, 2; 1975, 2; 1978, 1; 1980, 2
MISSIONARY PREPARATION: Bible Institute

FIELDS OF SERVICE:
Taiwan, the Taiwanese people, the Hakka, Mandarin languages and Fukien
    dialect, Evangelism, Church Planting
East Malaysia, the Ethnic Chinese people, the Mandarin, Fukien and Cantonese
    languages, Evangelism

All Indian Prayer Fellowship
Q-3 Green Park Extension
New Delhi, 110 016 INDIA

Dr. P.N. Kurien, Chief Officer
Organized 1957 - 1958
Interdenominational

PERSONNEL: 1980, 227; 1981, 377 (projected)
MISSIONARY PREPARATION: Bible Institute

FIELDS OF SERVICE:
India, various people, 44 languages, Evangelism
Nepal, various people, Nepali and Hindi languages, Evangelism
Sikkim, various peopls, tne Nepali and Hindi languages, Evangelism

---

Asia Evangelistic Fellowship
6 Farida Villa; TPSIU Rd. No. 1
Bandra, Bombay 400 050 INDIA

K.J. Joseph, Chief Officer
Organized 1960
Nondenominational

PERSONNEL: 1978, 10; 1980, 12 (20% growth)
MISSIONARY PREPARATION: Bible Institute

FIELDS OF SERVICE:
India, the Tamil people and language, Evangelism
India, the Gujarati people and language, the English language, Evangelism
India, the Hindustanis people, the Hindi and English language, Evangelism
India, the Maratis, Tamils and Malayalis people and languages, Evangelism

---

Christian Endeavor for Hill Tribes
K. Kotapadu Visakha District
Andhra Pradesh 531 034, INDIA

Henry E. David, Chief Officer
Organized February 13, 1974
Nondenominational

PERSONNEL: 1975, 5; 1978, 7; 1980, 6 (20% growth)
MISSIONARY PREPARATION: Practical Experience, Mission Related
Orientation (2 months)
FIELDS OF SERVICE:
India, the Sikhs and Punjabis people, the English, Hindi and Punjabi
    languages, Evangelism, Teaching
India, the Hindus and Tribal people, the English, Hindi and Nepali languages,
    Evangelism, Teaching

Church Growth Missionary Movement
36 Meiyappapuram, 3rd Street
Madurai 625 016, _INDIA_

Rev. Bose Meiyappan, Chief Officer
Organized June 29, 1975
Interdenominational

PERSONNEL: 1975, 7; 1978, 9; 1980, 11 (57% growth)
MISSIONARY PREPARATION: Bible Institute, Language Learning, Practical
Experience, Mission Related Orientation (1 year)
FIELDS OF SERVICE:
India, the Tamilnad villagers and their language, Church Planting
India, the Sourashtras people, the Sourashtra and Tamil language, Ch. Plant.
India, the Korkus and Lambadis people, the Korku, Hindi, Lambadi and
    Kannerese languages, Church Planting

Council of Baptist Churches in
    North East India
Panbazar, Gauhati - 781 001,
Assam, _INDIA_

Rev. K. Imotemjen Aier, Chief Officer
Organized 1950
Denominational

PERSONNEL: 1980, 44; 1981, 48 (projected)
MISSIONARY PREPARATION: Bible Institute

FIELDS OF SERVICE:
India, the Meitie people and language, Church Planting
India, the Adi Nishi people, local dialects, Church Planting
India, Nagaland tribes, local dialects, Church Planting

Diocesan Missionary Prayer Band
Santhapuram
P.O. Box 629 205
Tamil Nadu, _S. INDIA_

Rev. M. Rajian, Chief Officer
Organized July 31, 1962
Denominational

PERSONNEL: 1972, 18; 1975, 23; 1978, 26; 1980, 32 (78% growth)
MISSIONARY PREPARATION: Bible Institute, Language Learning, Seminary
Practical Experience
FIELDS OF SERVICE:
India, the TamilNadu Tribals, the Tamil language, Evangelism
India, the TamilNadu Tribals, the Oria language, Evangelism
India, the Orissa Tribals, the Hindi language, Evangelism, Medical

Dipti Mission
Sahibganj (S.P.)
Bihar 816 109 _INDIA_

D. Rajkumar, Chief Officer
Organized 1925
Interdenominational

PERSONNEL: 1972, 7; 2975, 5; 1978, 6; 1980, 7, 1981, 9 (projected)
MISSIONARY PREPARATION: Bible Institute, Language Learning, Practical
Experience
FIELDS OF SERVICE:
India, the Malto Tribes and their language, Evangelism, Church Planting

Evangelical Lutheran Church in   Bishop Rev. I.N. Roberts, Chief Officer
  Madhra Pradesh   Organized 1923
PO Box No. 30, Luther Bhavan   Denominational
Chhindwara, M.P. 480 001, INDIA

PERSONNEL: *1980, 10; 1981, 15 (projected)*
MISSIONARY PREPARATION: *Seminary, University*

FIELDS OF SERVICE:
India, the Hindus people and language, Evangelism
India, the Hindus people, the Hindi and Marati language, Evangelism

---

Evangelize Every Muslim in India   T. Babu Umar Pulavar, Chief Officer
P.B. 420   Organized 1976
Vellore 632 004, INDIA   Interdenominational

PERSONNEL: *1978, 3; 1980, 3*
MISSIONARY PREPARATION: *Mission Related Orientaiton*

FIELDS OF SERVICE:
India, the Musli people, the Tamil language, Evangelism
India, the Hindus people, the Hindi language, Evangelism

Fellowship of Evangelical Friends   Mr. D.T. Rajah, Chief Officer
PO Box 68, Jehova Jireh   Organized 1960
Isaac St., Nagercoil   Interdenominational
629 001, INDIA

PERSONNEL: *1972, 10; 1975, 20; 1978, 27' 1980, 31 (210% growth)*
MISSIONARY PREPARATION: *Practical Experience, Mission Related Orientation*
                                                    (3 months)
FIELDS OF SERVICE:
India, the Tamilnad people, the Tamil and Malayalam language, Evangelism
India, the "Kerala" people, the Malayalam language, Evangelism
India, the "Maharastra" people, the Tamil and Hindi language, Evangelism
India, the "Gujarat" people, the Tamil and Gujarathi language, Evangelism
India, the "Delhi" people, the Tamil and Hindi language, Evangelism

---

Friends Missionary Prayer Band   Mr. M. Patrich Joshua, Chief Officer
22 Anderson Road, Anyanvaram   Organized 1958
Madras 600 023, S. INDIA   Interdenominational

PERSONNEL: *1972, 16; 1975, 55; 1978, 113; 1980, 170 (963% growth)*
MISSIONARY PREPARATION: *Bible Institute, Language Learning, Pracitcal
Experience, Mission Related Orientation (1 week)*
FIELDS OF SERVICE:
India, the Hindu - V.P. people, the Hindi language, Evangelism, Ch. Planting
India, the Hindu slums, the Hindi and Tamil languages, Evangelism, Ch. Planting
India, the Bhil - M.P. people, the Bhil, Hindi and Malwi languages,
     Evangelism, Church Planting, Literature

163

Friends Missionary Prayer Band   *Mr. M. Patrick Joshua, Chief Officer*

(previous continued)

FIELDS OF SERVICE:
India, the Rajasthani people, the Hindi and Rajasthani languages, Evangelism,
   Church Planting
India, the Punjabis people, the Hindi language, Evangelism,Church Planting
India, the Sikhs people the Hindi language, Evangelism, Church Planting
India, the Maharashtra Hill Tribes, Marate, Hindi languages, Evang., Ch. Pl.
India, the Adivasis Hill Tribes - Gujarat, the Kukna language, Evangelism,
   Church Planting
India, the Lingayets, Irulas and Tamilian people, the Kanaris language,
   Evangelism, Church Planting

Full Gospel Young Men's Association *R. Stanley, Chief Officer*
PO Box 609, Vellore   *Organized November 1971*
Tamil Nadu 632 006, S. INDIA   *Interdenominational*

PERSONNEL: *1975, 8; 1978, 22; 1980, 27 (238% growth)*
MISSIONARY PREPARATION: *Bible Institute, Language Learning, Practical*
Experience, Mission Related Orientation (3 months)
FIELDS OF SERVICE:
India, the Tamilnadu Tribes, the Tamil language, Evangelism
India, the Orissa Tribes, the Oriya language, Evangelism
India, the Karnatake Tribes, the Kannadam and Marati language, Evangelism
India, the M. Pradash Tribes, the Hindi language, Evangelism

Gospel Echoing Missionary Society, *Rev. D. Dayanandhan, Chief Officer*
7 13th Cross Street, Chromepet   *Organized December 7, 1979*
Madras, 600 044 INDIA   *Interdenominational*

PERSONNEL: *1972, 3; 1975, 6; 1978, 13; 1980, 32 (966% growth)*
MISSIONARY PREPARATION: *Language Learning, Practical Experience*

FIELDS OF SERVICE:
N. India, the Bihari and Tamilian people, the Hindi and Tamil languages,
   Evangelism

Gospel Mission Society
c/o Kuki Christian Church -
  Dewlah Land
PO Imphal, Manipur, 795,001 *INDIA*

Rev. T. Lunkim, Chief Officer
Organized April 8, 1978
Nondenominational

PERSONNEL: *1978, 5; 1980, 9 (80% growth)*
MISSIONARY PREPARATION: *Bible Institute, Language Learning, Practical Experience, Mission Related Orientation (meeting needs)*
FIELDS OF SERVICE:
India, the Kukis people and language, Evangelism
India, the Nepalis people and language, Evangelism, Church Planting
India, the Cacharis people and language, Evangelism, Church Planting
India, the Meiteis people, the Manipuri language, Evangelism, Church Planting
Burma, the Kukis people and language, Evangelism, Church Planting
Burma, the Burmese people and language, Evangelism, Church Planting
Burma, the Nagal people, the Somra language, Evangelism, Church Planting

---

Independent Church of India
Sielmat, Churachandpur
Manipur, *INDIA*

Rev. D. Rudlngul, Chief Officer
Organized April 1, 1930
Denominational

PERSONNEL: *1972, 4; 1975, 4; 1978, 15; 1980, 20 (400% growth)*
MISSIONARY PREPARATION: *Seminary*

FIELDS OF SERVICE:
India, the Meiteis people, the Manipuri language, Evangelism
India, the Jamatia people, the Jamatia language, Evangelism

India Church Growth Mission
Pasumlai
Madurai, 625 004 *INDIA*

Rev. N. J. Gnaniah, Chief Officer
Organized October 1, 1978
Interdenominational

PERSONNEL: *1978, 6; 1980, 9 (50% growth)*
MISSIONARY PREPARATION: *Bible Institute*

FIELDS OF SERVICE:
India, the Tamil Nadu village people, the Tamil language, Church Planting
India, the Sourashtra people, the Sourashtra and Tamil language, Ch. Planting
India, the Nepalese people and language, Evangelism

Indian Evangelical Mission   Rev. Theodore Williams, Chief Officer
38 Langford Rd.   Organized January 15, 1965
Bangalore 560 025, INDIA   Interdenominational

PERSONNEL: 1972, 14; 1975, 33; 1978, 67; 1980, 88 (529% growth)
MISSIONARY PREPARATION: Bible Institute, Language Learning, Practical
Experience, Mission Related Orientation (1 year)
FIELDS OF SERVICE:
India, the Kuluis Caste Hindus people, the Kului and Hindi language,
    Church Planting
India, the Garhwalis people and language, the Hindi language, Ch. Planting
India, the Bhils Guharatis people and language, Church Planting
India, the Oriyas people and language, Church Planting
India, the Bhatris and Halgis people, the Bhatri and Hindi languages,
    Church Planting
India, the Nepalis, Bhutanese and Bengalis people and languages, Ch. Plant.
India, the Andaman Villagers, the Malaylis, Tamil and Hindi languages,
    Church Planting
India, the Nepalis people, the Nepali and Hindi languages, Church Planting
India, the Gonds, Yerukilas, Koyas, Reddis, Nilwanis, Lambadis people, the
    Gondi, Koya, Lambadi and Telugiu languages, Church Planting
India, the Afghan people, the Pushtu language, Church Planting
India, the Lowland people, the Gogodala and English languages, Evangelism
India, the Lingayats people, the Kannada language, Church Planting

---

Indian Evangelical Team   P.G. Vargis, Chief Officer
Indira Colony, Pathankot   Organized July 1973
145 001 INDIA   Nondenominational

PERSONNEL: 1972, 4; 1980, 69 (1625% growth)
MISSIONARY PREPARATION: Bible Institute, Language Learning, Mission
Related Orientation (8 months)
FIELDS OF SERVICE:
India, the Hindu and Moslem people, the Dogri language, Church Planting
India, the Hindu people, the Punjabi language, Church Planting
India, the Hindu people, the Hindi language, Church Planting
India, the Hindu and Moslem people, the Marathe language, Church Planting

Indian Inland Mission
V-20 Green Park Extension
New Delhi, 110 016, INDIA

Rev. Paul Pillai
Organized August 2, 1964
Nondenominational

PERSONNEL: *1972, 20; 1975, 37; 1978, 48; 1980, 52 (160% growth)*
MISSIONARY PREPARATION: *Bible Institute, Language Learning, Practical Experience, Mission Realted Orientation (4 Years)*
FIELDS OF SERVICE:
India, Hindu and Moslem people, Hindi and Urudu languages, Evang., Ch. Pl.
India, the Moslem people, the Kashmiri language, Evangelism, Ch. Planting
India, the Hindu people and language, Evangelism, Church Planting
India, the Sikhs people, the Punjabi language, Evangelism, Ch. Planting
India, the Karan people, the Urudu and Burmese languages, Evang., Ch. Pl.

Indian Missionary Movement
5 Waddell Rd. - Kilpank
Madras, 600 010, INDIA

A. Christopher, Chief Officer
Organized 1974
Interdenominational

PERSONNEL: *1972, 4; 1975, 4; 1978, 6; 1980, 8 (100% growth)*
MISSIONARY PREPARATION: *Bible Institute, Seminary, Practical Experience, Mission Related Orientation (1 year)*
FIELDS OF SERVICE:
India, the Harijan people, the Tamil language, Church Planting
India, the Andaman Island Villagers, the Oriya language, Church Planting
India the Bihar Villagers, Church Planting

Indian Missionary Society
11B Trivandrum High Rd.
Tirunelveli - 2
Tamil Nadu, 627 002 INDIA

Rev. Jason S. Dharmaraj, Chief Officer
Organized February 12, 1909
Denominational

PERSONNEL:*1972, 129; 1975, 133; 1978, 141; 1980, 150 (16% growth)*
MISSIONARY PREPARATION:

FIELDS OF SERVICE:
India, Paliar Tribe, the Tamil language, Evangelism
India, Andra Pradesh Hill Tribes, the Telegu language, Evangelism
India, the Adivaries people, the Hindi language, Evangelism
India, the Lambadies people, the Lambadi and Marathi language, Evangelism
India, the Adivaries people, the Griya language, Evangelism

Kashmir Evangelical Fellowship
Mission House, Udhampur
Jamma & Kashmir, 182 101 INDIA

P.M. Thomas, Chief Officer
Organized October 31, 1975
Nondenominational

PERSONNEL:*1972, 3; 1975, 16; 1978, 37, 1980, 45 (1400% growth)*
MISSIONARY PREPARATION: *Bible Institute, Language Learning, Mission Related Orientation (1 month)*
FIELDS OF SERVICE:
India, Moslem people, the Urdu and Hindi language, Church Planting
India, Hindu people, the Dogri and English languages, Church Planting
India, the Sikhs people, the Ladhaki language, Church Planting
India, the Buddhist people, the Tibetan Language, Church Planting

Kerala Tribal Mission　　　　　　　Mohan Kurian, *Chief Officer*
Old Muvattupuzha Rd.　　　　　　　*Organized June 16, 1977*
Perumbavoor, Kerala 683 542　　　*Nondenominational*
INDIA

PERSONNEL: *1978, 2; 1980, 7 (200% growth)*
MISSIONARY PREPARATION: *Bible Institute, Practical Experience, Mission Related Orientation (over 6 months)*
FIELDS OF SERVICE:
India, Tribal people, various languages, Church Planting

Manipur Presbyterian Mission　　　Rev. S. Lalkhuma, *Chief Officer*
P.O. Imphal　　　　　　　　　　　　*Organized January 1964*
Manipur, 795 001 INDIA　　　　　*Denominational*

PERSONNEL: *1972, 19; 1975, 22; 1978, 43; 1980, 67 (253% growth)*
MISSIONARY PREPARATION: *Language Learning, Seminary, Mission Related Orientation (1 year)*
FIELDS OF SERVICE:
India, the Meiteis people, the Manipuri language, Evangelism

Meitei Mission　　　　　　　　　　Rev. K.I. Aier, *Chief Officer*
(c/o C.B.C.N.E.I.)　　　　　　　　*Organized 1961*
Wangjing Thougal, Manipur, INDIA　*Denominational*

PERSONNEL: *1980, 1*
MISSIONARY PREPARATION: *Seminary, University, Mission Related Orientation*

FIELDS OF SERVICE:
India, Manipuri people, the Manipuri language, Evangelism

Mizoram Synod Mission　　　　　　Rev. V.L. Zaithanga, *Chief Officer*
P.O. Aizawl, Synod Office　　　　*Organized December 1961*
Mizoram, INDIA　　　　　　　　　　*Denominational*

PERSONNEL: *1972, 54; 1975, 84; 1978, 127; 180, 161 (198% growth)*
MISSIONARY PREPARATION:

FIELDS OF SERVICE:
India, the Hrangkhol people and language, Evangelism and Medical
India, the Karbis people and language, Evangelism and Medical
India, the Meitei people and language, Evangelism and Medical
India, the Oryia people and language, Medical
India, the Nepalis people and language, Preaching

168

Prayer Partners Fellowship
Grace Cottage   Kesavadasapuram
Patton, TVM-4
Kerala, _INDIA_

A.J. Joseph, Chief Officer
Organized August 1956
Interdenominational

PERSONNEL:1972, 16; 1975, 18; 1978, 24; 1980, 30 (88% growth)
MISSIONARY PREPARATION: Bible Institute, Mission Related Orientation
(3 months to 2 years)
FIELDS OF SERVICE:
India, Agriculturalists, the Malayalam and English languages, Evangelism
India, Tribal people, the Hindi, Punjabi and Urdu languages, Evangelism

---

Quiet Corner India
1/A Ramakrishnappa Rd.
Cox Town
Bangalore 560 005 _INDIA_

Thomas Samuel, Chief Officer
Organized October 14, 1974
Nondenominational

PERSONNEL: 1972, 5; 1975, 10; 1978, 15; 1980, 15 (200% growth)
MISSIONARY PREPARATION: Language Learning, Practical Experience, Mission
Related Orientation
FIELDS OF SERVICE:
India, the rural-tribal people, the Tamil, Kannada, Malayalam, Kurumbas and
Pania languages, Evangelism

St. Thomas Evangelical Church
of India
Tiruvalla, 5
Kerala, 689 105 _INDIA_

R.T. Rev. Bishop T.C. Cherian, Chief Off.
Organized January 26, 1961
Denominational

PERSONNEL: 1975, 80; 1978, 88; 1980, 116 (45% growth)
MISSIONARY PREPARATION: Bible Institute, Language Learning, Seminary, Univer.
Practical Experience, Mission Related Orientation (3 months)
FIELDS OF SERVICE:
India, the Hindi, Kurdu, Gurjarati, Maratti, Kanaries, Tamil and
Malayalam languages, Evangelism

Seekers of Lost Souls
P.O. Aizawl, Zarkawt
Mizoram 796 001 _INDIA_

Mr. Chhawnzinga, Chief Officer
Organized April 13, 1972
Interdenominational

PERSONNEL:1972, 7; 1975, 18; 1978, 36; 1980, 51 (629% growth)
MISSIONARY PREPARATION: Practical Experience

FIELDS OF SERVICE:
India, Bengalis, Hrangklawl, Sakechep and Chawrai people, various languages
Evangelism
India, the Adi people, the Assamese language, Evangelism
India, the Tripuri and Halam Tribes, Tripuri and Tribal languages, Evangelism

Tirap Mission　　　　　　　　　　*Rev. I. Longsa, Chief Officer*
P.O. Impur　　　　　　　　　　　*Organized March 17, 1974*
Nagaland, 798 615 <u>*INDIA*</u>　　*Denominational*

PERSONNEL: *1975, 6; 1978, 12; 1980, 27 (350% growth)*
MISSIONARY PREPARATION: *Bible Institute, Language Learning, Practical Experience*
FIELDS OF SERVICE:
India, the Tangsa people and language, Evangelism, Church Planting
India, the Nokte people and language, Evangelism, Church Planting
India, the Wancho people and language, Evangelism, Church Planting

---

Voice of Gospel　　　　　　　　*Daniel K.V., Chief Officer*
Trichur　　　　　　　　　　　　*Organized May 30, 1975*
Kerala 680 005 <u>*INDIA*</u>　　　*Interdenominational*

PERSONNEL: *1975, 4; 1978, 7; 1980, 10 (150% growth)*
MISSIONARY PREPARATION: *Mission Related Orientation (3-6 months)*

FIELDS OF SERVICE:
India, Tribal and Hindu people, the Malayalam language, Church Planting

---

Worldwide Gospel Mission　　　　*Mr. Phuveyi Dozo, Chief Officer*
Khermahal, Dimapur　　　　　　*Organized 1965*
Nagaland, 797 110 <u>*INDIA*</u>　*Interdenominational*

PERSONNEL: *1980, 73; 1981, 78 (projected)*
MISSIONARY PREPARATION: *Bible Institute, Seminary, Practical Experience*
FIELDS OF SERVICE:
India, the Assamese people, the Assemese and English languages, Evangelism
India, the Manipur tribal people, the Korem language, Evangelism
India, the Arunacahl tribal people, the English language and Adi dialect, Evangelism
India, the Nepalese people and language, Evangelism
India, the Mikiris and Kacharis people, the English, Assemese and Karbi languages, Evangelism
India-Burma border, tribal people, Konyak and Burmese languages, Evangelism

Zoram Baptist Mission   Rev. Dr. Chhangte Lal Hminga, Chief Off.
Serkawn P.O. Zotlang   Organized June 1967
Lungley District   Denominational
Mizoram 796 126 INDIA

PERSONNEL: 1972, 21; 1975, 33; 1978, 36; 1980, 49 (133% growth)
MISSIONARY PREPARATION: Mission Related Orientation

FIELDS OF SERVICE:
India, the Ragha and Assamese people and language, Church Planting
India, the Nepalis people, the Nepali and Hindi languages, Preaching
India, the Mizo sub-tribes, the Mizo Gqnate dialects, Church Planting
India the Korku people, the Korku and Hindi languages, Discipling
Bhutan, Nepalis, Bhutanis people, English, Hindi languages, Evangelism

---

Asia Pacific Christian Mission   Dr. Gideon Imanto Tanbunaan, Chief Off.
  International Indonesia   Organized September 12, 1979
PO Box 73, Bandung INDONESIA   Nondenominational

PERSONNEL: 1980, 6
MISSIONARY PREPARATION: Bible Institute, Practical Experience, Mission Rel.
Orientation, (1 year)
FIELDS OF SERVICE:
Indonesia, Cross- Cultural Evangelism

Christian Gospel Expansion
  Assistance Group
Jl. Pinangsia 1/8, Jakarta Barat
INDONESIA

PERSONNEL:
MISSIONARY PREPARATION:

FIELDS OF SERVICE:
Indonesia, Belitung Island, Evangelism
Kalimantan Barat, the Indonesian language, Evangelism

Christopherus, Yayasan   Andreas Christanaday, Chief Officer
Jl. Pringgading Dalam 2   Organized May 3, 1972
Semarang, INDONESIA   Interdenominational

PERSONNEL: 1980, 2
MISSIONARY PREPARATION: Bible Institute

FIELDS OF SERVICE:
Indonesia, the Javanese people, the Indonesian and English languages,
  Evangelism

171

Duta Sabda
Pandanaran 62
Semarang, INDONESIA

Tony A. Tanutama, Chief Officer
Organized August 1958
Interdenominational

PERSONNEL: *1972, 5; 1975, 2; 19783; 1980, 3*
MISSIONARY PREPARATION: Language Learning, Seminary

FIELDS OF SERVICE:

Fellowship of Baptist Churches of
  Indonesia
Tromol Pos 129
Manado, INDONESIA

Rev. Joutie Legoh, Chief Officer
Organized July 11, 1951
Interdenominational

PERSONNEL: *1975, 3; 1978, 15; 1980, 13 (30% growth)*
MISSIONARY PREPARATION: *Bible Institute, Practical Experience, Mission Related Orientation (2months)*
FIELDS OF SERVICE:
Indonesia, the Batak people, the Indonesia language, Church Planting
Indonesia, the Dayak people, the Dayak and Indonesian languages, Ch. Planting
Indonesia, the Jaya people, the Java and Indonesian languages, Ch. Planting

---

Gereja Christian Jakarta
Jalan Kartini 5/16C
Jakarta Pusat INDONESIA

PERSONNEL: *1980, 1; 1981, 6 (projected)*
MISSIONARY PREPARATION:

FIELDS OF SERVICE:

Gereja Injili Irian Jaya
Kotah Pos 38
Jayapura
Irian Jaya, INDONESIA

Amimban Elabi, Chief Officer

Denominational

PERSONNEL: *1980, 180*
MISSIONARY PREPARATION: *Bible Institute*

FIELDS OF SERVICE:
Indonesia, the Eau people and language, Evangelism and Church Planting
Indonesia, the Duvele people and language, Evangelism, Church Planting
Indonesia, the Ketengban people and language, Evangelism and Church Planting
Indonesia, the Yali people and language, Evangelism, Church Planting
Indonesia, the Koyon people, the Koyon and Indonesian languages, Evang. Ch. Pl
Indonesia, the Bare people, the Bare and Indonusian languages, Evang., Ch. Pl.
Indonesia, the lowland dwellers, the Indonesian language, Evangelism, Ch. Pl.

G.K.M.I.
  (Indonesian Mennonite Church)

PERSONNEL: *1980, 40*
MISSIONARY PREPARATION:

FIELDS OF SERVICE:
Indonesia, the Bali people, Evangelism, Church Planting
Indonesia, the Java people, Evangelism, Church Planting
Indonesia, the Kalimantan and Sumatra people, Evangelism, Church Planting

---

Kingmi Kraya Mission   *Rev. R.A. Yohanes Sakai, Chief Officer*
Kampung Baru Krayan   *Organized April 1973*
via Kotak Pos 18   *Denominational*
Tarakan, Kaltim, INDONESIA

PERSONNEL: *1972, 34; 1975, 52; 1978, 31; 1980, 67 (97% growth)*
MISSIONARY PREPARATION: *Bible Institute*

FIELDS OF SERVICE:

Korea Mission in Indonesia   *Rev. Paul M. Suh, Chief Officer*
PO Box 2355   *Organized June 22, 1972*
Jakarta, INDONESIA   *Interdenominational*

PERSONNEL: *1972, 2; 1975, 5; 1978, 18; 1980, 32 (1500% growth)*
MISSIONARY PREPARATION: *Language Learning, Seminary, Practical
Experience, Mission Related Orientation (6 months)*
FIELDS OF SERVICE:
Indonesia, the Javanese people and language, Church Planting
Indonesia, the Tapanulu people, the Batak language, Church Planting

Sangkakala Millsion Fellowship
Tromol Pos 262
Semarang, INDONESIA

Adi Sutanto, Chief Officer
Organized May 27, 1977
Interdenominational

PERSONNEL: *1978, 3; 1980, 9 (200% growth)*
MISSIONARY PREPARATION: *Bible Institute, Practical Experience*

FIELDS OF SERVICE:
*Indonesia, the Timorese people, the Timor and Indonesian languages, Church
     Planting*
*Indonesia, the Java people, the Javanese and Indonesian languages, Church
     Planting*

Yayasan Persekutuan Pekabaran
  Injil Indonesia (Indonesian
  Missionary Fellowship)
Jl. Trunijoyo No. 2, Batu, Malang, East Java, INDONESIA

Dr. Petrus Octavianus, Chief Officer
Organized 1961
Interdenominational

PERSONNEL: *1980, 206*
MISSIONARY PREPARATION: *Bible Institute, Language Learning, Practical
Experience*
FIELDS OF SERVICE:
Indonesia, West Kalimantan and South Sumatera people, Evangelism, Ch. Planting
Brazil, Brazilian people, Portuguese language, Evangelism, Church Planting
Bangladesh, the Bengali people and language, Evangelism, Church Planting
England, the English language, Evangelism, Church Planting
Suriname, Evangelism, Church Planting

Assemblies of God Asian Mission Ass.
3-15-20 Komagome, Toshima Ku
Tokyo 170 JAPAN

Dr. Akiei Ito, Chief Officer
Organized September 26, 1978
Denominational

PERSONNEL: *1978, 35; 1980, 82 (134% growth)*
MISSIONARY PREPARATION:

FIELDS OF SERVICE:
Taiwan, the Chinese people, Mandarin and Taiwanese languages, Ch. Palnting
Philippines, Mt. Tribal People, the Tagalog language, Evangelism
Thailand, the Thai people and language, Church Planting
U.S.A., the Japanese people, the Japanese and English languages, Ch. Planting
Germany, the Korean people and language, Church Planting
U.S.A., the Dorean people and language, Chruch Planting

Asia Evangelical Missionary
  Fellowship
Nishijin PO Box 88
Koyoto 602 *JAPAN*

Rev. Tomihide Noguchi, Chief Officer
Organized 1967

PERSONNEL:1972, 5; 1975, 6; 1978, 5; 1980, 5
MISSIONARY PREPARATION: Bible Institute, Mission Related Orientation

FIELDS OF SERVICE:
Taiwan, Teaching, Evangelism

Christ Gospel Mission
PO Box 218
Chuo Yokohama-shi, 220-91
JAPAN

Rev. Mindru Hayashi, Chief Officer
Organized October 1974
Nondenominational

PERSONNEL: 1975, 4; 1978, 5; 1980, 6 (50% growth)
MISSIONARY PREPARATION: Bible Institute, Practical Experience,
Mission Related Orientation (1 year)
FIELDS OF SERVICE:
Mongolia and Communist countries in Asia, Evangelism

Immanuel General Mission
3-4-1 Marunouchi Chiyodaku,
Tokyo 100 *JAPAN*

Rev. Hiroshi Asahina, Chief Officer
Organized October 21, 1945
Denominational

PERSONNEL: 1972, 8; 1975, 10; 1978, 10, 1980, 14 (75% growth)
MISSIONARY PREPARATION: Bible Institute, Language Learning, Seminary
University, Practical Experience
FIELDS OF SERVICE:
India, various Tamil Nadu people, the Tamil, Khanada and English languages,
  Preaching and Agriculture
Philippines, the Tagalog language, Church Planting
Papua New Guinea, the Pidgin and English languages, Church Planting
Kenya, the Swahili and English languages, Church Planting
Carribean, the English language, Church Planting
Taiwan, the Taiwanese language, Church Planting

175

Japan Alliance Church   Rev. Kozo Tamura, Chief Officer
255 Itsukaichi-Machi
Saiki Gun   Denominational
Kiroshima Ken, JAPAN

PERSONNEL: *1975, 9; 1978, 13; 1980, 15 (67% growth)*
MISSIONARY PREPARATION: Seminary

FIELDS OF SERVICE:
Brazil, the Portuguese language, Church Planting

Japan Antioch Mission   Rev. Minoru Okuyama, Chief Officer
17-2 Higashi Arai   Organized March 28, 1977
Omiya-Shi, 330 JAPAN   Interdenominational

PERSONNEL: *1978, 2; 1980, 5 (150% growth)*
MISSIONARY PREPARATION: Bible Institute, Mission Related Orientation (6 months)

FIELDS OF SERVICE:

Overseas Mission of the Liebenzeller   Rev. Masataka Tanabe, Chief Officer
  Church Alliance in Japan   Organized November 29, 1976
214 Kanagawa-ken, Kawasaki-shi   Interdenominational
Tamaku, Iknta, JAPAN

PERSONNEL: *1980, 1; 1981, 2 (projected)*
MISSIONARY PREPARATION: Bible Institute, Language Learning, Practical
Experience, Mission Related Orientation
FIELDS OF SERVICE:
Bangladesh, the farmers, the Banglanese language, Evangelism, Medicine

---

The Supporting Group for Miss   Miss Chikako Saito, Chief Officer
  Kimiko Goto, c/o Tokyo Oncho   Organized May 1977
  Kyokai
1-33-9 Ebisu Nishi, Shibuya-ku, Tokyo 150 JAPAN

PERSONNEL: *1978, 1; 1980, 1*
MISSIONARY PREPARATION: Seminary, Practical Experience

FIELDS OF SERVICE:
Singapore, the Japanese people and language, Evangelism

West Japan Evangelical Lutheran
  Church
2-2-11 Nakajima-Dori, Fukiai-ku
Kobe, 651, *JAPAN*

Rev. Shigeru Masaki, Chief Officer
Organized 1980
Denominational

PERSONNEL: *1980, 3*
MISSIONARY PREPARATION: *Bible Institute, Language Learning, Seminary,
University, Practical Experience, Mission Related Orientation (5 years)*
FIELDS OF SERVICE:
Indonesia, the Indonesian people and language, Evangelism

Assemblies of God
Yonjsan PO Box 28
Seoul 140 *KOREA*

Rev. Charles W. Butterfield, Chief
                      Officer

PERSONNEL: *1980, 16*
MISSIONARY PREPARATION:

FIELDS OF SERVICE:

Agape Missions
K.P.O. Box 421
Seoul, 110, *KOREA*

Young-Jae, Chief Officer
Organized May 1969
Interdenominational

PERSONNEL: *1980, 1; 1981, 7 (projected)*
MISSIONARY PREPARATION: *Bible Institute, Language Learning,
Seminary*
FIELDS OF SERVICE:
Norway, the English language, Evangelism

Dongsin World Mission
PO Box 56
Daegu 630 *KOREA*

Chang Ryum Kim, Chief Officer
Organized November 4, 1973
Denominational

PERSONNEL: *1975, 1; 1978, 2; 1980, 4 (300% growth)*
MISSIONARY PREPARATION: *Language Learning*

FIELDS OF SERVICE:
Japan, Philippines, West Germay and Taiwan, Evangelism

Ewha Mission Committee
No. 11-1 Dai-Hyun Dong
Seodaimun-Ku
Seoul, KOREA

Rev. Heung Ho Kim, Chief Officer
Organized 1959
Interdenominational

PERSONNEL: *1972, 1; 1981, 2 (projected)*
MISSIONARY PREPARATION: *University, Practical Experience*

FIELDS OF SERVICE:

Korea Christian Mission Society
Room 605 Youn Ji-Dong 136
Jong Ro-Ku
Seoul, KOREA

Shin-Myung Kang, Chief Officer
Organized January 31, 1966
Interdenominational

PERSONNEL: *1978, 7; 1980, 7; 1981, 10 (projected)*
MISSIONARY PREPARATION: *Seminary*

FIELDS OF SERVICE:
Indonesia, the Indonesian people and language, Evangelism, Teaching

---

The Korean Evangelical Church
(Foreign Mission Committee)
Gangnam-gu, Samseong-dong, 2 Gigu
Seong Gyol Center KOREA

Rev. Hong Shun Gyun, Chief Officer
Organized 1979
Denominational

PERSONNEL: *1980, 4*
MISSIONARY PREPARATION: *Seminary, Practical Experience, Mission Related Orientation*
FIELDS OF SERVICE:
Indonesia, the Indonesian people and language, the English language, Church Planting

---

Korea International Christian
Mission for Christ, Inc.
432 Changshin-dong,
Jongro-gu, Seoul, KOREA

Rev. Kim Se-Jin, Chief Officer
Organized June 20, 1962

PERSONNEL: *100% growth*
MISSIONARY PREPARATION: *Seminary, University, Mission Related Orientation*
(1 year)
FIELDS OF SERVICE:
Saudi Arabia, Saudi Arabian people, Evangelism
Indonesia, the Indonesian people, Evangelism

178

Korea International Mission   David J. Cho, Chief Officer
C.P.O. Box 3476   Organized March 10, 1968
Seoul, <u>KOREA</u>   100   Interdenominational

PERSONNEL:1972, 12; 1975, 12; 1978, 16; 1980, 24 (100% growth)
MISSIONARY PREPARATION: Bible Institute, Language Learning, SEminary,
University, Practical Experience, Mission Related Orientation (12 months)
FIELDS OF SERVICE:
Hong Kong, the Chinese people, Chinese, Korean language, Church Planting
Thailand, Thai people and language, Church Planting
Indonesia, the Indonesian language, Church Planting
U.S.A., the Laotian, Thai people, Thai language, Church Planting
W. Germany, German Korean people, German language, Evangelism, Pastoring

Mission to Moslem Area   Yoon Jin Chung, Chief Officer
c/o Hoo-Am Church   Organized 1976
238-Hoo Am-Dong, Yongsan-Ku   Interdenominational
Seoul, <u>KOREA</u> 140
PERSONNEL: 1975, 1; 1978, 4; 1980, 4 (300% growth)
MISSIONARY PREPARATION: Bible Institute, Language Learning, Practical
Experience, Mission Related Orientation
FIELDS OF SERVICE:
Libya, the Arabic alnguage, Church Planting
Saudia Arabia, the Arabic Language, Church Planting
Nigeria, the English language, Church Planting
Philippines, tribal languages, Church Planting

North Korea Mission Federation   Rev. Chang-in Kim, Chief Officer
C.P.O. Box 5385   Organized April 29, 1977
Seoul, <u>KOREA</u>   Interdenominational

PERSONNEL:1978, 8; 1980, 11 (38% growth)
MISSIONARY PREPARATION: Bible Institute, Language Learning, Seminary,
University, Practical Experience, Mission Related Orientation (6 months)
FIELDS OF SERVICE:
Hong Kong, Korean and Chinese people, English and Chinese languages, Evang.
Indonesia, Indonesian, Korean people, Indonesian, English languages,
    Evangelism, Teaching
Egypt, the Egyptian people, the English language, Evangelism, Teaching
Argentina, Argentine people, Spanish, English language, Evang., Teaching
Paraguay, the Korean and Paraguayan people, Spanish and English languages,
    Evangelism and Teaching
W. Germany, German Korean people, German and English languages, Evangelism
    Teaching
Australia, Korean Australian people, the English language, Evangelism

Overseas Missionary Fellowship
P.O. Box 1637,Kwanghwamun
Seoul, KOREA

Dr. Peter R.M. Pattisson, Chief Officer
Organized 1980
Interdenominational

PERSONNEL: *1980, 2*
MISSIONARY PREPARATION: *Bible Institute, Practical Experience,*
Mission related Orientation (3-6 months)
FIELDS OF SERVICE:

Presbyterian Church in Korea
  (Koryu)
P.O. Box 190
Busan, KOREA

Dr. Ho Jin Chun, Chief Officer
Organized September 20, 1955
Denominational

PERSONNEL: *1972, 2; 1975, 2; 1978, 4; 1980, 4 (100% growth)*
MISSIONARY PREPARATION: *Seminary, Practical Experience, Mission*
Related Orientation (2 years)
FIELDS OF SERVICE:
Taiwan, the Chinese people and language, Church Planting
Taiwan, the Taiwanese people and language, Church Planting

World Omega's Revival Mission
  Society
P.O. Box Sudaimun
Seoul, KOREA 120

Heaystone S. Choi, Chief Officer
Organized April 1974
Interdenominational

PERSONNEL: *1975, 15; 1978, 31; 1980, 35 (169% growth)*
MISSIONARY PREPARATION: *Seminary, Practical Experience, Mission*
Related Orientation (3 months)
FIELDS OF SERVICE:
Bangladesh, Bengali people, Bengali and English languages, Evang., Ch. Pl.
E. Malaysia, Iban people, Malay and English languages, Evang., Ch. Plant.
Brunei, Murut people, the Malay and English languages, Evang., Ch. Plant.
Israel, Arabian people, Hebrew and English languages, Evang., Ch. Plant.
W. Germany, Korean people, German and Korean language, Evang., Ch. Plant.
Paraguay, Paraguayan people, Spanish and Korean language, Evang., Ch. Pl.
Argentina, Korean people, Spanish and Korean languages, Evang., Ch. Plant.
Ecuador, Ecuadorean people, Spanish and Korean language, Evang., Ch. Plant.
U.S.A., the Korean people, English and Korean languages, Evang., Ch. Plant.

Malaysia India Evangelism
  Council
PO Box 689
Penang, MALAYSIA

Dr. Chris D. Thomas, Chief Officer
Organized December 3, 1976
Interdenominatiional

PERSONNEL: 1978, 21; 1980, 10 1981, 20 (projected)
MISSIONARY PREPARATION: Bible Institute, Practical Experience,
Mission Related Orientation (1-2 years)
FIELDS OF SERVICE:

The Christian and Missionary Alliance
  Church of the Philippines
PO Box 290, Tetuan,
Zamboanga City, PHILIPPINES 7801

Benjamin P. de Jesus, Chief Officer
Organized June 1962
Denominational

PERSONNEL: 1972, 4; 1975, 6; 1978, 11; 1980, 11 (175 % growth)
MISSIONARY PREPARATION: Seminary, Practical Experience, Mission
Related Orientation (2 years)
FIELDS OF SERVICE:
Indonesia, the Muslim and Chinese people, the Bahasa and Indonesian
    languages, Church Planting

Conservative Baptist Association
  of the Philippines
PO Box 1882
Manial PHILIPPINES

Rev. Oscar C. Baldemor, Chief Officer
Organized December 28, 1978
Denominational

PERSONNEL: 1978, 2; 1980, 3; 1981, 7 (projected)
MISSIONARY PREPARATION: Seminary or University

FIELDS OF SERVICE:
Bangladesh, Bengalis people, English and Bengali language, Teaching
Nepal, Nepalese people, English and Gorkhali language, Teaching
Guam, Filipino and Chamorros people, English, Filipino and Chamorro
    languages, Church Planting

The Evangelical Presbyterian
  Mission Ind.
ACPO Box 595
Quezon City, PHILIPPINES 3001

Rev. Hwal Young Kim, Chief Officer
Organized June 19, 1978
Denominational

PERSONNEL: 1978, 2; 1980, 5; 1981 9 (projected)
MISSIONARY PREPARATION:

FIELDS OF SERVICE:
Philippines, Church Planting

Grace Evangelical Mission
PO Box 21, Valenzuela,
Metro Manila PHILIPPINES

Rev. Hilarion A. Guste, Chief Officer
Organized September 30, 1978
Interdenominational

PERSONNEL: *1980, 5; 1981, 9 (projected)*
MISSIONARY PREPARATION: *Bible Institute, Seminary, Practical Experience*
FIELDS OF SERVICE:
Philippines, the Ilocano language, Church Planting
Philippines, the Zombal language, Church Planting

Jubilee Evangelical Church,
*   Mission Board*
35 Hemady Cor., Third Street
New Manila, Quezon City, PHILLIPINES

Alejandor Beltran, Chief Officer
Organized July 1970
Interdenominational

PERSONNEL: *1972, 10; 1975, 10; 1978, 12; 1980, 13 (30% growth)*
MISSIONARY PREPARATION: *Bible Institute, Seminary*

FIELDS OF SERVICE:
Philippines, the Filipino people, Evangelism, Church Planting
France, the Indo-Chinese refugees, Vietnamese, Laosian languages, Evang.,
Malaysia, the Malaysian people, the Malaysian, Chinese languages, Evangel.
Hong Kong, the Chinese people and language, Evangelism, Research

---

Missionary Diocese of Central
* Philippines (Philippine Episcopal*
* Church)*
PO Box 655, Manila PHILIPPINES

Rt. Rev. Manuel C. Lumpias, Chief Off.
Organized 1901
Denominational

PERSONNEL: *1972, 33; 1975, 47; 1978, 54; 1980, 56 (70% growth)*
MISSIONARY PREPARATION:

FIELDS OF SERVICE:
U.S.A., the American people, the English language, Pastoral
W. Malaysia, Native Malaysian people, Malaysian and English languages, Evang.
Australia, the Australian people, the English language, Chaplaincy
Germany, the German people and language, Student Evangelism
Philippines, the Filipino people, Tagalog and English languages, Evangelism
Philippines, Chinese people, Ilocano language, Evangelism
Philippines, American people, English language, Evangelism, Chaplaincy
Philippines, Canadian people, English language, Evangelism, Chaplaincy

Philippine Association of Baptists   Rev. Mariano Leones, Chief Officer
  for World Evangelism   Organized May 1957
PO Box 317   Denominational
Iloilo City, PHILIPPINES

PERSONNEL: *1972, 11; 1975, 11; 1978, 7; 1980, 8 (-36% growth)*
MISSIONARY PREPARATION: *Bible Institute, Practical Experience*

FIELDS OF SERVICE:
Thailand, the Thai people, the English and Thai languages, Evangelism

---

Philippine Evangelical Mission, Inc.   Rev. Cornelio R. Dalisay, Chief Off.
PO Box 4274   Organized Juen 12, 1979
Manila, 2800 PHILLIPINES   Nondenominational

PERSONNEL: *1980, 8; 1981, 20 (projected)*
MISSIONARY PREPARATION: *Bible Institute, Seminary*

FIELDS OF SERVICE:
Philippines, the Tagalog people, the Filipino language, Church Planting
Philippines, the Pangasinan people and language, Church Planting

---

Philippine General Council of the
  Assemblies of God
PO Box 3782   Denominational
Manila PHILIPPINES

PERSONNEL: *1980, 1*
MISSIONARY PREPARATION: *Bible Institute*

FIELDS OF SERVICE:

Philippines Missionary Fellowship   Rev. Evangelista Siodora, Chief Off.
PO Box 3349   Organized 1954
Manila, PHILIPPINES   Interdenominational

PERSONNEL: *1978, 72; 1980, 96 (33% growth)*
MISSIONARY PREPARATION: *Bible Institute, Seminary,*
Practical Experience
FIELDS OF SERVICE:

Philippine Native Crusade
PO Box 121, Tuguegarao
Cagayau, 1101 PHILIPPINES

Rev. Claudio R. Cortez, Chief Officer
Organized April 2, 1962
Nondenominational

PERSONNEL: 1980, 207
MISSIONARY PREPARATION: Bible Institute

FIELDS OF SERVICE:
Philippine, primitive tribal people, the Ilocano language, Evangelism

---

United Church of Christ in the
   Philippines
PO Box 718
Manila, PHILIPPINES

Bishop Estanislao Q. Abainza, Chief Off.
Organized May 25-27, 1948
Denominational

PERSONNEL: 1980, 116
MISSIONARY PREPARATION: Seminary, Practical Experience, Mission
Related Orientation
FIELDS OF SERVICE:

United Evangelical Church of the
   Philippines Mission Board
1242 Benavidez Street
Manila, PHILIPPINES

Rev. Wesley K. Shao, Chief Officer
Organized July 1969
Interdenominational

PERSONNEL: 1972, 37; 1975, 37; 1978, 38; 1980, 41 (11% growth)
MISSIONARY PREPARATION: Bible Institute, Seminary

FIELDS OF SERVICE:
Philippines, the Filipino tribal people, the Chinese language, Filipino
    dialects, Church Planting
Taiwan, the Chinese people and language, Evangelism
Hong Kong, the Chinese people and language, Evangelism
Singapore, the Chinese people and language, Evangelism
Indonesia, the Chinese people and language, Evangelism and Church Planting
France, the Vietnamese people and language, EVangelism and Church Planting

Asia Evangelistic Fellowship   Dr. G.D. James, Chief Officer
G.P.O. Box 579   Organized July 20, 1960
SINGAPORE   Interdenominational

PERSONNEL: *1972, 44; 1975, 50; 1978, 63; 1980, 80 (82% growth)*
MISSIONARY PREPARATION: *Bible Institute, Seminary, Practical Experience,*
Mission Related Orientation (1 year)
FIELDS OF SERVICE:
Singapore, Chinese and Indian people, English and Chinese languages, Evang.
Malaysia, Chinese and Indian people, English and Chinese languages, Evang.
Indonesia, the Indonesian people and language, Church Planting
Thailand, the Malaysian and Thai people and languages, Evangelism
India, Indian people, English, Tamil, Marathi languages, Evang., Ch. Planting
Philippines, the Filipino and Chinese people, the Tagalog and English
languages, Evangelism
Australia and New Zealand, the Chinese and Vietnamese people, the Chinese
and Vietnamese language, Evangelism

The Chen Li Church
76 Guillemard Rd.
SINGAPORE

PERSONNEL: *1980, 13*
MISSIONARY PREPARATION:

FIELDS OF SERVICE:

Overseas Missionary Fellowship
2 Cluny Rd.
REPUBLIC OF SINGAPORE

PERSONNEL: *1978, 24; 1980, 32; 1981; 39 (projected)*
MISSIONARY PREPARATION: *Bible Institute, Seminary, Practical Experience,*
Mission Related Orientation (8 weeks)
FIELDS OF SERVICE:
Thailand, the Thai people and language, Church Planting
Japan, the Japanese people and language, Church Planting
Pakistan, the Urdu people and language, Evangelism
Bangladesh, the Bengali people and language, Social Work
Philippines, the Filipino people, the Tagalog language, Church Planting
Indonesia, Indonesian people, Japanese and Indonesian languages, Teaching,
Training
Taiwan, the Chinese people, the Hokkien language, Teaching
Hong Kong, the Chinese, the Cantonese language, Reasearch

The Tabernacle Ltd.   Mr. Seah Hok Heng David, Chief Officer
RMS 210/212 Bible House   Organized January 5, 1975
Armenian St. SINGAPORE 0617   Nondenominational

PERSONNEL: 1975,2; 1978, 6; 1980, 12; 1981,(500% growth)
MISSIONARY PREPARATION: Practical Experience

FIELDS OF SERVICE:
Philippines, slum dwelling people, English and Cebuano languages, Ch. Planting
Thailand, the Chinese and tribal people, the Mandarin, Thai and tribal
     languages, Church Planting

The Burning Bush Mission   Lillian R. Dickson, Chief Officer
PO Box 46-46   Organized 1968
Taipei 104, TAIWAN R.O.C.   Denominational

PERSONNEL: 1972, 16; 1975, 10; 1978, 8; 1980, 8 (-50% growth)
MISSIONARY PREPARATION: Seminary, Mission Related Orientation (4 weeks)

FIELDS OF SERVICE:
Malaysia, the Iban people and language, Church Planting

The Chinese Baptist Convention
   Overseas Mission
47-1 Huai Mein Street, Taipei, TAIWAN

PERSONNEL: 1980, 2
MISSIONARY PREPARATION:

FIELDS OF SERVICE:
Korea
Malaysia

The Chinese Missions Overseas
Chung Shan North Rd., Sec. 2
131 3/F
Taipei, TAIWAN R.O.C.

PERSONNEL: 1980, 1
MISSIONARY PREPARATION:

FIELDS OF SERVICE:
Thailand

Mission of Taipei Ling Liang Church Rev. Nathaniel Chow, Chief Officer
24 Ho-ping East Road, Sec. 2   Organized December 26, 1976
Taipei, TAIWAN   R.O.C.   Nondenominational

PERSONNEL: *1980, 4; 1981, 9*
MISSIONARY PREPARATION: *Bible Institute, Language Learning, Seminary,*
University, Practical Experience, Mission Related Orientation (1-2 years)
FIELDS OF SERVICE:
Japan, the Japanese people and language
Hong Kong, the Chinese people, the Cantonese language
Korea, the Korean people, the Chinese language
Taiwan, the Chinese people and language

Latin American Respondents (no survey information)

Christian and Missionary Alliance
Pampa 2975
1428 Buenos Airea, ARGENTINA
Rev. Guellermo Gitz

Evangelical Methodist Church of
Argentina
240, 10B
Buenos Airea, ARGENTINA

Laguna Yacre Evangelical Mission
Bacacay 3450
Capital Federal, ARGENTINA
Dr. Aldolfo Meliman

Brazilian Council of the African
Evangelical Fellowship
Rua Alexandre MacKenzie 60
Rio de Janeiro, R.J. BRAZIL

Brazil's Korean Church
C.P. 18861 - Aeroporto
0100 Sao Paulo, S.P., BRAZIL
Rev. Moon Whong

Brazilian Presbyterian Church -
Board of Foreign Missions
c/o Calvary Presbyterian Church
18.106 Sorocaba, S.P., BRAZIL
Rev. Elson Bittencourt

Independent Presbyterian Church
Board of Missions
C.P. 300
01.000 Sao Paulo, S.P., BRAZIL

Missionary Church, Board of
Missions
C.P. 618
Maringa, P.A., BRAZIL
Pr. Ayrton Justos

National Baptist Convention
C.P. 400
Belo Horizonte, MG, BRAZIL
Pr. Rosivaldo Araujo

The Navigators
C.P. 2925
80.000 Curitiba, Parana, BRAZIL
Sr. Aldo Berndt

Priscilla and Aquilla Mission
Travessa Ipatinga, 30
39.800 Teofilo Otonia, MG
BRAZIL

Pro-Redemption of the Indians
Mission
C.P. 4
Dourados, Moto Grosso do Sul
BRAZIL
Rev. Martim Blek

REMI
C.P. 68
35.100 Gov. Valdares, MG
BRAZIL
Armando da Penha

Transmission
C.P. 1206
30.000 Belo Horizonte, MG
BRAZIL
Pr. Rui C. Santiago

University Biblical Alliance
(InterVarsity)
C.P. 30.505
01.000 Sao Paulo, SP, BRAZIL

Faith Christian Missions
Apartado Aereo 1505
Barranquilla, COLOMBIA
Enrique Mendoza

Panamerican Mission of Colombia
Apartado Aereo 53425
Bogota, COLUMBIA
Ignacio Guevara

The Church of God of the Prophecy
Apartado 1792
Santo Domingo, DOMINICAN REPUBLIC
Rev. Felix Santiago
Denominational

O.C.S.
Casilla 4829
Quito, ECUADOR
James G. Carpenter

LATIN AMERICAN COUNTRIES (Continued)

SI Amen
Casilla 8507
Guayaquil, ECUADOR
  Rev. Jose Arauz Brito

Great Final Day
Apartado 1213
Guatemala City, GUATEMALA
  Rev. Hernandez

Mount Sinai
Apartado 1213
Guatemala City, GUATEMALA
  Rev. Antonio Lima

The Nazarene Church
c/o Alfonso Barrientos
Apartado 11, Coban
Alta Verapaz, GUATEMALA

Strictel English Baptist
Jacmel, HAITI
West Indies

Missionary Association of the
  Aymaro Indians
La Paz, BOLIVIA

PERSONNEL:
MISSIONARY PREPARATION:

FIELDS OF SERVICE:
U.S.A., the Navajo people, the English and Navajo languages, Evangelism,
  Church Planting

Alabama   *Gidalfo Sales Figueira, Chief Officer*
C.P. 1067   *Organized July 16, 1976*
66.000 Belem, PA BRAZIL   *Denominational*

PERSONNEL: *1976, 10; 1978, 20; 1980, 25 (150% growth)*
MISSIONARY PREPARATION: *Bible Institute, Practical Experience*

FIELDS OF SERVICE:
Brazil, the Backland people, the Portuguese language, Evangelism, Discipling

---

Antioch Mission   *Pr. Jonathan Ferreira dos Santos, Chief*
C.P. 582   *Organized 1975*   *Officer*
01000 Sao Paulo, S.P., BRAZIL   *Interdenominational*

PERSONNEL: *1980, 4; 1981, 8*
MISSIONARY PREPARATION: *Bible Institute, Practical Experience, Mission*
Related Orientation (6 months)
FIELDS OF SERVICE:
Portugal, the Portuguese Catholic people, the Portuguese language, Church
  Planting

Assembly of God in the Amazon   *Pr. A.P. Vasconcelos*
C.P. 22   *Organized January 1, 1973*
69.000 Manaus, AM, BRAZIL   *Denominational*

PERSONNEL: *1980, 21*
MISSIONARY PREPARATION: *Bible Institute, Language Learning, Practical*
Experience, Mission Related Orientation (3 years)
FIELDS OF SERVICE:
Bolivia, the Spanish language, Evangelism
Brazil, the Portuguese language, Evangelism

190

Brazilian Assemblies of God Timoteo Ramos de Oliveira, Chief Off.
  National Missions
Estrada Vicente de Carvalho, 1083
20.000 Rio de Janeiro, R.J. BRAZIL

PERSONNEL: *1980, 82*
MISSIONARY PREPARATION:

FIELDS OF SERVICE:
Bolivia, Uruguay, Chile, Ecuador, Colombia and Paraguay, the Spanish
    language, Evangelism
U.S.A., the English and Spanish languages, Evangelism
Portugal, the Portuguese language, Evangelism
Argentina, Belgium and Venezuela, the Spanish language, Evangelism
England, the English language, Evangelism
French Guiana, Evangelism
Rondonia, the Portuguese language, Evangelism

Brazilian Baptist Convention Pr. Waldemiro Tymchak, Chief Officer
  Foreign Mission Board Organized 1907
C.P. 40.022 Denominational
20.000 Rio de Janeiro, R.J. BRAZIL

PERSONNEL:*1975, 45; 1978, 62; 1980, 70 (56% growth)*
MISSIONARY PREPARATION: *Seminary, Practical Experience*

FIELDS OF SERVICE:
Paraguay, the Paraguaian people, the Spanish language, Evangelism
Uruguay, the Uruguain people the Spanish language, Evangelism
Argentina, the Argentinian people, the Spanish language, Evangelism
Bolivia, the Bolivian people, the Spanish language, Evangelism
Venezuela, the Venezuelan people, the Spanish language, Evangelism
Portugal, the Portuguese people and language, Evangelism
Azores, the Spanish people and language, Evangelism
Mozambique, Evangelism
France, the French language, Evangelism
Spain, the Spanish language, Evangelism

Braziliam Baptist Convention   Paulo Roberto Seabra, Chief Officer
   Home Mission Board
Rua Barao do Bom Retiro, 1241   Denominational
20.000 Rio de Janeiro, R.J. _BRAZIL_

PERSONNEL: *1980, 300*
MISSIONARY PREPARATION:

FIELDS OF SERVICE:
Brazil, the Brazilian people, the Portuguese language, Evangelism, Church
   Planting

Brazilian Methodist Church,   Rev. Francisco Antonio Correia, Chief
   Missions Department   Officer
Rua Visconde de Porto Seguro, 442   Denominational
Santa Amaro, S.P. _BRAZIL_

PERSONNEL: *1980, 30*
MISSIONARY PREPARATION:

FIELDS OF SERVICE:
Colombia, Panama, Ecuador and Bolivia, the Spanish language, Evangelism,
   Church Planting
Brazil, the Portuguese language, Evangelism, Church Planting

Caiua Evangelical Mission   Rev. Orlando Andrade, Chief Officer
C.P. 4   Organized August 28, 1928
79.800 Dourados, Mato Grosso do   Denominational
Sul, _BRAZIL_

PERSONNEL: *1980, 30; 1981, 36 (projected)*
MISSIONARY PREPARATION: *Bible Institute, Language Learning, Seminary,*
University (at times). Practical Experience, Mission Related Orientation
FIELDS OF SERVICE: *(3 months)*
Brazil, the Caiua, Guarani, Terena, Kadivev, Amotina and Bakairi people,
   the Portuguese and Caiva languages, Evangelism

Evangelical Church of Lutheran   Rev. P. Heimberto Kunkel, Chief Off.
   Confession in Brazil
C.P. 2876   Denominational
90.000 Porto Alegre, R.S. _BRAZIL_

PERSONNEL:
MISSIONARY PREPARATION: *Language Learning, Seminary*

FIELDS OF SERVICE:
Brazil, the Kaingang Tribe people, Evangelism, Pastoral

Evangelism Mission to the   Rev. Zacarias Matos Monteiro, Chief Off.
  Brazilian Indians   Organized November 1967
C.P. 3.030   Interdenominational
66.000 Belem, PA, BRAZIL

PERSONNEL: 1972, 3; 1975, 6; 1978, 6; 1980, 7 (133% growth)
MISSIONARY PREPARATION: Bible Institute, Seminary

FIELDS OF SERVICE:
Brazil, Guajajara Indians, Portuguese, Guajajara languages, Church Planting
Brazil, Kayapo Indians, Portuguese, Kayapo languages, Church Planting
Brazil, Waiwai Indians, Portuguese, Waiwai languages, Church Planting

---

Gipsy Missionary Work in Brazil   Dr. Evaldo A. dos Santos, Chief Officer
R. das Acacias, #193 (Pituga)
Salvador, Baia 40.000 BRAZIL   Interdenominational

PERSONNEL: 1980, 1; 1981, 3
MISSIONARY PREPARATION: Bible Institute, Mission Related Orientation

FIELDS OF SERVICE:
Portugal, the Gipsy people, the Portuguese dialects, Evangelism

---

Missionary Expansion Fund   Rev. Gesse Teixeira de Carvalho, Chief
Estrada do itamarati, 313   Officer
C.P. 421   Denominational
Petropolis, R.J., BRAZIL   25.600

PERSONNEL: 1980, 23; 1981, 28
MISSIONARY PREPARATION:

FIELDS OF SERVICE:
Portugal, the Portuguese people and language, Evangelism
Brazil, the Braziliam people and language, Evangelism

Presbyterian Church   Rev. Joed Lamonica, Chief Officer
C.P. 453   Organized November 9, 1969
09.500 Sao Caetano do Sul, SP   Denominational
BRAZIL

PERSONNEL: 1978, 6; 1980, 2 (-67% growth)
MISSIONARY PREPARATION:

FIELDS OF SERVICE:
Brazil, the Protuguese language, Evangelism, Church Planting

Union of Brazilian Congregational   Rev. Antonio Limeira Neto, Chief Officer
  Evangelical Churches
  Dept. of Mission   Denominational
Rua Sao Luis Gonzaga 1132, 20.000 Rio deJaneiro, RJ, <u>BRAZIL</u>

PERSONNEL: *1980, 10*
MISSIONARY PREPARATION:

FIELDS OF SERVICE:
Brazil, the Portuguese language, Evangelism, Church Planting

Worldwide Evangelization Crusade   Rev. Robert George Harvey, Chief Officer
C.P. 1206   Organized May 4, 1963
30.000 Belo Horizonte, MG   Interdenominational
<u>BRAZIL</u>

PERSONNEL: *1978, 3; 1980, 4 (33% growth)*
MISSIONARY PREPARATION: *Bible Institute, Language Learning, Practical*
Experience, Mission Related Orientation (4 months)
FIELDS OF SERVICE:
Italy, the Sards people, the Italian language, Evangelism, Church Planting
Guine-Bissau, the Mancanha Tribe, the Portuguese and Criole languages,
  Evangelism, Church Planting

Wycliffe Translators of Brazil   Dr. Gilberto Pickering, Chief Officer
C.P. 14-2205
70.000 Brasilia, DF,   Interdenominational
<u>BRAZIL</u>

PERSONNEL: *1975, 2; 1978, 2; 1980, 4 (100% growth)*
MISSIONARY PREPARATION: *Bible Institute, Language Learning, Practical*
Experience, Mission Related Orientation
FIELDS OF SERVICE:
Brazil, Tribal peoples, Surui and Paumari languages, Linguistic, Evangelism

---

Christian Brethren   Carlos Machacon, Chief Officer
Apdo. Aereo 4248   Organized September 29, 1976
Cartagena, <u>COLOMBIA</u>   Denominational

PERSONNEL: *1980, 4*
MISSIONARY PREPARATION:

FIELDS OF SERVICE:
Columbia, rural people, Spanish language, Evangelism

```
Colombian Christian Alliamce        Jose Rafael Lopez H., Chief Officer
Apartado Aereo 678                  Organized March 9, 1942
Armenia Quindio, COLOMBIA           Denominational
```

PERSONNEL: *1978, 10; 1980, 8 (-20% growth)*
MISSIONARY PREPARATION: *Bible Institute, Language Learning, Seminary,*
Practical Experience
FIELDS OF SERVICE:
Brazil, Amazon Tribal people, Portuguese language, Evangelism, Church Plant.
Colombia, the Spanish language, Evangelism, Church Planting
Colombia, tribal people, Spanish dialect, Evangelism, Translation
Colombia, tribal people, Spanish language, Evangelism, Church Planting

---

Mission of the Motilone Indians   *Bruce E. Olson, Chief Officer*

COLOMBIA

PERSONNEL: *1980, 3*
MISSIONARY PREPARATION:

FIELDS OF SEkVICE:
Colombia, the Yukos people and language, Evangelism
Colombia, the Guajigos people and language, Evangelism
Colombia, the Cuivas people and language, Evangelism

```
Ecuadorian Evangelical Missionary   Sr. Washington Leon, Chief Officer
   Association                      Organized November 19, 1968
Casilla 5185                        Nondenominational
Quito, ECUADOR
```

PERSONNEL: *1972, 5; 1975, 5; 1978, 11; 1980, 12 (140% growth)*
MISSIONARY PREPARATION: *Bible Institute, Practical Experience*

FIELDS OF SERVICE:
Ecuador, tribal people, the Spanish language, Evangelism, Teaching
Ecuador, the Shuar people and language, Evangelism, Teaching
Ecuador, the Quechua people and language, Evangelism, Teaching

---

```
The Calvary                         Pr. Eliu Castillo, Chief Officer
Av. Ferrocarril Y 2a.C., Zona 9     Organized 1963
Guatemala City, GUATEMALA           Denominational
```

PERSONNEL: *1980, 18*
MISSIONARY PREPARATION:

FIELDS OF SERVICE:
Colombia, Honduras, Mexico and U.S.A., the Spanish language, Evangelism

Elim Christian Mission
48 Av. 4-21, Zona 7
Colonia El Rosario
Guatemala City, GUATEMALA

Dr. Otoniel Rios P. Chief Officer
Organized 1968
Denominational

PERSONNEL: 1980, 6
MISSIONARY PREPARATION:

FIELDS OF SERVICE:
El Salvador
Mexico
U.S.A.

Prince of Peace National Association
Apartado 786
Guatemala City, GUATEMALA

Rev. Jose A. Coellar, Chief Officer
Organized March 25, 1955
Denominational

PERSONNEL: 1980, 3; 1981, 5 (projected)
MISSIONARY PREPARATION: Bible Institute, Language Learning

FIELDS OF SERVICE:
Colombia, the Spanish language, Evangelism
Mexico, the Spanish language, Evangelism

Baptist National Convention
Esq. Mina y Heroes
Mexico 3, D.F. MEXICO

Dr. Librado Ramos, Chief Officer

PERSONNEL: 1980, 2
MISSIONARY PREPARATION:

FIELDS OF SERVICE:
Honduras, the Spanish language, Evangelism

Chiapas Mission
c/o Reformed Church in America
Apartado 8, San Cristobal de las
  Casas, Chiapas, MEXICO

Rev. Harold Brown, Chief Officer
Organized 1943
Denominational

PERSONNEL:1972, 18; 1975, 20; 1978, 18; 1980, 16   (-11% growth)
MISSIONARY PREPARATION: Bible Institute, Language Learning, Seminary,
University, Practical Experience, Mission Related Orientation (3 months)
FIELDS OF SERVICE:
Mexico, the Tzgtzil Indians, the Tzotzil language, Evangelism, Teaching
Mexico, the Ch'ol Indians and their language, Teaching
Mexico, the Tojolobal Indians, the Spanish and Tojolobal languages, Evang.

Youth for Christ　　　　　　　　Moises Zegarra A., Chief Officer
Apartado 3801
Lima 1, _PERU_　　　　　　　　　Interdenominational

PERSONNEL: _1980, 41_
MISSIONARY PREPARATION: _Bible Institute, Mission Related Orientation (1 year)_

FIELDS OF SERVICE:
Argentian, Brazil, Chile, Colombia, Uruguay and Peru, the Young people,
the Spanish language, Evangelism

International Missionary　　　　Mr. Kingsley Bailey, Chief Officer
　Fellowship, Ltd.　　　　　　　Organized April 2, 1962
Box 929 - Kingston 10　　　　　　Interdenominational
Jamaica, _WEST INDIES_

PERSONNEL: _1972, 23; 1975, 26: 1978, 26; 1980, 26 (13% growth)_
MISSIONARY PREPARATION: _Bible Institute, Mission Related Orientation (1 year)_

FIELDS OF SERVICE:
Dominican Republic, the Nationals, the English language, Evangelism, Pastoring
Haiti, the Nationals, the Creole French language, Evangelism, Postoring, Medical
St. Vincent, the English language, Evangelism
Indonesia, the English language, Evangelism, Pastoring
Bolivia, the Indians, the Spanish language, Camps, Evangelism
Nigeria, the Nationals, the English language, Evangelism, Pastoring
Ghana, the Nationals, Evangelism

Oceanian Respondents (no survey information)

First Church of God
P.O. Box 20850
GMF, GUAM 96921

General Baptist Church of Guam
P.O. Box 595
Aqana, GUAM 96910

Palau Evangelical Church
P.O. Box 3664
Aqana, GUAM 96910

Assemblies of God in Fiji
P.O. Box 3697
Suva, FIJI ISLANDS
Rev. Alipate Cakau

Diocese of Polynesia
P.O. Box 25
Suva, FIJI ISLANDS

Assemblies of God Mission
Ambunti, E.S.P.
PAPUA NEW GUINEA

United Church in Papua, New Guinea
and Solomon Islands
P.O. Box 3401
Port Moresby, PAPUA NEW GUINEA
Rev. Leslie Bogeto
Denominational

Methodist Church in Tonga
P.O. Box 57
Nukualofa, TONGA ISLANDS
Rev. Dr. Viliami Mongoloa

Methodist Church in Fiji
G.P.O. Box 357
Suva, FIJI ISLANDS

Rev. Paula Niukula and
Rev. Daniel Nastapha, Chief Officers
Organized 1975
Interdenominational

PERSONNEL: *1980, 38*
MISSIONARY PREPARATION: *Seminary, Practical Experience, Mission*
Related Orientation (3 months)
FIELDS OF SERVICE:
Papua New Guinea
Australia
England

Evangelical Lutheran Church
P.O. Box 80
Lae, PAPUA NEW GUINEA

Rev. Getake Gam, Chief Officer

Denominational

PERSONNEL: *1980, 45: 1981, 50 (projected)*
MISSIONARY PREPARATION:

FIELDS OF SERVICE:

Good News Lutheran Church
P.O. Box 111
Wabag, Enga Province
PAPUA NEW GUINEA

Mr. Mark Yapao, Chief Officer
Organized May 1960
Denominational

PERSONNEL: *1972, 28; 1975, 27; 1978, 22; 1980, 24 (-14% growth)*
MISSIONARY PREPARATION: *Seminary, Practical Experience, Mission*
Related Orientation
FIELDS OF SERVICE:
Papua New Guinea, Yangis people, Enga, Pidgin languages, Church Planting
Papua New Guinea, Nete people, Enga language, Church Planting
Papua New Guinea, Hewa people, Ipili, Hewe languages, Church Planting
Papua New Guinea, Penale people, Pidgin language, Church Planting
Papua New Guinea, Hewa people, Duna, Pidgin languages, Church Planting
Papua New Guinea, Tambul people, Enga, Pidgin languages, Church Planting
Papua New Guinea, Urban people, Pidgin language, Evangelism

Highland Christian Mission
Okapa via Goroka,
PAPUA NEW GUINEA

Dr. Stuart H. Merriam, Chief Officer
Organized March 15, 1964
Interdenominational

PERSONNEL: 1972, 5; 1975, 6; 1978, 12; 1980, 12 (140% growth)
MISSIONARY PREPARATION:

FIELDS OF SERVICE:
Papua New Guinea, the Fore people, the Fore and English languages,
Christian Education

Samoa Congregational Church
Tamaligi, WESTERN SAMOA

Rev. Elder Tuuau, Chief Officer
Organized August 1830
Interdenominational

PERSONNEL: 1972, 5; 1975, 4; 1978, 6; 1980, 10 (100% growth)
MISSIONARY PREPARATION: Bible Institute

FIELDS OF SERVICE:
Africa, Students, the English language and African dialects, Teach., Preach.
Marshall Islands, Village, English languge and dialects, Teaching, Preaching
New Guinea, Village, English language and dialects, Teaching, Preaching
Fiji, Samoan people, English language and dialects, Teaching, Preaching

---

Youth With a Mission
P.O. Box 2608
Pago Pago, AMERICAN SAMOA 96799

Sosene T. Le'au, Chief Officer
Organized February 1, 1974
Interdenominational

PERSONNEL: 1975, 4; 1978, 4; 1980, 25 (525% growth)
MISSIONARY PREPARATION: Mission Related Orientation (10 months)

FIELDS OF SERVICE:
Hong Kong, refugees, the English language, Evangelism
Hawaii, the Hawaiian people, the English language, Evangelism

---

Church of Melanesia, Board of
   Mission
P.O. Box 19
Honiara, SOLOMON ISLANDS

B.J. LePine-Williams, Chief Officer
Organized September, 1979
Denominational

PERSONNEL: 1978, 100; 1980, 120 (20% growth)
MISSIONARY PREPARATION: Practical Experience, Mission Related
Orientation (2 years total)
FIELDS OF SERVICE:
Fiji, the Pidgin language, Evangelism
Papua New Guinea, the Pidgin language, Evangelism
Australia, the Aboriginies, the Pidgin language, Evangelism

South Sea Evangelical Church
P.O. Box 16
Honiara, SOLOMON ISLANDS

Rev. Jezreel Filoa, Chief Officer
Organized 1904
Denominational

PERSONNEL: *1978, 12; 1980, 10 (-17% growth)*
MISSIONARY PREPARATION: *Bible Institute, Practical Experience*

FIELDS OF SERVICE:
Papua New Guinea, various peoples, the Pidgin language, Evangelism, Church
Planting

Western Countries Respondents (no survey information)

ABC Central Asia Mission
47 Tranmere Road
Hamilton, NEW ZEALAND

New Zealand Evangelical Missionary Alliance
427 Queen Street, P.O. Box 68-140
Auckland, NEW ZEALAND

Chinese Christian Mission
3503 Petaluma Blvd. N.
Petaluma, California 94952
  Rev. Thomas Wang
  1961, Nondenominational

Chinese for Christ
922 N. Edgemont St.
Los Angeles, CALIFORNIA 90029
  Rev. Calvin Chao
  1959, Nondenominational

India Mission for Evangelism
1514 Portland Ave.
St. Paul, MINNESOTA 55104
  Rev. Chacko P. Varghese
  1975, Nondenominational

Nora Lam Ministries
5672 Almaden Expressway
San Jose, CALIFORNIA 95118
  Rev. Nora Lam Sung
  1971, Nondenominational

Tokyo Gospel Mission
1402 Magnolia
Norman, OKLAHOMA 73069

CHIEF
P.O. Box 2600
Orange, California U.S.A. 92669

Rev. Tom Claus, Chief Officer
Organized 1975
Interdenominational

PERSONNEL: *1980, 3*
MISSIONARY PREPARATION: Bible Institute, Seminary, Practical
Experience
FIELDS OF SERVICE:
U.S.A., various Indian tribes and their languages, Evangelism, Church Plant*

Evangelize China Fellowship
617 Parkman Avenue
Los Angeles, CA 90026   U.S.A.

Dr. Andrew Gih, Chief Officer
Organized 1947
Interdenominational

PERSONNEL: *1978, 300*
MISSIONARY PREPARATION:

FIELDS OF SERVICE:

India Evangelical Mission, Inc.
9915 Marquam Dr.
Route 3
Molalla, Oregon 97038   U.S.A.

Rev. G.V. Mathai, Chief Officer
Organized 1966
Nondenominational

PERSONNEL: *1980, 4*
MISSIONARY PREPARATION:

FIELDS OF SERVICE:
India

The Navigators
    (Third World Missionaries)
P.O. Box 20
Colorado Springs, Colorado 80901   U.S.A.

Donald McGilchrist (in U.S.A.), Chief
                                Officer
Interdenominational

PERSONNEL: *1980, 26; 1981, 29*
MISSIONARY PREPARATION:

FIELDS OF SERVICE:
India, Australia, Argentina, Canada, Egypt, Indonesia, Japan, Jordan and
    Taiwan, Evangelism

APPENDIX III

Major Research and Study Centers Involved in Third World Evangelization

Asian Center for Theological
  Studies
187 Choong Jeongro 3 ka
Seodaemoon-ku
Seoul 120 KOREA

Asia Outreach
G.P.O. Box 3448
HONG KONG

Bolivia Center for World Mission
Casilla 20100
La Paz, BOLIVIA

China Research Center Christian
  Communication, Ltd.
144 Boundary Street
P.O. Box 5364
Kowloon, HONG KONG

China Research Center of China
  Evangelical Seminary
15, Lane 5, Hsing Fu Street
Shihlin, Taipei, TAIWAN

Chinese Church Research Center
  of China Graduate School of
  Theology
5 Devon Road
Kowloon, HONG KONG

Chinese Coordination Center of
  World Evangelism
P.O. Box 98435
Tsimshatsui
HONG KONG

Christian Research Institute
116 Surrey Drive
Wayne, NH 07470 USA

Christian Research, Inc.
2624 First Avenue S.
Minneapolis, MN 55408

Church Growth Association of
  India
P.O. Box 768
Kilpauk, Madras 110 048
New Delhi, INDIA

Church Growth Institute of Japan
c/o Reverend John Masuda
4-13-16 Sakuragaoka
Setagaya-ku
Tokyo 156 JAPAN

Church Growth Society of Taiwan
191, Lane 309, East Gate Road
Tainan, TAIWAN 700

Daystar Communications
P.O. Box 44400
Nairobi, KENYA

East-West Center for Missions
  Research and Development
Dr. David Cho
CPO Box 2732
Seoul 100 KOREA

Evangelical Missions Information
  Service
Box 794
Wheaton, IL 60187

Far Eastern Gospel Crusade
Box 513
Farmington, MI 48024

Glenmary Research Center
4606 East-West Highway
Washington, DC 20014

Henry Martyn Institute of
  Islamic Studies
P.O. 153, Chirag Ali Lane
Hyderbad 50000 A.P., India

Institute of Chinese Studies
1605 E. Elizabeth Street
Pasadena, CA 91104

Institute for Tribal Studies
1605 E. Elizabeth Street
Pasadena, CA 91104

Mr. Patrick Johnstone
c/o MV Logos
64 Tweedy Road
Bromley, Kent 8RI 3NJ
ENGLAND

Missions Advance Research and
  Communication Center (MARC)
919 West Huntington Drive
Monrovia, CA 91016

Missionary Research Library
3041 Broadway
New York, NY 10027

Missions Research Center
Dallas Theological Seminary
3909 Swiss Avenue
Dallas, TX 75204

Missions Training Resource Center
221 E. Walnut, Suite 271
Pasadena, CA 91101

Overseas Ministries Study Center
P.O. Box 2057
Ventnor, NJ 08406

Samuel Zwemer Institute
Box 365
Altadena, CA 91001

Thailand Church Growth Committee
G.P.O. Box 432
Bangkok, THAILAND

Theological Research and Communi-
  cation Institute
E537 Greater Kailash II
New Delhi 110-048, INDIA

Unit of Research
P.O. Box 40230
Nairobi, KENYA

Wycliffe Summer Institute of
  Linguistics
2500 Camp Wisdom Road
Dallas, TX 75211

BIBLIOGRAPHY

Abraham, Valston
Personal interview on February 25, 1980.

Adeyemo, Tokunbo
"The African Church Struggle into Her Third Century".
Christianity Today. Volume XXIII, No. 19. Washington, D.C.:
July 20, 1979.

Aihara, Paul
"The Foreign Missions Work of The Immanuel General Mission,
Japan". Pasadena: Unpublished paper for Dr. Paul Pierson at
the School of World Mission, on February 27, 1980, for the
class "The Historical Development of the Christian Movement."

Akangbe, Stephen
"Three Major Ways That North American Mission Agencies Can
Effectively Assist National Churches in the Evangelization of
Their Countries". Overland Park, Kansas: Unpublished paper,
presented at the 1973 *EFMA/IFMA Study Conference*, November 27-30.

Akpan, Rev. O.M.
Personal letter dated February 18, 1980.

Allen, Roland
Missionary Methods: St. Paul's or Ours? Grand Rapids: Wm. B.
Eerdmans Publishing Co., 1962.

Allen, Roland
The Spontaneous Expansion of the Church. Grand Rapids: Wm. B.
Eerdmans Publishing Co., 1962.

Anderson, Gerald H., ed.
Asian Voices in Christian Theology. Maryknoll: Orbis Books,
1976.

Anderson, Gerald H., ed.
The Theology of the Christian Mission. Nashville and New York:
Abingdon Press, 1961.

Anderson, Gerald H., and Thomas F. Stransky, eds.
Mission Trends No. 1. Grand Rapids: Wm. B. Eerdmans Publishing
Co. and New York: Paulist Fathers, 1974.
Mission Trends No. 2, 1975
Mission Trends No. 3, 1976
Mission Trends No. 4, 1979
Mission Trends No. 5, 1980

Anderson, J.N.D.
Christianity and Comparative Religion. Downers Grove: Inter
Varisty Press, 1970.

Angali-I, Dr.
Personal letter dated February 2, 1980.

Appiah-Kubi, Kofi and Sergio Torres, eds.
African Theology En Route. Maryknoll: Orbis Books, 1979.

Artless, Stuart W.
The Story of the Melanesian Mission. London: The Melanesian
Mission, 1937.

Association of Church Mission Committees
Evaluation, A Research Report Based on the Preliminary Report
E.F.M.A./I.F.M.A./A.C.M.C. Task Force on Evaluation. Pasadena:
The Association of Church Missions Committees, 1978.

Assmann, Hugo
Theology For A Normad Church. Maryknoll: Orbis Books, 1975.

Bavinck, J.H. (Translated by David H. Freeman)
An Introduction to the Science of Missions. Philadelphia: The
Presbyterian and Reformed Publishing Co., 1960.

Beaver, R. Pierce, ed.
A Directory of Indian, Aleut, and Eskimo Churhces. Monrovia:
Missions Advanced Research and Communication Center, 1979.

Beaver, R. Pierce, ed.
The Gospel and Frontier Peoples. Pasadena: Wm. Carey Library,
1973.

Beaver, R. Pierce, ed.
The Missionary Between the Times. New York: Doubleday, 1968.

Bellamy, Wilfred A.
"How Can North American Mission Agencies More Effectively Assist
National Churches in the Evangelization of Their Countries?"
Overland Park, Kansas: Unpublished paper presented at the 1973
EFMA/IFMA Study Conference, November 27-30.

Beyerhaus, Peter
Missions: Which Way? Grand Rapids: Zondervan Publishing House,
1971.

Beyerhaus, Peter
Shaken Foundations: Theological Foundations for Missions.
Grand Rapids: Zondervan Publishing House, 1972.

Beyerhaus, Peter and Henry Lefever
The Responsible Church and The Foreign Mission. Grand Rapids:
Wm. B. Eerdmans Publishing Co., 1964.

Blauw, Johannes
The Missionary Nature of the Church. Grand Rapids: Wm. B.
Eerdmans Publishing Co., 1962.

Boberg, J.T. and James A. Scherer, eds.
Mission in the Seventies. Chicago: Chicago Cluster of Theological Schools, 1972.

Brierley, Leslie
Personal letter to Edward C. Pentecost, Peter Larson and James
Wong dated October 26, 1973.

Browning, Neal
"Made in Japan Missionaries", *Japan Harvest.* Greenville: Japan
Overseas Missionary Association, Spring, 1975.

Buhlmann, Walbert
The Coming of the Third Church. Maryknoll: Orbis Books, 1976.

Castillo, Met
"Missiological Education: The Mission Vitamin in Mission
Strategy". *Asia Pulse.* Wheaton: Evangelical Missions Infor-
mation Service, Volume VII, Number 2, May 1976.

Chinese and Western Leadership Cooperation Seminar. Compendium.
Hong Kong: Chinese Coordination Centre of World Evangelism,
1980.

Christianity Today editorial
"In Search of Africa". Carol Stream, Illinois: Volume 23,
No. 19, July 20, 1979.

Clark, Dennis E.
The Third World and Missions. Waco: Word Books, 1971.

Coggins, Wade T. and E.L. Frizen, eds.
Evangelical Missions Tomorrow. Pasadena: Wm. Carey Library,
1977.

Cook, Harold R.
Historic Patterns of Church Growth. Chicago: Moody Press,
1971.

Costas, Orlando E.
*The Church and Its Mission: A Shattering Critique from the
Third World*. Wheaton: Tyndale House Publishers, 1974.

Costas, Orlando E.
The Integrity of Mission. New York: Harper and Row, 1979.

Danker, Wm. J. and Wi Jo Kang
*The Future of the Christian World Mission: Studies in Honor of
R. Pierce Beaver*. Grand Rapids: Wm. B. Eerdmans Publishing
Co., 1971.

Davidson, Basil
A History of West Africa to the Nineteenth Century. Garden
City: Doubleday and Co., 1966.

Davis, Raymond J.
"A National Missionary Movement". Winona Lake, Indiana:
Unpublished paper presented at the 1963 *EFMA/IFMA Joint Con-
ference*, September 30 to October 3.

Dayton, Edward, ed.
*Mission Handbook: North American Protestant Ministries Over-
seas, 11th Edition*. Monrovia: Missions Advanced Research and
Communications Center, 1976.

Dayton, Edward, ed.
That Everyone May Hear. Monrovia: Missions Advanced Research
and Communications Center, 1976.

Dayton, Edward and C. Peter Wagner, eds.
Unreached Peoples '80. Elgin: David C. Cook Publishing Co.,
1980.

Dayton, Edward and Samual Wilson, eds.
Unreached Peoples '82. Elgin: David C. Cook Publishing Co.,
1982.

Douglas, Donald E.
Evangelical Perspectives on China. Farmington: Evangelical
China Committee, 1976.

Douglas, J.D., ed.
Let the Earth Hear His Voice. Minneapolis: World Wide Publications, 1975.

Dussel, Enrique
Ethics and the Theology of Liberation. Maryknoll: Orbis Books,
1978.

Dussel, Enrique
History and the Theology of Liberation. Maryknoll: Orbis
Books, 1976.

Engel, James and H. Willert Norton
What's Gone Wrong With the Harvest? Grand Rapids: Zondervan
Publishing House, 1975.

Engstrom, Ted. W.
"Airing of Mission Tensions". *World Vision Magazine.* Monrovia:
World Vision International, Vol. 15, No. 10, November, 1971.

Engstrom, Ted W.
What in the World is God Doing? Waco: Word Books, 1978.

"Epic Evangelistic Event Witnessed in South Korea".
Wheaton: *EP News Service.* September 13, 1980.

Fife, Eric S. and Arthur Glasser
Missions in Crisis. Downers Grove: Inter Varsity Press, 1961.

Fox, Charles E.
Lord of the Southern Islands. London: A.R. Mowbray and Co.,
1958.

Frigoli, Bruno
The Visit to Farmington. Unpublished, No date; Accompanied
Memorandum by C. Peter Wagner.

Gerber, Virgil, ed.
Missions in Creative Tension: The Green Lake '71 Compendium.
Pasadena: Wm. Carey Library, 1971.

Glasser, Arthur F.
"The New Overseas Missionary Fellowship". Winona Lake, Indiana: Unpublished paper presented at the 1965 *EFMA Retreat*, October 4-7.

Glasser, Arthur F., Paul G. Hiebert, C. Peter Wagner, Ralph D. Winter
Crucial Dimensions in World Evangelization. Pasadena: Wm. Carey Library, 1976.

Glover, Robert H.
The Progress of World Wide Missions, revised and enlarged by J. Herbert Kane. New York: Harper Brothers, 1960.

Goddard, B.L., ed.
The Encyclopedia of Modern Christian Missions: The Agencies. Camden: Nelson and Sons, 1967.

Gort, Jerald D.
"Jerusalem 1928: Mission Kingdom and Church." *International Review of Mission* LXVII: 267. Geneva: Commission on World Mission and Evangelism, July 1978.

Gospel Light Magazine. India: Vol. 4, No. 7, November 1979.

Grassi, Joseph A.
A World to Win. New York: Maryknoll Books, 1965.

Green, Michael
Evangelism in the Early Church. Grad Rapids: Wm. B. Eerdmans Publishing Co., 1970.

Gutierrez, Gustavo
A Theology of Liberation. Maryknoll: Orbis Books, 1973.

Hall, Billy
Introducing International Missionary Fellowship. Alexandria, Jamaica, West Indies: International Missionary Fellowship, n.d.

Hamilton, Donald A., ed.
Missions Policy Handbook. Pasadena: The Association of Church Missions Committees, 1977.

Handy, Robert T.
A History of the Churches in the United States and Canada. New York: Oxford University Press, 1977.

Hargrave, Robert L. Jr.
The Nadars of Thailand. Los Angeles: University of California Press, 1969.

Harr, Wilbur C.
Frontiers of the Christian World Mission Since 1938. New York: Harper, 1962.

Hay, Alexander Rattray
The New Testament Order for Church and Missionary. Buenos Aires: New Testament Missionary Union, 1947.

Henry, Carl F. H. and Stanley Mooneyham, eds.
One Race, One Gospel, One Task, Volumes I and II. Minneapolis: World Wide Publications, 1967.

Hoekstra, Harvey T.
The World Council of Churches and the Demise of Evangelism. Wheaton: Tyndale Publishing House, 1979.

Holms III, Urban T.
The Future Shape of Ministry. New York: Seabury Press, 1971.

Howard, David M. ed.
Declare His Glory Among the Nations. Downers Grove: Inter Varsity Press, 1977.

Howard, David M. ed.
The Great Commission Today. Downers Grove: Inter Varsity Press, 1976.

Howells, William
The Heathens. The Natural History Library. Garden City: Doubleday and Co., 1948.

IDOC (Joel Underwood, ed.)
In Search of Mission: Future of the Missionary Enterprise Project. New York: IDOC North America, 1974.

Ishiguro, N.
Kansai Mission Research Center News Report. Kobe: KMRC Preparatory Committee, 1980.

James, Preston E.
Latin America. New York: The Odyssey Press, 1942

Johnston, Arthur
The Battle for World Evangelization. Wheaton: Tyndale House Publishers, 1978.

Johnstone, P.J.
Operation World: A Handbook for World Intercession. Kent, England: STL Publications, 1978.

Kane, J. Herbert
  A Global View of Christian Missions. Grand Rapids: Baker Book
  House, 1971.

Kane, J. Herbert
  Christian Missions in Biblical Perspectives. Grand Rapids:
  Baker Book House, 1974.

Kane, J. Herbert
  Winds of Change in the Christian Mission. Chicago: Moody Press,
  1973.

Kato, Byang H.
  "Evangelical Structures That Should Affect the Church Nationally
  and Internationally". Overland Park, Kansas: Unpublished paper
  presented at the 1973 *EFMA/IFMA Study Conference*, November 27-30.

Kent, Homer A. Jr.
  Jerusalem to Rome. Grand Rapids: Baker Book House, 1972.

Kim, Samuel
  "Problems of the Third World Missionaries". Pasadena: Unpub-
  lished paper presented to C. Peter Wagner at the School of
  World Missions, Fuller Theological Seminary, May 17, 1973.

Koyama, Kosuke
  Waterbuffalo Theology. Maryknoll: Orbis Books, 1976.

Kraemer, Hendrik
  The Christian Message in a Non-Christian World. New York and
  London: International Missionary Council, 1938.

Larson, Robert
  "The New International Missionary". *World Vision Magazine*.
  Monrovia: World Vision International, May 1975.

Latourette, Kenneth Scott
  Christianity in a Revolutionary Age, Five Vols. New York: Harper,
  1958-1962.

Latourette, Kenneth Scott
  Christianity Through the Ages. New York: Harper and Row, 1965.

Latourette, Kenneth Scott
  History of the Expansion of Christianity, Seven Vols. New York:
  Harper, 1939-1941.

Lausanne Covenant
  Sponsored by the Lausanne Committee for World Evangelization.
  Wheaton: LCWE, 1974

Lindsell, Harold
"Precedent - Setting in Missions Strategy", *Christianity Today*.
Vol. 10, No. 15. Carol Stream, Illinois: April 29, 1966.

Lindsell, Harold, ed.
The Church's Worldwide Mission. Waco: Word Books, 1966.

Maslow, Abraham
Religions, Values and Peak-Experiences. New York: Penguin
Books, 1964.

McGavran, Donald A., ed.
Church Growth and Christian Mission. New York: Harper and
Row, 1965.

McGavran, Donald A., ed.
Crucial Issues in Missions Tomorrow. Chicago: Moody Press,
1972.

McGavran, Donald A., ed.
The Clash Between Christianity and Culture. Washington D.C.:
Canon Press, 1974.

McGavran, Donald A., ed.
The Evangelical - Conciliar Debate. Pasadena: Wm. Carely
Library, 1977.

McGavran, Donald and Norman Riddle
Zaire, Midday in Missions. Valley Forge: Judson Press, 1979.

Moffett, Eileen and Samuel
Personal prayer letter from Presbyterian Missions in Seoul,
Korea, December 2, 1971.

Moore, Basil, ed.
The Challenge of Black Theology in South Africa. Atlanta:
John Knox Press, 1973.

Nanfelt, Peter N.
Personal letter dated June 16, 1980.

Neill, Stephen
A History of Christian Missions. Baltimore: Penguin Books
Inc., 1964.

Neill, Stephen
Call to Mission. Philadelphia: Fortress Press, 1970.

Neill, Stephen
Concise Dictionary of the Christian World Mission. Nashville:
Abingdon Press, 1971.

Neill, Stephen
"Mission in the 1980". *Occasional Bulletin of Missionary
Research.* Ventor: Overseas Ministries Study Center, January,
1979.

Nelson, Marlin L.
Reading in Third World Missions. Pasadena: Wm. Carey Library,
1976.

Nelson, Marlin L.
The How and Why of Third World Missions. Pasadena: Wm. Carey
Library, 1976.

Nevius, John L.
Planting and Development of Missionary Churches. Nutley, New
Jersey: The Presbyterian and Reformed Publishing Co.

Newbigin, Leslie
Open Secret. Grand Rapids: Wm. B. Eerdmans Publishing Co.,
1978.

Nida, Eugene A.
Customs and Culture: Anthropology for Christian Missions.
Pasadena: Wm. Carey Library, 1975.

Nida, Eugene A.
Message and Mission. Pasadena: Wm. Carey Library, 1973.

O Estado de Sao Paulo, editorial
"The Population in the year 2000: 6 Billion and 200 Million".
Sao Paulo: September 5, 1980.

Ogot, B.A. and J.A. Kieran
Zamani: A Survey of East African History. London: Longmans,
Green and Co., 1968.

Oliver, Roland and Anthony Atmore
Africa Since 1800. Oxford: Cambridge University Press, 1969.

O'Meara, Most Reverend Edward T.
"Ecclesial Basic Communities". *World Mission,* Vol. 30, No. 2
Washington D.C.: Society for the Propaganda of the Faith,
Summer, 1979.

Padilla, C. Rene
"Being God's Church in Latin America", *Christianity Today,* Vol.
24, No. 6. Carol Stream, Illinois: March 21, 1980.

Pentecost, Edward C.
"How Can North American Mission Agencies Effectively Cooperate With and Encourage Third World Mission Sending Agencies?" Overland Park, Kansas: Unpublished paper presented at the 1973 *EFMA/IFMA Study Conference,* November 27-30.

Perez, Pablo
"How Can North American Mission Agencies Effectively Cooperate With and Encourage Third World Mission Sending Agencies?" Overland Park, Kansas: Unpublished paper presented at the 1973 *EFMA/IFMA Study Conference,* November 27-30.

Peters, George W.
A Biblical Theology of Missions. Chicago: Moody Press, 1972.

Peters, George W.
Indonesia Revival. Grand Rapids: Zondervan Publishing House, 1973.

Peters, George W.
Saturation Evangelism. Grand Rapids: Zondervan Publishing House, 1973.

Philippine Native Crusade
Newsletter. Cagayan 1101, Philippines: dated February 1980.

Pobee, John S.
Toward An African Theology. Nashville: Abingdon Press, 1979.

The Presbyterian Journal
"Ghana Sends Missionaries to Atlanta Presbytery", September 2, 1975.

Ransom, Charles W., ed.
Renewal and Advance. London: Edinburgh House Press, 1948.

Reapsome, James
"Third World Missions". *His Magazine,* Vol. 40, No. 8. Downers Grove: Inter Varsity Christian Fellowship, May 1980.

Reapsome, James
"So Send I You to the U.S.?" *Eternity.* Philadelphia: August 1979.

Reed, William R.
New Patterns of Church Growth in Brazil. Grand Rapids: Wm. B. Eerdmans Publishing Co., 1965.

Sangu, Bishop James
Cited in *Mission Intercom*, No. 49. Washington D.C.: U.S.
Catholic Mission Council, November 1975.

Sawyerr, Harry
"The First World Missionary Conference: Edinburgh 1910".
International Review of Mission, LWVII: 267. Geneva: Com-
mision on World Mission and Evangelism, July, 1978.

Scherer, James A.
Missionary, Go Home! Englewood Cliffs: Prentice-Hall, Inc.
1964.

Seia, Robin
Personal correspondence, n.d.

Song, Choan-Seng, ed.
Doing Theology Today. Madras: Christian Literature Society,
1976.

Stott, John R.W.
Christian Mission in the Modern World. Downers Grove: Inter
Varsity Press, 1975

Sudan Interior Mission Press Release
"Asian Christians Serving in Africa". Scarborough, Ontario:
Sudan Interior Mission, April 17, 1980.

Teng, Philip
Quoted in *Missionary News Service*. Wheaton: Evangelical Missionary Information Service, Vol. 22, No. 18, September 15,
1975.

Thiessen, John Caldwell
Survey of World Missions. Chicago: Moody Press, 1955.

Time Magazine
"Faith in Africa", January 21, 1980.

Time Magazine
"Toward a Troubled 21st Century", August 4, 1980.

Tippett, Alan R.
Church Growth and the Word of God. Grand Rapids: Wm. B.
Eerdmans Publishing Co., 1970.

Tippett, Alan R.
God, Man and Church Growth. Grand Rapids: Wm. B. Eerdmans
Publishing Co., 1973.

Tippett, Alan R.
Solomon Islands Christianity: A Study in Growth and Obstruc-
tion. London: Lutterworth Press, 1967.

Torres, Sergio and Virginia Favella, eds.
The Emergent Gospel. Maryknoll: Orbis Books, 1976.

Traub, Margaret
"Relief for the Oppressed in the Village Called Africa".
Christianity Today, Vol. 23, No. 19. Carol Stream, Illinois:
July 20, 1979.

Tsucliya, Philip
"A Black Fishing Net With White Corks - The Story of the
Melanesian Brotherhood". Pasadena: Unpublished paper written
at the School of World Mission, for the class of History III,
Number 653, taught by Ralph D. Winter, Spring Quarter, 1973.

U.S. News and World Report
"What is the Third World", Vol. 78, No. 13, March 31, 1975.

Wagner, C. Peter, ed.
Church/Mission Tensions Today. Chicago: Moody Press, 1972.

Wagner, C. Peter, ed.
Stop the World I Want to Get On. Glendale: Gospel Light Press,
1974.

Wagner, C. Peter
Memorandum. An unpublished paper of the Strategy Working Group
of The Lausanne Continuation Committee, October 13, 1977.

Wagner, C. Peter
Quoted in *Moody Monthly,* Vol. 80, No. 1. Chicago: Moody Bible
Institute, September, 1979.

Wagner, C. Peter
"The People Approach to World Evangelism". Pasadena: Initial
and unpublished presentation of the Strategy Working Group for
the Consultation on World Evangelization, Pattaya, Thailand on
Tuesday, June 19, 1980.

Wakatama, Pius
Independence for the Third World Church. Downers Grove: Inter
Varsity Press, 1976.

Webster, Warren
"Reaching the Unreached". *Impact,* Vol. 37, No. 1. Wheaton:
Conservative Baptist Foreign Mission Society, January, 1980.

Westing, Harold J., ed.
I'd Love to Tell the World: The Challenge of Missions. Denver:
Accent Books, 1977.

Williams, Theodore
"Bombay Consultation Papers Released". *MNS Pulse,* Vol. 25, No.
12. Wheaton: Missionary News Service - June 15, 1978.

Williams, Theodore
Quoted in "Indigenous Missions in India" by Rev. F. Herangkluma,
in *India Church Growth Quarterly,* Vol. 1, No. 4. Madras: India
Church Growth Association of India, October-December, 1979.

Wills, A.J.
An Introduction to the History of Central Africa. London: Oxford
University Press, 1964.

Wilson, J. Christy Jr.
Today's Tentmakers. Wheaton: Tyndale House Publishers, 1979.

Wilson, Samuel
"World Vision Partnership in Church Planting", in *MARC Newsletter.*
Monrovia: World Vision International, September, 1980.

Winter, Ralph D.
"1980: Year of Three Missions Congress". *Evangelical Missions
Quarterly,* Vol. 16, No. 2. Wheaton: Evangelical Missions
Information Service, Inc., April 1980.

Winter, Ralph D.
"Penetrating the Last Frontiers", a graph. Pasadena: U.S.
Center for World Mission, 1978.

Winter, Ralph D.
"The Highest Priority: Cross-Cultural Evangelism", *Let the Earth
Hear His Voice,* J.D. Douglas, ed. Minnesota: World Wide Publica-
tions, 1975.

Winter, Ralph D.
"The Missionary Anomaly". Pasadena: School of World Mission
taped lecture, No. 4, to course No. 651, "The Historical Development of the Christian Movement".

Winter, Ralph D.
"The Planting of Younger Missions", *Reading in Third World Missions,* Marlin L. Nelson, ed. Pasadena: Wm. Carey Library, 1976.

Winter, Ralph D.
The 25 Unbelievable Years, 1945-1969. Pasadena: Wm. Carey
Library, 1970.

Winter, Ralph D. and R. Pierce Beaver
  The Warp and the Woof: Organizing for Mission. Pasadena: Wm.
  Carey Library, 1970.

Wolpert, Stanley
  A New History of India. New York: Oxford University Press,
  1977.

Wong, James and Peter Larson, Edward Pentecost
  Missions From the Third World. Singapore: Church Growth Study
  Center, 1972.

Wong, Paul
  "Serving Among American Indians". *Challenger.* Petaluma,
  California: Chinese Christian Mission, January 1979.

Worldteam
  What Does it Mean to be a World Christian? Miami: Worldteam,
  1978.

Wylie, Mrs. MacLeod
  The Gospel in Burma. Calcutta: G.C. Hay and Co., 1859.

FOOTNOTES

Chapter 1

1. Theodore Williams, "Bombay Consultation Papers Released,"
    MNS Pulse, Wheaton, Missionary News Service, Vol. 25, No. 12,
    June 15, 1978, p. 2.

2. Ralph D. Winter, "The Missionary Anomaly," Pasadena: School
    of World Mission, Class Lecture #4 of taped course *The Histor-
    ical Development of the Christian Movement* (SWM 651)

3. Robert T. Handy, *A History of the Churches in the United States
    and Canada,* New York, Oxford University Press, 1977, p. 278-279.

4. Edward Dayton, ed., *Mission Handbook: North American Protes-
    tant Ministries Overseas, 11th ed.,* Monrovia, Calif., Missions
    Advance Research and Communication Center (MARC), 1976, p. 58.

5. Edward Dayton, *That Everyone May Hear,* Monrovia, Calif., Mis-
    sions Advance Research and Communication Center (MARC), 1976,
    p. 58.

6. Ralph D. Winter, *Hidden People, 1980,* U.S. Center for World
    Mission, poster 1980.

7. "Missions: From All Six to All Six," *Christianity Today*, Washington, D.C., November 22, 1974, p. 40.

8. Ralph D. Winter, "The Planting of Younger Missions," *Reading in Third World Missions*, Marlin L. Nelson, ed., Pasadena, Calif.: Wm. Carey Library, 1976, p. 55.

9. "What is the Third World?", *U.S. News and World Report*, 78:13, March 31, 1975, p. 59.

10. Dennis E. Clark, *The Third World and Missions*, Waco, Texas, Word Books, 1971, p. 14.

11. Walbert Buhlmann, *The Coming of the Third Church*, Maryknoll, New York, Orbis Books, 1976, p. 3, (emphasis mine).

12. Ibid., p. 5.

13. C. Peter Wagner, *Stop the World I Want to Get On*, Glendale, Calif., Gospel Light Press, 1974, p. 107.

14. Bishop James Sangu cited in *Mission Intercom*, Washington, D.C., U.S. Catholic Mission Council, no. 49, November, 1975, p. 1.

15. Philip Teng quoted in *Missionary News Service*, Wheaton, Evangelical Missionary Information Service, 22:18, September 15, 1975, p. 1.

16. Eileen and Samuel Moffett, personal prayer letter of December 2, 1971, Seoul, Korea, Presbyterian Missions.

17. Leslie Brierley, unpublished letter to Edward C. Pentecost, James Wong and Peter Larson, October 26, 1973.

18. "Ghana Sends Missionary to Atlanta Presbytery," *The Presbyterian Journal*, September 3, 1975, p. 6.

19. Valston Abraham (Indian evangelist from Kerala), a personal interview, February 25, 1980.

20. Edward Dayton, ed., *Mission Handbook*, p. 59.

21. Theodore Williams quoted in "Indigenous Missions in India" by Rev. F. Herangkluma, in *India Church Growth Quarterly*, Madras, Indian Church Growth Association of India, 1:4, October-December, 1979.

22. Neal Browning, "Made in Japan Missionaries," *Japan Harvest*, Greenville, Spring, 1975, p. 25.

23. C. Peter Wagner, *Stop the World I Want to Get On*, p. 111-112.

24. C. Peter Wagner quoted in *Moody Monthly*, Chicago, 80:1, September, 1979, p. 139.

25. *Christianity Today*, Washington, D.C., August 17, 1979, p. 50.

26. Ralph D. Winter, *The 25 Unbelievable Years*, p. 61.

27. "Faith in Africa," *Time Magazine*, 115:3, January 21, 1980, p. 50.

28. *Crusade Magazine*, December, 1976.

29. *Gospel Light Magazine*, India, 4:7, November, 1979, p. 24.

39. Robin Seia in personal correspondence; also from personal letters from the Burmese Baptist Convention.

31. P. J. Johnstone, *Operation World*, Bromley, England, S.T.L. Publishers, 1978, pp. 98, 159, 223, 235.

32. Max Warren, quoted by Gerald H. Anderson in "Introductions," *Asian Voices in Christian Theology*, Gerald H. Anderson, ed., Maryknoll, New York, Orbis Books, 1976, p. 7

Chapter 2

1. Johannes Blauw, *The Missionary Nature of the Church*. Grand Rapids: William B. Eerdmans Publishing Co., 1962, p. 9.

2. C. Peter Wagner, "The People Approach to World Evangelism", Initial presentation of the Strategy Working Group at the Consultation on World Evangelization, Pattaya, Thailand, Tuesday, June 19, 1980, p. 8.

3. Warren Webster, "Reaching the Unreached", *Impact*. 37.1 January 1980, Wheaton: Conservative Baptist Foreign Mission Society, p. 13.

4. C. Peter Wagner, *Stop the World I Want to Get On*. Glendale, Calif.: Gospel Light Publishers, 1974, pp. 110-111.

5. Kenneth S. Latourette, *A History of the Expansion of Christianity*. Vol. IV. Grand Rapids: Zondervan, 1970, p. 18.

6. Harry Sawyerr, "The First World Missionary Conference: Edinburgh 1910", *International Review of Mission.* LXVII:267, July 1978, p. 272.

7. Ibid., p. 257.

8, Ralph D. Winter, "1980: Year of Three Missions Congresses", *Evangelical Missions Quarterly.* James W. Reapsome, ed., 16:2, April, 1980, Wheaton: Evangelical Missions Information Service, Inc., p. 84.

9. Sawyerr, "The First World Missionary Conference: Edinburgh 1910", p. 265.

10. Charles Wesley Ransom, "The Whitby Meeting of the International Missionary Council", *Renewal and Advance,* by Charles W. Ransom, ed., London: Edinburgh House Press, 1948, p. 3.

11. Jerald D. Gort, "Jerusalem 1928: Mission Kingdom and Church", *International Review of Mission.* LXVII:267, July 1978, p. 275.

12. Ibid., p. 282.

13. Ransom, "The Whitby Meeting of the International Missionary Council," p. 3.

14. Evert Jansen Schoonhoven, "Tambaram 1938", *International Review of Mission,* p. 300.

15. Ibid., p. 307.

16. "One Race, One Gospel, One Task", closing statement of the World Congress on Evangelism, *One Race, One Gospel, One Task,* Vol. I., Carl F.H. Henry and Stanley Mooneyham, eds., Minneapolis: World Wide Publications, 1967, p. 5.

17. Harold Lindsell, "Precedent-Setting in Missions Strategy", *Christianity Today,* 10:15, April 29, 1966, p. 43.

18. "The Call to the Congress", *The Church's Worldwide Mission.* Harold Lindsell, ed., Waco, Texas: Word Books, 1966, p. 3 (emphasis mine).

19. Ibid., pp. 274-279.

20. "Attendance Summary", *Missions in Creative Tension.* Vergil Gerber, ed., Pasadena, Calif.: Wm. Carey Library, 1971, p. 337.

21. Pius Wakatama, *Independence for the Third World Church.* Downers Grave, Ill.: Intervarsity Press, 1976, p. 106.

22. Ted W. Engstrom, "Airing of Mission Tensions", *World Vision Magazine*. 15:10, November, 1971, p. 28.

23. Hector Espinoza, "Grim Facts About Green Lake '71", *Church Growth Bulletin*. 7:4, March 1972, p. 206.

24. Warren Webster, "Mission in Time and Space", *Church/Mission Tensions Today*. C. Peter Wagner, ed., Chicago: Moody Press, 1972, p. 104.

25. Ibid., p. 105.

26. Ralph D. Winter, "The Planting of Younger Missions", *Church/ Mission Tensions Today,* pp. 131-132.

27. Ibid., p. 139.

28. James Wong, Peter Larson, Edward Pentecost, *Missions From the Third World*. Singapore: Church Growth Study Center, 1972, pp. 15-17.

29. Billy Graham, "Why Lausanne?", *Let the Earth Hear His Voice*. J.D. Douglas, ed., Minneapolis: World Wide Publications, 1975, p. 33.

30. Stephen J. Akangbe, "Third World Missions", *Let the Earth Hear His Voice,* p. 1302.

31. Ibid.

32. Pius Wakatama, p. 21.

33. Quoted in interview by Robert Larson, "The New International Missionary", *World Vision Magazine*. May 1975, Monrovia: World Vision Inc., p. 14.

Chapter 3

1. Leslie Newbigin, *The Open Secret*. Grand Rapids: Wm. B. Eerdmans Publishing Co., 1978, p. 31.

2. Shoki Coe, "Contextualizing Theology", *Mission Trends No. 3*. Gerald H. Anderson and Thomas F. Stransky, eds., Grand Rapids: Wm. B. Eerdmans Publishing Co. and New York: Paulist Fathers, 1976, p. 29.

3. Yoshinobu Kumazawa, "Where Theology Seeks to Integrate Text and Context", *Mission Trends No. 3,* p. 203.

4. C. Rene Padilla, "Being God's Church in Latin America", *Christianity Today*. Vol. XXIV, No. 6, March 21, 1980, Washington, D.C., p. 54.

5. Ibid.

6. Tokunbo Adeyemo, "The African Church Struggle into Her Third Century", *Christianity Today*. Volume XXIII, No. 19, July 20, 1979, Washington, D.C., p. 17.

7. *Christianity Today*. "In Search of Africa", Vol. XXIII, No. 19, July 20, 1979, Washington, D.C., p. 9.

8. Choan-Seng Song, "Theology of the Incarnation", *Asian Voices in Christian Theology*. Gerald H. Anderson, ed., Maryknoll: Orbis Books, 1976, pp. 150-151.

9. Kosuke Koyama, *Waterbuffalo Theology*. Maryknoll: Orbis Books, 1976, p. 3ff.

10. Gerald H. Anderson, *Asian Voices in Christian Theology*, p. 3.

11. Harvey Perkins, Harry Daniel, Asal Simandjuntak, "Let My people Go", *Mission Trends No. 3*, p. 195.

12. Ibid., pp. 202-203.

13. John S. Mbiti, "Theological Impotence and the Universality of the Church", *Mission Trends No. 3*, p. 18.

14. In a personal letter to the author by the Right Reverend Bishop Alber Yawoah.

15. Marie-Louise Martin, "Does the World Need Fantastically Growing Churchs?", *The Conciliar-Evangelical Debate*. Donald A. McGavran, ed., Pasadena, Calif.: Wm. Carey Library, 1977, p. 151.

16. Bongamjalo Goba, "Corporate Personality: Ancient Israel and Africa", *The Challenge of Black Theology in South Africa*. Basil Moore, ed., Atlanta: John Knox Press, 1973, p. 69.

17. Christopher Mwoleka, "Trinity and Community", *Mission Trends No. 3*, p. 151.

18. John S. Pobee, *Toward an African Theology*. Nashville: Abingdon Press, 1979, p. 49.

19. Margaret Traub, "Relief for the Oppressed in the Village Called Africa", *Christianity Today*. Vol. XXIII, No. 19, July 20, 1979, p. 10.

20. Most Reverend Edward T. O'Meara, "Ecclesial Basic Communities", *Worldmission*. Vol. 30, No. 2, Summer 1979, p. 2.

21. Choan-Seng Song, "Love of God-and-Man in Action", *Doing Theology Today*. Choan-Seng Song, ed., Madras: Christian Literature Society, 1976, pp. 42-43.

22. Kosuke Koyama, *Waterbuffalo Theology*, p. 93.

23. Enrique Guang, "Missionary Action is an 'In-the-Meantime'", *Evangelical Missions Tomorrow*. Wade T. Coggins and E. L. Frizen, eds., Pasadena, Calif.: Wm. Carey Library, 1977, p. 40.

24. J. R. Chandran, "Development of Christian Theology in India: a Critical Survey", *The Emergent Gospel*. Sergio Torres and Virginia Favella, eds., Maryknoll: Orbis Books, 1976, p. 166.

25. Enrique Dussel, *Ethics and Theology of Liberation*. Maryknoll: Orbis Books, 1977, p. 89.

26. Ibid., p. 94.

27. Urban T. Holmes III, *The Future Shape of Ministry*. New York: Seabury Press, 1971, p. 229.

28. Joseph A. Grassi, *A World to Win*. New York: Maryknoll Books, 1965, p. 159.

29. Abraham Maslow, *Religious Values and Peak-Experiences*. New York: Penguin Books, 1964, pp. 30-31.

30. Ibid.

31. Hugo Assmann, *Theology for a Nomad Church*. Maryknoll: Orbis Books, 1975, p. 67.

32. Orlando E. Costas, *The Integrity of Mission*. New York: Harper and Row, 1979, pp. XII-XIII.

33. D.S. Amalorpavadass, "The Indian Universe of a New Theology", *The Emergent Gospel*, p. 148.

34. Jung Young Lee, "The Yin-Yang Way of Thinking", *Mission Trends No. 3*, p. 34.

35. John S. Pobee, *Toward an African Theology*, p. 26.

36. Harvey T. Hoekstra, *The World Council of Churches and the Demise of Evangelism*. Wheaton: Tyndale Publishing House, 1979, p. 133.

37. Kofi Appiah-Kubi, "Indigenous African Christian Churches: Signs of Authenticity", *African Theology En Route*. Kofi Appiah-Kubi and Sergio Torres, eds., Maryknoll: Obis Books, 1979, p. 118.

Chapter 4

1. James Reapsome, "Third World Missions", *His Magazine*. Vol. 40, No. 8, May 1980, Downers Grove: Inter Varsity Christian Fellowship, p. 21.

2. Donald A. McGavran and Norman Riddle, *Zaire, Midday In Missions*. Valley Forge: Judson Press, 1979, p. 20.

3. James Reapsome, "Third World Missions".

4. Stephen Neill, "Mission in the 1980's", *Occasional Bulletin*. January, 1979, Ventnor, p. 27.

5. Marlin Nelson, *The How and Why of Third World Missions*. Pasadena, Calif.: Wm. Carey Library, 1976, p. 199.

6. *Ibid.*

7. C. Peter Wagner, *Stop the World I Want to Get On*. Glendale: Gospel Light Publications, 1974, p. 107.

8. Ralph D. Winter, "The Highest Priority: Cross-Cultural Evangelism", *Let the Earth Hear His Voice*. J.D. Douglas ed. Minnesota: World Wide Publications, 1975, p. 220.

9. Ralph D. Winter, "The Warp and the Woof of the Christian Movement", *The Warp and the Woof: Organizing for Mission*. By Ralph D. Winter and R. Pierce Beauer. Pasadena: Wm. Carey Library, 1970, p. 52-62.

10. Ralph D. Winter, "The Two Structures of God's Redemptive Mission", *Crucial Dimensions in World Evangelization*. By Arthur F. Glasser, Paul G. Hiebert, C. Peter Wagner, Ralph D. Winter. Pasadena: Wm. Carey Library, 1976, p. 341.

11. N. Ishiguro, ed., *Kansai Mission Research Center News Report*. Kobe: KMRC Preparatory Committee, 1980, p. 1.

Chapter 5

1. In a personal letter to the author, dated March 28, 1980.

2. In a personal letter to the author, dated February 29, 1980.

3. Peter Larson, Edward Pentecost and James Wong, ed., *Missions from the Third World*. Singapore: Church Growth Study Center, 1972, p. 80.

4. Ibid., p. 17, 18.

5. Ibid., p. 30.

6. Ibid.

7. Edward R. Dayton, ed., *Mission Handbook: North American Protestant Ministries Overseas*. 11th Edition. Monrovia: MARC, a division of World Vision International, 1976, p. 37.

8. Ibid.

9. Ibid.

10. Larson, Pentecost, and Wong, ed., *Missions from the Third World*, p. 17, 18.

11. Ibid.

12. P.J. Johnstone, *Operation World*. Kent, England: STL Publications, 1978, p. 108.

13. Ibid., p. 218.

14. Larson, Pentecost, and Wong, ed., *Missions from the Third World*, pp. 37-39.

15. Ibid., p. 31.

16. Ibid., p. 17, 18.

17. Dayton, ed., *Mission Handbook*, p. 36.

18. P.J. Johnstone, *Operation World*, p. 24.

19. Ibid., p. 218.

20. Ibid., p. 98.

21. P.J. Johnstone, *Operation World*. Kent, England: STL Publications, 1978, p. 223, 235.

22. Ibid., p. 258.

23. C. Peter Wagner and Edward R. Dayton, eds., *Unreached Peoples '80*. Elgin, Illinois: David C. Cook Publishing Co., 1980, p. 7.

Chapter 6

1. Marlin Nelson, *The How and Why of Third World Missions*. Pasadena, Wm. Carey Library, 1976, p. 122.

2. In a personal letter, dated July 28, 1980.

3. In a personal letter from Dr. Angali-I, dated February 2, 1980.

4. In a personal letter from Dr. Angali-I, dated February 2, 1980 (emphasis his).

5. "World Vision Partnership in Church Planting" in MARC Newsletter, Samuel Wilson, Director. Monrovia: World Vision International, September 1980, p. 1.

6. *Chinese and Western Leadership Cooperation Seminar Compendium*, Hong Kong, Chinese Coordination Centre of World Evangelism, March, 1980, p. 67-68.

7. Ibid., p. 135.

8. "Toward a Troubled 21st Century", *Time Magazine*, August 4, 1980, p. 53.

9. Ibid.

10. "The Population in the Year 2000: 6 Billion and 200 Million", *O Estado de Sao Paulo*, September 5, 1980, p. 34.

Chapter 7

1. Paul Wong, "Serving Among American Indians", *Challenger*. Petaluma, California: Chinese Christian Mission, January, 1979, p. 3.

2. C. Peter Wagner, *Memorandum*. A paper to the Strategy Working Group of The Lausanne Congress on World Evangelism, October 13, 1977.

3. *Navaho-Aymara; Aymara-Navaho*, n.d., attached to *Memorandum*. Page 1 only.

4. Wagner, *Memorandum*, p. 2.

5. Bruno Grigoli, *The Visit to Farmington*. Unpublished, n.d., attached to *Memorandum*, p. 1.

6. Ibid.

7. Ibid.

8. James Reapsome, "So Send I You to the U.S.?", *Eternity*. Philadelphia, August, 1979, p. 40.

9. Mrs. MacLeod Wylie, *The Gospel in Burma*. Calcutta: G.C. Hay and Co., 1859, p. 41.

10. Ibid., p. 50.

11. Ibid., pp. 50-51.

12. Ibid.

13. Peter Larson, James Wong, Edward Pentecost, "Historical Perspectives", in *Reading in Third World Missions*. Marlin L. Nelson, ed. Pasadena: Wm. Carey Library, 1976, p. 85.

14. Philip Tsuchiya, "A Black Fishing Net With White Corks - The Story of the Melanesian Brotherhood". Unpublished paper written at the School of World Mission, 1973, p. 1.

15. Ibid., p. 4.

16. Alan R. Tippett, *Solomon Islands Christianity: A Study in Growth and Obstruction*. London: Lutterworth Press, 1967, p. 50.

17. Tsuchiya, "A Black Fishing Net...", pp. 7-8.

18. Charles E. Fox, *Lord of the Southern Islands*, London: A.R. Mowbray and Co., 1958, p. 263.

19. Tsuchiya, "A Black Fishing Net...", p. 8.

20. Stuart W. Artless, *The Story of the Melanesian Mission*. London: The Melanesian Mission, 1937, p. 37.

21. Tippett, *Solomon Islands Christianity...*, p. 51.

22. Tsuchiya, "A Black Fishing Net...", p. 1.

23. Personal letter from Peter N. Nanfelt, June 16, 1980.

24. Paul Aihara, "The Foreign Missions Work of the Immanuel General Mission, Japan". Unpublished paper for Dr. Paul Pierson at the School of World Mission, February 27, 1980, for the class 'The Historical Development of the Christian Movement', p. 2.

25. Ibid., p. 4.

26. Ibid., p. 9.

27. Ibid., p. 12.

28. Ibid., p. 10.

29. Ibid., p. 14.

30. Ibid., p. 10.

31. Billy Hall, *Introducing International Missionary Fellowship*.
    Alexandria, Jamaica, West Indies: International Missionary
    Fellowship, n.d., p. 2.

32. Ibid., p. 7.

33. "Epic Evangelistic Event Witnessed in South Korea". Wheaton:
    EP News Service, September 13, 1980, p. 4.

34. "Asian Christians Serving in Africa". Scarborough, Ontario:
    Sudan Interior Mission Press Release, April 17, 1980.

35. Ibid.

36. In a personal letter dated September 24, 1980.

Chapter 8

1. C. Peter Wagner and Edward R. Dayton, editors, *Unreached Peoples
   '80*. Elgin, Illinois, David C. Cook Publishing Co., 1980, p. 331,
   329.

2. Ibid., p. 350, 347.

3. Edward R. Dayton and Samuel Wilson, editors, *Unreached Peoples
   '82*. Elgin, Illinois, David C. Cook Publishing Co., 1982, p. 173.

4. Ralph D. Winter, "Penetrating the Last Frontiers". Pasadena:
   U.S. Center for World Mission, graph 1978.

5. "Philippine Native Crusade", Newsletter of February 1980.
   Caqayan 1101, Philippines, p. 2.

6. Stephen J. Akangbe, "Three Major Ways That North American Mission Agencies Can Effectively Assist National Churches in the
   Evangelization of Their Countries". Unpublished paper, presented
   at the 1973 *EFMA/IFMA Study Conference*, Overland Park, Kansas,
   November 27-30, p. 2.

7. Met Castillo, "Missiological Education: The Missing Vitamin in Mission Strategy". *Asia Pulse*. Wheaton: Evangelical Missions Information Service, Volume VII, Number 2, May 1976, p. 3.

8. J. Christy Wilson, Jr., *Today's Tentmakers*. Wheaton: Tyndale House Publishers, 1979, p. 142.

9. Ibid., p. 17.

10. Quoted by Wilfred A. Bellamy, "How Can North American Mission Agencies More Effectively Assist National Churches in the Evangelization of Their Countries?" Unpublished paper presented at the 1973 *EFMA/IFMA Study Conference*, Overland Park, Kansas, November 27-30, p. 2.

11. Pablo Perez, "How Can North American Mission Agencies Effectively Cooperate with and Encourage Third World Mission Sending Agencies?" Unpublished paper presented at the 1973 *EFMA/IFMA Study Conference*, Overland Park, Kansas, November 27-30, p. 11.

12. Samuel Kim, "Problems of the Third World Missionaries". Unpublished paper presented to C. Peter Wagner at the School of World Mission, Fuller Theological Seminary, May 17, 1973, p. 4.

13. In a personal letter by Rev. O.M. Akpan, dated February 18, 1980.

14. Byang H. Kato, "Evangelical Structures That Should Affect the Church Nationally and Internationally". Unpublished paper presented at the 1973 *EFMA/IFMA Study Conference*, Overland Park, Kansas, November 27-30, pp. 8-9.

15. Edward C. Pentecost, "How Can North American Mission Agencies Effectively Cooperate With and Encourage Third World Mission Sending Agencies?" Unpublished paper presented at the 1973 *EFMA/IFMA Study Conference*, Overland Park, Kansas, November 27-30, p. 5.

16. Emilio Castro, "Structures For Mission" in *Mission Trends No. 1*. Gerald A. Anderson and Thomas F. Stronsky, editors. Grand Rapids: Wm. B. Eerdmans Publishing Co., 1974, p. 161.

17. Arthur F. Glasser, "The New Overseas Missionary Fellowship". Unpublished paper presented at the 1965 *EFMA Retreat* at Winona Lake, Indiana, October 4-7, p. 15.

18. Raymond J. Davis, "A National Missionary Movement". Unpublished paper presented at the 1963 *EFMA/IFMA Joint Conference* at Winona Lake, Indiana, September 30 to October 3, p. 23.

19. Charles R. Tabor, "Evangelizing the Unreached Peoples: What to Do and How to Do It", in *The Gospel and Frontier Peoples*, R. Pierce Beaver, ed. Pasadena: Wm. Carey Library, 1973, p. 127.

You Can Help

The information contained in this book represents the most complete listing of Third World Mission Societies available anywhere. Yet it *still* contains error and ommissions. Furthermore, the data are in constant need of revision. Therefore, you can help make the next Third World mission directory even more precise by sharing your experience and knowledge. Perhaps already you are familiar with one or more of the many non-western missionary sending activities near you. After reading this book and reacting to it, the simple form below may be used as a guide for your participation. In gratitude, you will be listed as one of the informants in the next directory. Your participation is highly desired and valued.

Please send all comments directly to the author:

Lawrence E. Keyes
c/o Sepal
C.P. 30,548
01000 Sao Paulo, S.P. Brazil

| 1 | This information concerns | 2 | This information is based based upon: |

1 This information concerns
[ ] an up-date of already
     listed information
[ ] a new listing
[ ] a corrective comment
[ ] a personal opinion
[ ] _____

2 This information is based based upon:
[ ] personal research
[ ] personal experience
[ ] secondary sources
[ ] _____

3 Information: _____

_____

_____

_____

_____

_____

Continued on Next Page

Information (continued)

_____

_____

_____

_____

_____

_____

_____

_____

_____

_____

_____

_____

_____

_____

_____

_____

_____

_____

_____

_____

_____

Thank you *very much* for helping up-date
Third World mission information

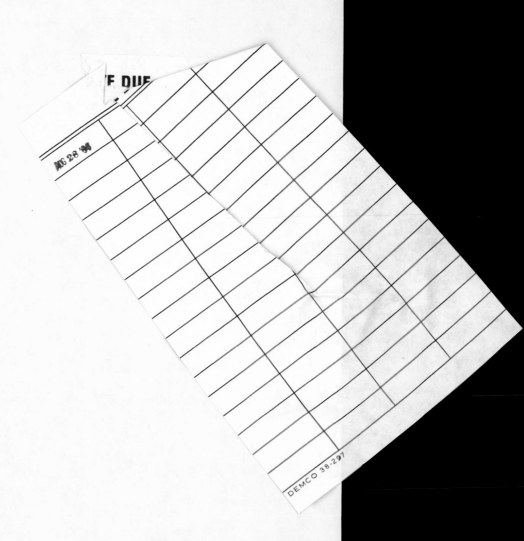